The Rise of China, Inc.

Leveraging its absolute power, low human rights advantage, and tolerance by other countries, the Chinese Communist Party has transformed China into a giant corporation. Living and working is not a right but a privilege granted by the party. State-owned firms are business units or subsidiaries, private firms are joint ventures, and foreign firms are franchisees of the party. 'China, Inc.,' enjoys the agility of a firm and the vast resources of a state. Meanwhile, foreign firms competing with Chinese firms can find themselves matched against the mighty Chinese state. *China, Inc.* will interest many readers: it will compel business scholars to rethink state-firm relationships; assist multinational business practitioners in formulating effective strategies; aid policymakers in countering China's expansion; and inform the public of the massive corporate organization China has become and how democracies can effectively deal with it.

SHAOMIN LI is Professor and Eminent Scholar at Old Dominion University. His research has appeared in *Harvard Business Review*, *The Economist*, *The Wall Street Journal*, and *The Financial Times*. He is author of *Bribery and Corruption in Weak Institutional Environments* (Cambridge University Press, 2019).

The Rise of China, Inc.

How the Chinese Communist Party
Transformed China into a Giant
Corporation

SHAOMIN LI
Old Dominion University

CAMBRIDGE
UNIVERSITY PRESS

CAMBRIDGE
UNIVERSITY PRESS

University Printing House, Cambridge CB2 8BS, United Kingdom

One Liberty Plaza, 20th Floor, New York, NY 10006, USA

477 Williamstown Road, Port Melbourne, VIC 3207, Australia

314–321, 3rd Floor, Plot 3, Splendor Forum, Jasola District Centre,
New Delhi – 110025, India

103 Penang Road, #05–06/07, Visioncrest Commercial, Singapore 238467

Cambridge University Press is part of the University of Cambridge.

It furthers the University's mission by disseminating knowledge in the pursuit of
education, learning, and research at the highest international levels of excellence.

www.cambridge.org
Information on this title: www.cambridge.org/9781316513873
DOI: 10.1017/9781009076210

First published 2022

Printed in the United Kingdom by TJ Books Limited, Padstow Cornwall

A catalogue record for this publication is available from the British Library.

Library of Congress Cataloging-in-Publication Data
Names: Li, Shaomin (Sociologist), author.
Title: The rise of China, Inc : how the Chinese Communist Party transformed China into a
    giant / Shaomin Li, Old Dominion University, Virginia.
Description: Cambridge, United Kingdom ; New York, NY : Cambridge University Press, 2022. |
    Includes bibliographical references and index.
Identifiers: LCCN 2021037856 (print) | LCCN 2021037857 (ebook) | ISBN 9781316513873
    (hardback) | ISBN 9781009074926 (paperback) | ISBN 9781009076210 (epub)
Subjects: LCSH: Zhongguo gong chan dang. | Capitalism–Political aspects–China. | Economic
    development–Political aspects–China. | China–Commerce. | China–Foreign economic
    relations. | China–Politics and government–1949- | China–Economic policy–1949- |
    BISAC: BUSINESS & ECONOMICS / International / General
Classification: LCC HC427.95 .L55285 2022 (print) | LCC HC427.95 (ebook) |
    DDC 330.951–dc23
LC record available at https://lccn.loc.gov/2021037856
LC ebook record available at https://lccn.loc.gov/2021037857

ISBN 978-1-316-51387-3 Hardback
ISBN 978-1-009-07492-6 Paperback

To people who have made great efforts in improving China as a society and a more responsible member of the international community.

Contents

Acknowledgments

I would like to thank the Department of Management at Old Dominion University's Strome College of Business for providing an open and supportive environment.

This book is the result of decades of observation on China, especially over the past four years, during which time the friction between China and the democratic countries has intensified substantially. Many people have helped me during the brainstorming and writing process, and the following colleagues and friends are more than deserving of a big "thank you": Mahdi Forghani Bajestani, Matthew Farrell, David Selover, Samuel Wilson, and Wei Zhang. I benefited greatly from their lively discussions, thoughts on my drafts, and timely and dependable support.

I have presented the theme of this book at various seminars and conferences, including the 2020 Old Dominion University's Strome Business College Seminar, the 2019 China Goes Global Conference, and the 2019 World Affairs Council's Great Decisions Series. I want to thank the organizers and participants of these events for their valuable feedback that helped me improve my book.

At Cambridge University Press, I would like to thank my editor, Valerie Appleby, for her guidance and advice. It was Valerie's enthusiastic encouragement and support that enabled me to fully develop my ideas into this book. My appreciation also goes to Toby Ginsberg and Joshua Penney, who guided me through the manuscript preparation and production process at Cambridge University Press. Finally, I thank the anonymous referees for their constructive comments and suggestions.

As always, my deepest gratitude goes to my family: my wife, Amy, whose unwavering support allowed me to concentrate on writing my book – Thank you, Amy! And our daughter, Diana, a recent PhD herself, who provided not only serious critiques of my writing but also her trademark humor to make me more productive – Thank you, Dr. Li!

1 Introduction

Who Lost China?

In February, 2018, a picture was posted by Mercedes-Benz on Instagram showing a white Mercedes car on a beach, with an inspirational quote from the Dalai Lama: "Look at the situations from all angles, and you will become more open." Little did Mercedes know that this well-meaning quote could cause such a national fury that might wreak havoc on Mercedes' market in China.[1]

It would be an understatement to say that the fate of Mercedes-Benz in China has undergone drastic changes over the past fifty years. In Mao's China in the 1970s, Mercedes cars were a rarity, and only the very top government officials rode in them. During that period, my family and I lived in a government-military compound in the capital city of Hebei Province, Shijiazhuang. The compound also housed some ten villas for provincial heads and generals. Of the ten top officials, only one general had a Mercedes sedan, which was given to him as a used car. Back then most Mercedes cars in China were brought from Chinese embassies in foreign countries after the ambassadors used them first. The chauffeur of the general in the compound was generous in blowing the car's distinctive horn. Hearing the horn and seeing the car was a big privilege for me to brag about with my friends who did not get to live in the compound.

Today, China is the largest market for Mercedes-Benz in the world, buying 204,684 Mercedes cars in 2020, surpassing Mercedes' home market, Germany (95,265), and the United States (78,078) (Automotive World, 2021). It is small wonder that Mercedes is extremely attentive to what China thinks of its brand. But how

---

[1] P. Li and A. Jourdan, 2018. Mercedes-Benz Apologizes to Chinese for Quoting Dalai Lama. *Reuters*, February 6 (www.reuters.com/article/us-mercedes-benz-china-gaffe/mercedes-benz-apologizes-to-chinese-for-quoting-dalai-lama-idUSKBN1FQ1FJ): Accessed December 13, 2020.

Mercedes has achieved its success and why such success is so fragile not only requires far more explanation but is also merely a small drop in the ocean of China's evolution and its relationship with the world, which I will examine in this book.

1.1   ENGAGING CHINA

The year 1976 was a watershed year in Chinese history: Mao Zedong died. Mao, the founder and chairman of the Chinese Communist Party (CCP), ruled the People's Republic of China with absolute power and a revolutionary policy from its founding in 1949 until his death (see Figure 1.1). Under Mao's reign, the society experienced ceaseless political purges, and the economy was so severely damaged that even obtaining life's bare necessities was a constant daily struggle. It is safe to say that no one in China cared about how Mercedes promoted its

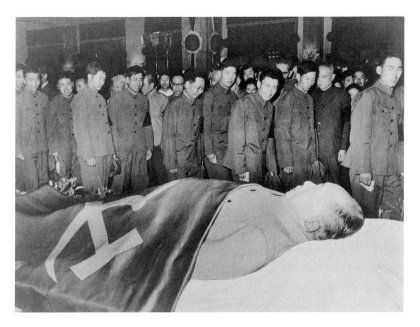

FIGURE 1.1 Members of the People's Liberation Army paying respects to the remains of Mao Zedong (September 12, 1976).
Source: Getty Images

cars: Needless to say, the people had no access to such information even if they cared.

Therefore, his death presented a historic opportunity for the country to change course. In order to save the near-bankrupt economy, the CCP under the leadership of Deng Xiaoping adopted a pragmatic approach to downplay communist ideology and introduce capitalism to China, albeit in a limited fashion. Deng and his associates, who had neither the experience nor the capital necessary for the development of markets, realized that they needed help from rich capitalist countries.

That required China to improve its international standing, which had been badly damaged by Mao's revolution. So, Deng and his associates reversed Mao's confrontational stance against the United States, which Mao accused of "American imperialism," and its allies, or "imperialist running dogs,"[2] according to Mao's phraseology. They eagerly sought trade and investment from these countries. This strategic shift would allow China to acquire much-needed foreign currencies, technologies, and management know-how (see Chapter 2 for more discussion on this topic).

The democracies welcomed China's move with great enthusiasm. They began to trade with and invest in China as early as the late 1970s, even though China was still a communist state with a protected economy. In addition to the economic benefit for them from engaging with China, their enthusiasm was also built on the hope that with China's economic development, a middle class would emerge, and they would demand democracy. Such a conviction – known as the "engagement approach" (Dobbins & Wyne, 2018) – was based on the experience of democratization in Europe several hundred years ago, especially in England, where the newly formed middle class, in order to protect their personal and property rights, demanded the rule of law and representation in politics (Chen, 2013; Moore, 1966).

---

[2] "Running dog" is a literal translation of the Chinese pejorative 走狗 (zou gou), meaning someone who follows the orders of those more powerful and often evil. Mao Zedong used "imperialist running dogs" to refer to the allies of the United States.

The engagement approach reached a high point when China applied for membership to the World Trade Organization (WTO) in the late 1990s and early 2000s. Against concerns about China's political repression and economic protectionism, engagement advocates in the democracies, especially in the United States, successfully persuaded other countries to admit China to the WTO. Then US president Bill Clinton, an ardent supporter of China's WTO bid, explained his rationale and hope as follows:

> By joining the W.T.O., China is not simply agreeing to import more of our products; it is agreeing to import one of democracy's most cherished values: economic freedom. The more China liberalizes its economy, the more fully it will liberate the potential of its people – their initiative, their imagination, their remarkable spirit of enterprise. And when individuals have the power, not just to dream but to realize their dreams, they will demand a greater say.
>
> *(Clinton, 2000)*

Multinational corporations eagerly followed this call. Jerry Yang, the founder CEO of Yahoo!, recalled in 2007,

> As our young company grew quickly in the late 1990s, the U.S. government, including Congress, made the decision to normalize trade relations with China. Since then, and across Democratic and Republican administrations, the U.S. government has encouraged American businesses – including technology companies – to engage with China, an enormous market and one focused on modernization. With this backdrop, Yahoo! made the choice like many other companies across many other industries to engage in the Chinese market by establishing local operations and providing services to Chinese citizens.
>
> *(Yang, 2007)*

When doing business in China, Yang met a little-known entrepreneur by the name of Jack Ma (Ma Yun in Chinese) and invested in his startup. As Yang put it, "Yahoo! became a shareholder in a Chinese company called Alibaba" (Yang, 2007).

After four decades of rapid economic growth, China's economy has reached US$23 trillion (based on purchasing power parity), larger than that of the United States (US$21 trillion), with a per capita income of US$16,700 and a huge middle class (estimated to be 400 million people). Jack Ma's Alibaba has grown into a US$668 billion global behemoth, while Yahoo!'s core business was sold for less than US$5 billion in 2017.

Despite its extraordinary economic achievement, China has yet to become a responsible member of the international community. Domestically, the CCP has failed to open many sectors of China's economy as promised on entering the WTO. And to the great disappointment of engagement supporters, democracy and the rule of law have not followed the emergence of the middle class in China. Internationally, the CCP imposes its ideology and practices on other countries and firms. As shown in the opening paragraph of this chapter, a well-intentioned inspirational quote from the Dalai Lama, a highly respected global figure and Nobel Peace Prize laureate, could cause one of the best-known brands in the world to be shunned in China.

I.2 TIMES HAVE CHANGED

In the spring of 1989, the death of the reform-minded Chinese leader Hu Yaobang triggered a large-scale pro-democracy demonstration in Beijing's Tiananmen Square. On June 4, 1989, the CCP ordered the military to open fire on the demonstrators, resulting in the Tiananmen Massacre (see Chapter 2). The world focused on China, and the major democracies were debating how to react to the brutal crackdown. The question that I heard most from policy-makers in the democracies was, "How can we democratize China?"

Back then, the question did not seem unrealistic at all. The Chinese economy was small, the Chinese army was not known to have much capability other than killing its own people, and most important of all, the Chinese people seemed ready for a change. So, for the mature democracies, ending the dictatorship in China appeared to be within reach.

Fast-forwarding thirty years, China is now a global superpower economically, militarily, and in international affairs. Instead of converging with the rule of law and democracy, it challenges existing international law and order and undermines the political and economic systems of the democracies. And now the question regarding China asked by leaders of the democracies has become, "How can we protect our democracy from China?"

1.3 "WHO LOST CHINA?"

What went wrong? Why did the emergence of the middle class in China fail to lead to democratization? Why does China's "peaceful" rise (as the CCP claims) fail to give peace of mind to the democracies? What should the democracies do to protect their way of life from the CCP's expansion? In the global marketplace, how should firms from other countries compete with Chinese firms, which are often intricately intertwined with the Chinese state?

In the above-quoted speech supporting China's accession to the WTO, President Clinton criticized the United States' wavering stance on China in the past and joked, "Who lost China?", implying he had found the right policy on China – engagement. Now we know that was an overstatement. The question of "Who lost China?" not only remains but more than ever needs to be addressed.

Indeed, numerous scholars have been trying to explain China's economic success. One of the main genres in this effort is to identify the major institutional forces behind China's economic success, namely, how its political and economic systems affect China's economic performance. There are two opposing views in this debate. One emphasizes the role of the state, and the other the market. The first view, which has been termed "the China model view" or the "Beijing consensus," believes that China's rapid economic growth is the result of the unique model that China has been following, characterized by one-party rule, state intervention in economic activities, dominance of state-owned enterprises (SOEs), and well-designed industrial policies (Lin, 2012). The second perspective, or "the universal model view," argues that the way in which China achieved its economic development is just the same as the method used by Western democracies earlier – relying on "the power of the market" (Zhang, 2019). They further argue that China has benefited from what they call "the latecomer's advantage," namely, that "China could avoid many detours and directly share the technological achievements that others have already obtained" (Zhang, 2019).

Both views have merits, and it is not my focus in this book to discuss which one has more merit. What I want to emphasize here is that they are not intended to (and are therefore unable to) address the questions I raised earlier, because these scholars study China's economic performance from a *China-centric* perspective. More specifically, their concern is what political and economic policies are best for the development of the Chinese economy. For example, the China model view attributes China's economic success to well-designed industrial policies. We need to ask how those policies affect *other countries*. The universal model view believes that China's rise is no different from the rise of other developed countries. This comparison may not be appropriate as most of the other developed countries were small and democratic, and were less interdependent. The universal model view admits that China's rise benefited from taking technologies from other countries, which I agree with. But the question is, did China do it truly through free market exchanges, or by some other means, against the technology-holders' interests?

As China has become the world's largest economy, intentionally or not, its mere existence causes great anxiety among and affects all the countries in the world. And scholars in China have begun to realize it too. They believe that given China's important position in a highly globalized world, all countries are stakeholders in what China does, and they therefore have the right to comment on and influence China. Qin Hui, a well-known scholar in China, commented that "due to globalization, the China factor is becoming bigger and bigger. If you don't understand China, you can't even talk about the United States ... China's problem does not only affect China " (Qin, 2020).

In this sense, we need to examine China's rise *from the perspective of other countries*, and this is what I attempt to achieve in this book. I will examine how certain institutional factors in the past four decades have shaped today's China, how China exerts its powerful impact on the world, and how the world has responded and should respond to it. In developing the themes of my book, I was motivated by two observations. The first is that in contrast to the engagement view (i.e., that economic development ushers in liberalization), the CCP has been steadfastly increasing its power over the past four decades along with the rise of the standard of living in China. The second is the growing integration of the CCP with the Chinese people and businesses. These two trends have enabled the CCP to run the entire country like a giant corporation. And, as I will elaborate on in the book, such a new form of organization, with unprecedented resources and flexibility, will have enormous and far-reaching effects on the world in both state affairs and business operations.

I.4   A GLANCE AT MY BOOK

This book has three parts. In Part I, "The Advantage of Low Human Rights," I explain the political, economic, legal, and cultural factors that paved the path for China's economic development and global expansion.

In Chapter 2, I start with an explanation about the CCP, the most important force in shaping China, with its features that are often overlooked but deserve our attention. For example, unlike political parties in democratic countries, in which citizens are free to participate or leave, the CCP is a Leninist party, which closely resembles a secret society with select and exclusive membership. I build my case concerning how the low human rights environment was created by the CCP, and how it has lowered the costs for the party to push through its policies. I show why the middle class in China today, unlike its counterpart in European history, has failed to push for democracy.

In Chapter 3's analysis of the development of China's legal system, I introduce a framework of two contrasting governance systems – rule-based (relying on public laws) and relation-based (relying on *guanxi* [personal connections]) – and show that people and firms in China rely on the latter to protect their socioeconomic exchanges and interest. An important reason that Chinese people rely on relation-based governance is not because they love the traditional *guanxi* culture but rather because the law is not impartially enforced. However, relation-based governance is not always inferior to rule-based governance: When markets are small and local, the former can be more efficient.

Chapter 4 sheds light on an important factor that has greatly contributed to China's economic performance, and yet is often over-looked: culture. The essence of this chapter is that recent history and the current political economic system of China have created a culture that is strongly materialistic and conducive to productivity growth in China. The combination of Mao Zedong's law-defying spirit and Deng Xiaoping's call to get rich has provided a business culture of poor quality and safety standards.

In a rare historical moment from the last quarter of the twentieth century and the early twenty-first century, these unique political, economic, legal, and cultural factors all coexisted in China. The outcome of the interaction among these factors is the emergence of what I call China, Inc.

In Part II, "The Rise of China, Inc.," I build my case on how the CCP runs the entire country like a giant corporation, the competitive advantages of such an arrangement, and how China, Inc., achieved dominance in key industries.

Chapter 5 presents evidence on the emergence of China, Inc. Since the late 1970s when the CCP embarked on reforms, it has tried to loosen or tighten its control to varying degrees. Eventually, the CCP realized that for its own benefit, it had to increase its control as much as possible. Following this conviction, the CCP has been building what it calls *juguo tizhi* (举国体制), "the system of mobilizing the entire country as a whole." In China, living, working, and doing business are not rights but privileges granted by the party-state. To a great degree, state-owned firms are business units, state-related firms are subsidiaries, Chinese-owned private firms are joint ventures, and foreign firms are franchisees of the party, with the party leader being the CEO of China, Inc. This perspective identifies a key and unique feature of the Chinese political economy: The government and firms are highly integrated to allow China, Inc., to have a firm's agility and a state's resources and power.

Building on the theme that the CCP runs China as a corporation, Chapter 6 shows how the Chinese government formulates and executes its industrial policy like a corporate strategy. The general pattern of China's industrial policy is that first, the CCP identifies certain industries and determines them to be high priorities. Once an industry is designated as strategically important, the party-state will mobilize all necessary resources from across the country to develop this industry. The party-state will also pick some domestic firms as national champions, and at the same time erect barriers against foreign firms entering the industry. With a large, protected domestic market, designated firms will be able to quickly realize scale economies and lower unit production costs. Once a designated domestic firm becomes efficient, the party-state will support it as it goes out and dominates the world market. Three cases are used to show how China's industrial policy has worked. They are electric vehicle batteries, solar panels, and high-speed rail.

Part III, "China, Inc.'s Achilles' Heel and the World's Response," covers the following related topics: the built-in structural weakness of China, Inc., that requires it to have an expansionary global strategy, the effects of the strategy and how other countries have reacted to it, and my policy and strategic suggestions for democratic countries and multinational corporations.

In Chapter 7, I first present a fundamental issue that China, Inc., faces: On the one hand, to maintain the low rights environment in

China, the CCP needs to suppress political participation and discussion in China; on the other hand, to benefit from global trade and investment, the CCP needs to keep China open, which exposes Chinese people to the ideas of democracy and human rights. In its attempt to resolve this issue, the CCP has been using its huge resources to buy support and silence criticism internationally. In doing so, the CCP has reversed the traditional pattern of bribery from individuals and firms bribing state officials to the state (in this case, the Chinese government) bribing elites, firms, and officials in other countries and international agencies. A particularly effective strategy of the CCP to draw supporters and silence criticism is the "Russian doll" method of wrapping the CCP's core interest within layers of Chinese-ness: Chinese state, Chinese culture, and pan-China. As the chapter will show, using this strategy, the CCP nudges foreigners who admire Chinese culture closer to the party, and labels its critics as anti-China.

Chapter 8 documents the changing attitudes of democratic countries toward the CCP's global expansion. In 2020, global favorable views of China have sunk to a new low, according to a survey by Pew Research Center. This chapter provides evidence and analyses to aid the democracies' efforts in dealing with China in its current form. The evidence and analyses show that China under the CCP's dictatorship freely entering other countries poses a greater danger to the democracies than a closed China. The chapter will show that for its political, economic, and social needs, the CCP relies on the democracies more than vice versa. Even though the CCP attacks the values of the democratic countries, it wants to be recognized and respected by the latter. Furthermore, the democracies, especially the United States, serve a vital role for the CCP – acting as an unappreciated opposition party, which, ironically, benefits the CCP.

Chapter 9 focuses on policy considerations for the governments of the democracies and strategic implications for multinational corporations and business executives. Since China needs the democracies more, the latter should stand firm on their demand for China to make meaningful changes. The key to achieve this for the major democracies is to form a coalition focusing on China. I will specify the principles for such a coalition to be effective. I propose a "tit for tat, delink-ready strategy" to policy-makers in the democracies. For their interactions with China to be effective, the democracies must be prepared to drastically reduce links with the Chinese economy, and be willing to use delinking as an option. While delinking is not the goal of the democracies, being ready to use it is a credible threat to push the CCP to change.

For multinational corporations and business executives, this book provides new and unique views on China's political, economic, legal, and cultural systems, such as the China, Inc., perspective and the rule-based versus relation-based framework. Finally, for management scholars, the China, Inc., perspective encourages them to rethink the theory of the firm. Where is the boundary of China, Inc.? What new patterns can we find between firms of different ownerships in China if we view them as different subunits of China, Inc.?

PART I The Advantage of Low Human Rights

2 The Political Foundation of China's Competitiveness and Its Failure to Democratize

> The force at the core leading our cause forward is the Chinese Communist Party. The theoretical basis guiding our thinking is Marxism-Leninism.
>
> Mao Zedong, 1954[1]

> The Chinese Communist Party is China's highest political leading force ... From east, west, south, north to center, from the party, the government, the military, the people to academics, the party leads all.
>
> Xi Jinping, 2018[2]

2.1 THE CHINESE COMMUNIST PARTY IS NOT A "PARTY" BUT A SECRET SOCIETY

The most important concept to understand when examining China is that of the CCP. Political parties in democracies, such as the Democratic Party and the Republican Party in the United States, compete in elections according to the laws, and all citizens are free to join[3]: as their namesake means, literally, let's *party*! If one does not like it, one can leave or switch to another party. In contrast, the CCP is not a party that people can freely join or leave; it is founded based on the principles established by the Russian revolutionary leader Vladimir Lenin (1870–1924). Drawing on the *Communist Manifesto* (Marx and Engels, 1848 (1906)), Lenin believed in communist

---

[1] Z. Mao, 1972. *Quotations from Chairman Mao Tsetung*. Peking: Foreign Languages Press.

[2] (quoted from BBC 2018a. People's Congress Session Ends: Xi Jinping Emphasizes "the Party Leads Everything." *BBC*, March 20 (www.bbc.com/zhongwen/simp/chinese-news-43468026): Accessed October 18, 2020).

[3] Since the two parties do not have formal membership, to "join" means to participate in their activities or to support them.

revolution with the goal of overthrowing capitalism and establishing communism. To achieve this goal, the communists had to establish the dictatorship of the proletariat, which could only be realized by a "revolutionary vanguard party," consisting of the most class-conscious and politically advanced section of the proletariat. In 1921, Mao Zedong and his comrades, encouraged by the victory of the Russian Soviet revolution in 1917, founded the CCP with the following key characteristics.

First, the party's theoretical foundation and core ideology is communism. According to the 2017 version of the Constitution of the Chinese Communist Party, it

> uses Marxism-Leninism ... as its guides to action. Marxism-Leninism reveals the laws governing the development of the history of human society. Its basic tenets are correct and have tremendous vitality. The highest ideal of communism pursued by Chinese Communists can be realized only when socialist society is fully developed and highly advanced. The development and improvement of the socialist system is a long historical process. By upholding the basic tenets of Marxism-Leninism ..., China's socialist cause will ultimately be victorious.
>
> *(Chinese Communist Party, 2017)*

Essentially, according to the communist ideology, there is a known destiny that humankind is predetermined to reach – communism, and the communist party is the only political force that can and must lead humankind to reach it.

Second, the CCP is an organization with exclusive and selective membership. This sets it apart from political parties in the democracies. For example, the Democratic and Republican Parties in the United States do not have a clearly defined "membership." American citizens are free to claim which party they belong to and voluntarily vote for it in elections. In contrast, the CCP's membership is clearly defined. No one can claim he/she is a CCP member without an explicit, lengthy, and elaborate process of admittance. And the bar is quite high: "Members of the Communist Party of China are vanguard fighters of the Chinese working class who possess Communist consciousness. Members of the Communist Party of China must ... be ready to make any personal sacrifice, and dedicate their lives to realizing communism" (Chinese Communist Party, 2017).

Applicants for membership of the party "must complete an application form and be recommended by two full party members." They will be put on a *kaoyan* (observation and test) period to earn the status of "the eager and active party applicant." The length of *kaoyan* is usually one year. If the eager and active applicant successfully passes the test and observation period, then he/she can be admitted to the party, take the oath under the CCP flag, and become a probationary member. The probation period is usually one year. The admission rate is low. For example, in 2014, there were about 22 million applicants, of which only 2 million were accepted to join the party. As McMorrow observed, the CCP's acceptance rate is "on par with the Ivy League" (McMorrow, 2015).

Once one becomes a CCP member, there is no turning back. The party requires its members to "fight for communism for their entire life," unless, of course, the party expels them, which often leads to jail or even execution. Exiting the party of one's free will is severely discouraged and thus punished, in a similar way to when a member of a mafia organization leaves (Catino, 2015).

An important mechanism to control members is the "democratic life meeting." This meeting of various scales is held by all levels of party organizations and branches regularly (weekly or monthly depending on the scale). In the meeting, all members engage in criticism and self-criticism. The official goal of the meeting is to purify members' thoughts, discover and criticize deviant thoughts and activities, and take actions against members who fail the party (Baidu, undated-b). A unique feature of these meetings is that the accused member must undergo self-criticism, in which they are expected to admit their alleged wrongdoings, apologize to the CCP, and denounce and humiliate themselves harshly.

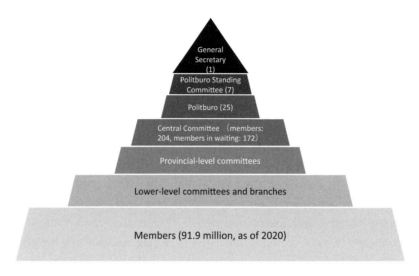

FIGURE 2.1 CCP's organizational hierarchy as of 2020.
Source: Made by author partially based on data from People.cn (2020)

Third, the CCP is highly centralized with a strict hierarchy. The lower-level party organizations obey higher-level party organizations. At the lowest level is the "primary-level Party organization" (commonly known as a "party branch"). All basic *danweis* ("units" – organizations where people work), such as firms (including private firms and foreign firms operating in China), schools, and companies of the People's Liberation Army (PLA), should each form a party branch if they have three or more party members. Party branches obey the higher-level party committees all the way to the general secretary at the top, as shown in Figure 2.1. The politburo (political bureau) is the highest-ranking committee in the party, a unique feature for communist parties, past and present. In the CCP, there is a committee within the politburo known as the standing committee of the politburo. Members of the standing committee enjoy the highest prestige in the party next to the general secretary.

Since 2012, Xi Jinping has been the general secretary of the CCP. His power is nearly absolute, as there are no known checks and balances on his power within the CCP: or within the country,

FIGURE 2.2 Xi Jinping attends a ceremony at Tiananmen Square, Beijing (2019).
Source: Getty Images

for that matter. He dictates China (see Figure 2.2). A natural question then is "how is such a powerful position filled?"

Unlike dynasties or monarchies in which succession is based on blood ties, or democracies in which succession is by vote, no one, including the incumbent party leader and politburo members, knows how the next general secretary is selected or how long their term will be.

On paper, this position is elected (Chinese Communist Party, 2017): every five years, party members elect the party congress, who then elect the central committee, which in turn elects the members of the politburo, its standing committee, and the general secretary. But it is well known that the candidates are pre-determined and everyone is instructed on whom to "vote" for. The right candidates are produced in secret through intense negotiations by current and, sometimes, retired party leaders. Once the candidates are determined, the party leaders will back them and persuade representatives and committee members to vote for them. If a member does not vote as instructed, the consequences will be dire. Thus, new top leaders usually receive unanimous votes.

Since Xi Jinping assumed the position of general secretary, he has put many high-ranking party officials in prison, many for life sentences, and has ordered at least one official, Lai Xiaomin, to be executed (Associated Press, 2021). On paper, their charges are usually corruption. But many China observers believe that the real reason he purged these cadres is that they failed to show personal loyalty to him (*The Economist*, 2014). The more political rivals he purges, the more power he has; but at the same time, the more dangerous his position will be. These purged officials or their allies and families would take any opportunity to seek revenge. In this vicious cycle, as some observers describe vividly with a Chinese idiom, one "rides the tiger and cannot get off." Once Xi steps down, he may get eaten (*Wall Street Journal*, 2014).

Obviously, to be designated for and "elected" to this most powerful and feared position in the party, the candidate needs support from the other powerful people in the party. But once he/she assumes the top post, the general secretary can put any of these powerful people who have supported him in jail. So, realizing this, why would these powerful people "vote" for anyone to take the job? This is the most difficult issue for the dictatorship of the CCP: succession is extremely uncertain and casts a long shadow on all involved in the process.

Finally, the CCP has four functional organs or departments: Organization, Propaganda, United Front Work, and International Liaison. While the function of the Organization Department is straightforward – managing human resources for the party – the other three need more explanation. The International Liaison Department is the "foreign affairs ministry" of the CCP. It develops and manages relationships with political parties in foreign countries. It originally focused on other communist and socialist parties, but has now expanded to nearly all types of political parties worldwide. The most interesting and by far the most noteworthy are the Propaganda and United Front Work Departments.

The Propaganda Department (the official English translation according to the CCP is the Publicity Department) is in charge of shaping the ideology of China and influencing the world's public attitudes. Propaganda refers to "communications to the public that are designed to influence opinion" (Dictionary.com, 2005). While all political parties use propaganda, what distinguishes the CCP from political parties in the democracies are the following: (1) It has the unchecked and absolute power to control and regulate information flows in China. The Propaganda Department publishes guidelines on what information is correct and what information is incorrect and therefore must be banned. Anyone who communicates the incorrect information, such as advocating for American-style democracy or upholding universal human rights, will not only be silenced but may also be imprisoned. (2) It has vast resources with which to operate. Based on several indirect estimates, the Propaganda Department's annual budget is more than US$7 billion (Diresta, Miller, Molter, Pomfret, and Tiffert, 2020; Tatlow, 2020). This is also expected to grow rapidly. For example, a report shows the increase in the budget for the Propaganda Department from 2014 to 2015 was 433 percent (Yang, 2015). It is revealed that in 2018, the department invested US$6 billion to create a giant media outlet named "Voice of China" that integrated three global media empires owned by the party: China Global Television Network, China Radio International, and China National Radio (Yip, 2018).

While governments and political parties in other countries have had propaganda ministries/departments, the United Front Work Department (UFWD) is a unique invention of the Chinese Communist Party. The UFWD is in charge of mobilizing non-CCP people, both in and outside China, to form a broad united alliance to support the CCP's cause (Chinese Communist Party, 2020). It identifies people with influence and status, such as politicians, academics, professionals, businesspeople, and opinion leaders, and directly or indirectly reaches out to them, mobilizing them by promoting the great cause of the CCP. A big part of the UFWD's strategy is to use incentives with resources (such as free trips to China, grants, investment opportunities, and consulting fees) and fame (including awards, key-note speeches, or audiences with CCP leaders in the Zhongnanhai compound, for example). In other words, the CCP essentially bribes people with influence to work for its cause worldwide (see Chapter 7). The UFWD was created in the 1920s during the Chinese Civil War (1927–1949) between the CCP and the Nationalist Party (Kuomintang or KMT) and played an instrumental role in the communists' victory in 1949. Mao placed it at the top of "the three magic weapons" of the CCP, above armed struggle and party-building (Mao, 1939). After nearly a century of practice, the CCP has become very effective at recruiting elites globally to support the party. While many targets go along with the CCP because of the resources they receive from the party, others have become active CCP supporters. Often the targets are so indoctrinated by the CCP that the party's viewpoints have become their own. They speak for the CCP without realizing it (Diresta et al., 2020). In cultivating relations with people of interest, the CCP is also very skilled and subtle. Many targeted people are unaware that they have been worked because the resources the CCP gives them are so spontaneous or indirect that they may even feel that they are doing a favor to the CCP rather than the other way around. For example, a CCP agent cultivating a relationship with a target may casually mention to the target: "I have a friend who is looking to buy lumber from your country, do you happen to know anyone who is in the business?" Or, on learning the target's brother is a shoemaker, the CCP agent may reply: "What a coincidence! A friend of mine in China is looking for a foreign partner in the shoe business! It would be great if you could introduce your brother to him."

The budget of the UFWD was more than US$2.6 billion in 2019, larger than the Chinese Foreign Ministry's, according to Ryan Fedasiuk of Georgetown University (Tatlow, 2020). In recent years, the CCP has increasingly relied on the UFWD for its overseas expansion and has substantially increased its capacity by adding 40,000 cadres to it (Groot, 2016).

The Propaganda Department and the United Front Work Department form the organizational structure to support and implement what scholars call "China's propaganda ecosystem" that controls ideology in China and promotes the CCP's views worldwide, with a total budget exceeding US$10 billion (Diresta et al., 2020, p. 41).

There are many similarities between the CCP and secret organizations such as the mafia. First, the mafia fosters personal loyalty to the boss by destroying public trust (Gambetta, 1988; Li and Filer, 2007). For example, in mafia-controlled markets such as a horse market, the mafia boss would allow subordinates to cheat by selling unhealthy horses as good ones to earn loyalty from them (Gambetta, 1988). It is well-known that CCP leaders allow subordinates who are personally loyal to them to violate rules (such as taking bribes) or make mistakes without consequences (Wedeman, 2017). Second, like the mafia (Catino, 2015), the CCP resorts to extralegal measures to enforce the boss's will and punish violators. The CCP has an all-feared internal organization that disciplines and punishes members known as "Zhong Ji Wei," which stands for "The Central Commission for Discipline Inspection" (CCDI). The CCDI can arrest and detain any CCP members without legal warrants. A running joke in China is that a person by the name Zhong Ji Wei returns to his hotel drunk and cannot remember his room number. He then knocks on every door in the hotel and calls for his roommate to let him in: "I am Zhong Ji Wei! Open the door!" Fearing arrest, every guest jumps out of their room window (Sohu.com, 2017). Third, like the mafia, the CCP uses thugs to do extralegal work. This is especially prevalent in land acquisitions by the party-state. People without an ID are used to threaten and drive owners out of their homes and demolish their properties (Human Rights Watch, 2004). Fourth, both the mafia and the CCP keep their information and operations secretive. In particular, the CCP's decision-making process and its senior officials' health conditions are top secret. It is reported that when the Propaganda Department gives orders to ban certain news items, it does not want to leave any written evidence and only gives oral orders, such as by phone (Chen, 2007; Lu, 2011). Fifth, similar to the mafia's use of illegal actions, the CCP does not follow the laws. There have been cases in which the CCP took a wanted person's family members hostage to force the target to turn themselves in (Voice of America, 2020). In one case the target lived in the United States, and the CCP sent agents illegally to the United States to harass and threaten them and even suggested that they commit suicide (U.S. Department of Justice, 2020a).

2.2 THE PARTY IS THE STATE, IS CHINA, AND IS ANYTHING CHINESE

In 1942, seven years before it assumed power, the CCP set out its position in China: "The party must lead all organizations, including the military, the government, and all civilian organizations"(Yang, 2020). This principle was put into action as soon as the CCP overthrew the Nationalist Party government and established the People's Republic of China (PRC) in 1949. Since then, "the party leads all" (or "the party leads everything") has become the most fundamental principle of the CCP. The party founder Mao Zedong reiterated this principle in 1962 and 1973, and the current party general secretary Xi Jinping has reaffirmed it many times (Wikipedia, 2020h). In 2017, the CCP added this to its Constitution as its guiding political principle. In 2018, the Constitution of the People's Republic of China added a phrase stating that "the leadership of the Chinese Communist Party is the most fundamental feature of the socialism with Chinese characteristics" (Wikipedia, 2020h). According to the CCP Constitution, the party "shall uphold its absolute leadership over the People's Liberation Army and other people's armed forces." (Chinese Communist Party, 2017). The party's omnipresent leadership can be seen from the following institutional arrangements.

The PRC's political system has two subsystems: the party system led by the CCP's Central Committee (which reports to the politburo and to the general secretary), and the government system headed by the State Council. The CCP has the highest power, with the party general secretary assuming the position of chairman of the state.[4] The CCP formulates the overall strategy for the country, and the State Council implements it. For all the important state functions, the CCP sets up two parallel agencies in charge: one is in the CCP organization and the other belongs to the State Council. For example, the CCP's Propaganda Department is in charge of information control, but when it comes to dealing with foreign affairs such as holding news conferences, it will appear under the name of "the State Council Information Office." Another example is that the CCP has its Military Committee, and the Chinese Government has its own Military Committee in parallel. This practice is known as "one agency, two names" (Wikipedia, 2020g). While not all governmental agencies follow the "one agency, two names" arrangement, all the important agencies and organizations follow it.

In addition to the "one agency, two names" arrangement, in every government agency or entity, there is a core group of party officials who control the agency on behalf of the party. The name of the core group of party officials varies depending on the size and level of the agency or entity. Large or higher-level organizations have party committees, and small and lower-level organizations have party branches. For example, all universities in China have a committee of the CCP as the leadership, with the secretary of the party committee as the top leader. The university president must follow the orders of the party secretary. In every rural village, there is a party branch, and the branch secretary calls the shots on everything.

The result of the "party-leads-all" system is that the party not only eclipses the state, but it becomes one with it to create a "party-state," or "one-party state." In such a political system, only one political party has the right to form the government, and that right

---

[4] This top state position, zhuxi, is translated by the CCP as "president," but the precise translation is "chairman."

is codified by the law (the constitution). Any resident in China who wants to be successful in their career must join or at least maintain a good relationship with the party. While historically party-states existed in noncommunist countries such as Nazi Germany, Fascist Italy, and Militarist Japan during World War II, contemporary party-states are mainly found in communist or former communist countries, including the former Soviet Union, and the current communist countries such as North Korea, Cuba, Vietnam, and China.

The party-state is more intrusive than a state. In this sense, the party is larger than the state, as it controls private social spaces that the state usually cannot or does not control. Though people's thoughts and private lives are supposedly individual freedoms according to China's constitution, the party-state can regulate and interfere with how people think and communicate privately. No one can escape the party-state's grip.

A comparison with the democratic system will help us further understand the party-leads-all system. As illustrated in Figure 2.3, in the mature democracies, all entities are subject to the rule of law, the government is limited, and the existence of people and firms is, to a

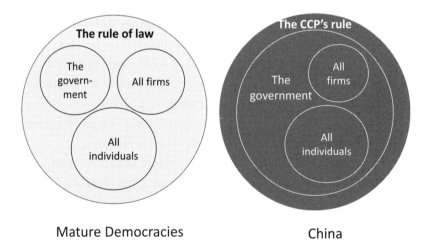

FIGURE 2.3 Political institutions: Mature democracies versus China.
Source: Li and Farrell (2020c)

great extent, independent of the government, whereas in China, the party is omnipresent and, through the government, rules over everything (see Chapter 5).

For the CCP, monopolizing power is its ultimate goal, and the party uses any and all means to achieve it. This is reflected in a book of Xi Jinping's works titled *On the Party's Leadership on All Works*, edited and published by the CCP in 2019, which includes seventy articles and speeches by Xi Jinping on the importance of the party's leadership (Xinhuanet.com, 2019). As I will show in this book, everything the party does, from developing the economy to participating in global trade and investment, must serve the purpose of maintaining its perpetual absolute rule.

To defend and advance one-party rule, the CCP has developed an effective strategy that combines the use of propaganda and the united front work. The former creates ideological arguments, while the latter implements it by mobilizing support worldwide. Ideologically, the CCP turns the relationship between the people and the state (government) upside down: instead of the common notion in the democratic countries that the people support the state, the CCP creates and promotes the view that the state provides the livelihood and resources to the people. So, as a result, the people must be grateful for the state's generosity (Shaomin Li, 1988). The CCP also promotes the view that the people in China overwhelmingly choose the CCP as their leader of their own volition. A frequently used expression by CCP propaganda is that "the Chinese people choose the Chinese Communist Party to lead them ... The Chinese Communist Party and the Chinese people are in the same boat, live and die together, and are connected by blood and flesh" (Xiao, 2020). So, without a visible gap, the ideological persuasion has been smoothly transformed into an ethnic and cultural appeal: the party is not only the state but also China, the Chinese people, and Chinese culture and heritage (see Chapter 7). Organizationally, the CCP uses its united front networks to recruit and mobilize people of Chinese origin worldwide to denounce any negative expression relating to anything Chinese, because doing so ultimately supports the CCP (Fan, 2020) (See Chapter 7 for detailed discussion on this topic).

2.3   THE LOW HUMAN RIGHTS ADVANTAGE

Under such a powerful party-state, China has witnessed high economic growth over the past four decades. While there is little dispute about China's high economic performance, little consensus exists on how to explain it. As briefly mentioned in Chapter 1, the institutional theorists, who study how political and economic systems affect economic performance, offer two main competing explanations. The first school (or "the China model view") emphasizes the advantage of state interventions in China's economic growth (Lin, 2012; Stiglitz, 2008). They attribute China's rapid economic growth to the one-party system: its efficiency in allocating resources, its reliance on large state-owned enterprises (SOEs), and its visionary industrial policies. In contrast, the second school (or "the universal model view") believes that the high growth of China's economy is primarily due to the weakening of the role of the party-state and liberalization and marketization (Li, Li, and Zhang, 2000; Zhang, 2019). They argue that newly allowed individual choices, combined with emerging market opportunities, are the keys to releasing productivity and creativity that are much needed for economic growth. China's intellectuals, who are accustomed to the "left-leaning vs right-leaning" categorization, labelled the first school as "leftists" for its emphasis on the role of the government, and the second "rightists" for its championing of the free market and individual liberty (Qin, 2007).

In fact, both schools overlook another important factor: a powerful ruling party that suppresses many fundamental rights of the people (Qin, 2007). According to this perspective, neither the leftists nor the rightists correctly pinpoint the key factor that distinguishes China's economic advantage over the democracies. It is true that China has the traditional advantage of less developed countries in having abundant low-cost labor. However, what sets China apart from other economies, developed or less developed, is China's low human rights advantage. According to the Rule of Law Index developed by the World Justice Project, China's Fundamental Rights Score is the third lowest in the world (126th out of 128 countries) with a value of 0.29 (0 = lowest and 1 = highest). Its Constraints on Government Powers Score is among the lowest (ranked 123rd out of 128 countries) with a value of 0.32 (0 = lowest, 1 = highest) (World Justice Project, 2020). The CCP deprives people of their rights for political participation, suppresses their opinions, persecutes all faiths that are not communist[5] (Smith, 2019b), and disregards social justice (Li, 2013a). Instead, the party promotes a materialistic culture and directs people's energy in a race to "get rich first" (Deng, 1985) (see Chapter 4 for more detailed discussion). This, aided by a collective memory of poverty imprinted by decades of Mao's economic deprivation, has released tremendous productive power on a scale unrivalled in the contemporary world.

Of course, if China had remained closed, such power would not have achieved much productively. However, China opened its doors to the world, and the world embraced China. Globalization and China's admission into the World Trade Organization have enabled it to find a very productive use of its power. Under the low rights advantage, China has been able to arbitrarily and forcibly lower the transaction costs of key economic inputs: labor, land, capital, and nonrenewable resources. The CCP can easily ban resource holders such as farmers or workers from bargaining and take away their entitlements in order to facilitate foreign investment and privatization. Under the CCP's dictatorship and low welfare policy, China does not have the headaches present in the democracies of serving diverse needs of different constituencies. These may include the burden of the high-welfare states, strong unions that scare investors away, or farmers and environmental protection groups to keep a check on the commercialization of land. Everything can be cleared for investment and economic growth. The negative consequences of such unbridled

---

[5] Since the CCP demands absolute submission of the people, it cannot allow any religion that demands the same.

capital accumulation and economic growth, such as capital shortage and overcapacity, can be temporarily mitigated by injecting resources from outside via foreign investments and product sales abroad. Such an economic development model powered by a huge low-cost labor force with minimal consumption ability, which otherwise would have been unsustainable if China were closed, is balanced by two powerful forces: the insatiable appetite for cheap consumer goods and an over-supply of capital seeking high returns in the mature democracies. While China's domestic friction between the CCP and the people due to the low rights condition is alleviated since the economy grows fast (thanks to the two forces), the preexisting problems in the mature democracies are actually exacerbated. In democracies that are more free-market oriented such as the United States, the workers (especially those in the manufacturing industries that face increasing competition from China) are pressured to accept pay cuts in order to keep their jobs. In contrast, in democracies that offer high welfare such as the Scandinavian countries, the influx of immigrants who have lost their jobs as a result of competition from China worsens the tension between the new settlers and old dominions. For both free-market and high-welfare countries, competition from China makes their job market and welfare burden worse off. Naturally, more and more of them become less receptive to Chinese products and erect higher trade barriers. Furthermore, China's ability to attract the most foreign direct investment in the world greatly diverts attention away from less developed countries and reduces their chances of obtaining capital, technologies, and management know-how.

Interestingly, policymakers and researchers explain China's economic success according to their own preferences (Qin, 2007; Zhang, 2019). The left-leaning camp marvels at China for strong and decisive government intervention, while the right-leaning camp praises its minimal social welfare burden. Ironically, in the democracies, neither left-leaning nor right-leaning governments can replicate the iron-fisted, rights-crushing policy to bulldoze through houses and farms to build, mine, and develop.

Even more ironic is that the right–left debate on China's political economy has missed an important point: the tug of war between the right-leaning camp and the left-leaning camp has prevented either side from gaining any power and resources redistributed by the party-state. For example, when the left-leaning camp has the upper hand, the CCP will gladly increase government power without correspondingly increasing government accountability. In 2020, the government initiated a healthcare reform that moved a large portion of the individual allowance to the state to give itself more discretion in using the funds. But this new centralization was not accompanied by any new services from the state (Xin, 2020). When the right-leaning camp gains favor, the CCP will happily reduce already low government accountability without granting more individual freedom. Since the 1980s, the party-state has gradually reduced its responsibility to provide jobs to university graduates, but it still does not allow graduates or anyone else to freely migrate into major cities with necessary residents' rights, such as working on local-preferred jobs, purchasing an apartment, or sending their children to school (Zhang, 2013a). As the well-known social critic Professor Sun Liping commented, no matter whether the public policy turns left or right, the same powerful group always gains and the same weak group always loses (Sun, 2009). In the process of left–right swings, the CCP shrinks social spaces from both sides and grabs more power. Some scholars (Qin, 2007) call this pattern "inchworm contraction": when one end contracts, the other does not expand (see Figure 2.4).

In terms of economic competition, the relationship between China and the mature democracies is reminiscent of the rivalry between the North and the South in the United States before the Civil War (Qin, 2007). Economists Robert Fogel and Stanley Engerman (Fogel and Engerman, 1995 (1974)) contended that the use of slaves and the so-called gang system of labor (closely monitored small work groups) enabled the Southern slave farms to be more productive and profitable than the free farms in the North. The implication of their findings is that if both sides were to compete freely

FIGURE 2.4 Inchworm contraction.
Upper panel: inchworm in a normal movement.
Lower panel: inchworm in a contracting movement.
Source: Author

without the military intervention of the North, the totally inhumane slavery system would have an edge and even defeat the North economically, as the South could freely adopt technologies and attract capital from the North. Today, the mature economies face similar competition from China: China outcompetes the democracies, and, more importantly, the low rights system of China will not go away on its own (see Chapter 8 for more discussions on this topic).

2.4 THE PARTY'S HIGH PRIORITY: ECONOMIC DEVELOPMENT

In the past four decades, the CCP has given economic development very high priority. However, this strategy was formulated by the CCP after a long and turbulent period of revolution and political movements, during which the Chinese people paid a heavy price.

In 1949, after decades of civil war, the Communists, led by Mao Zedong, defeated the Nationalists (Kuomintang), and established the People's Republic of China on the principles of Marxism and Leninism. From the onset of the PRC to the end of Mao's reign in 1976, the CCP focused on continuing the proletarian revolution and political movements. Economic policies were formulated for this goal as well, such as the rapid collectivization of agriculture and nationalization of industries. Unfortunately, these measures failed to deliver economic growth because they took away incentives for people to work. But politically, they helped the CCP consolidate power and control the masses by removing their means of production. With the economy worsening, the CCP's political repression intensified with numerous political purges. According to Li Honglin, a noted political historian in China, from 1949 to 1966, the party had at least nineteen such nationally recognized purges (Li, 1999a). One of the biggest purges was the Anti-Rightist Movement (1957–1959), in which party officials, scholars, writers, artists, and other intellectuals who expressed views different from the party were punished. While the number of victims has been kept secret by the CCP, researchers estimate that it is between one and two million or even higher (Wikipedia, 2020a). In spite of (or maybe because of) the many former colleagues persecuted through these efforts, Mao did not feel secure. In 1966, an increasingly paranoid Mao waged the Great Proletarian Cultural Revolution, during which many people were killed. As always, the CCP has never published the number of victims. Various estimates put the number of deaths between hundreds of thousands and 20 million (Strauss and Southerl, 1994). The Cultural Revolution was also pushing the economy toward total collapse. In 1976 Mao died, presenting a historic moment for China to alter his ultra-leftist course. Chapter 1 briefly mentioned how the CCP leaders seized the opportunity. Here I will elaborate in more detail.

The post-Mao CCP, under the leadership of Deng Xiaoping, Hu Yaobang, and Zhao Ziyang, made an appreciable transition from waging political campaigns to focusing on economic development. Such a shift was desperately needed not just for the economy but also the party's rule to survive.

They took a pragmatic approach and followed the developmental strategy of "feeling the stones to cross the river" (People.cn, 2018), a rare admission that they did not have a clear strategy. Their trial-and-error approach precipitated what is known as the "Thought Liberation Movement" (Li, 1999a), which encouraged the party-state to change communist economic practices and adopt some capitalist measures, as the latter provide stronger incentives for people to work.

A debate soon broke out between the traditional communists and the reform-minded liberal communists on whether China was embracing capitalism, a loaded label that could end any communist official's career. Deng Xiaoping, the *de facto* supreme leader of the communist party, used the following analogy to defend adopting some capitalistic measures in the reform: "it does not matter whether it is a black cat or a white cat; as long as it catches mice, it is a good cat" (Deng, 1962).[6] His clever comment, which eventually became his trademark, effectively defused the debate on capitalism versus socialism and freed the country to seek efficient ways to run the economy.

After some exploration, the reformists adopted two key policy measures. Domestically, they decentralized power from Beijing to incentivize local governments to create more output. Internationally, they opened the door for foreign investments in an attempt to obtain much-needed capital, technologies, and managerial expertise.

This two-pronged strategy worked. From 1978 to 1988, China's GDP grew 2.6 times, averaged 9.6 percent growth per year, and GDP per capita increased from 379 yuan (US$126) to 1,355 yuan (US$451) (National Bureau of Statistics of China, 1997, p. 42). While the reform measures boosted the economy, they also brought rampant corruption as a result of the collusion of government officials and newly emerging private entrepreneurs.

In December 1986, a student demonstration broke out at the University of Science and Technology of China in the city of Hefei, located in the southern central province Anhui. The triggering event was the CCP's manipulation of a local election. It is common knowledge that all elections are ultimately controlled by the CCP, so normally no one would voice any objection. But these young, naive students were outraged and started demonstrating. In response, the

---

[6] This is a phrase that is attributed to Deng, and Deng used it many times. The first time he was publicly heard using it was in 1962, and he used yellow cat instead of white cat. Since the late 1970s, his "black cat, white cat" phrase has been widely viewed as the key theoretical foundation for China's reform.

general secretary, Hu Yaobang, showed uncharacteristic sympathy toward the students and angered the party's old guard. The next year, Deng Xiaoping and other high-ranking party members, including Bo Yibo and Song Renqiong, summoned Hu to a "democratic life meeting" (see description earlier in this chapter). The meeting lasted several days, during which Hu was ferociously attacked and humiliated. He was forced to perform a harsh "self-criticism" (see Section 2.1 on "self-criticism") and to step down. The sacking of Hu by the old guard deepened existing social problems rather than resolving any of them. Nationwide, the common people's perception of corruption heightened and public discontent was brewing (Li, 1999a). The majority of the people felt that Hu was mistreated and sympathized with him.

In April 1989, Hu Yaobang suffered a heart attack and died. A huge crowd immediately gathered in Beijing's Tiananmen Square to mourn him, and over the course of a month it grew to one million people by May 20th (Xiao, 2019). The public mourning eventually turned into a mass demonstration demanding the eradication of corruption and the introduction of democracy. Quickly gaining momentum, the demonstration grew out of control and greatly worried the CCP. On June 4th, the People's Liberation Army marched in Beijing and opened fire on the demonstrators (mostly college students), creating what is known as the 1989 June 4th Tiananmen Crackdown.

After the crackdown, many Chinese were dispirited and scared; participants in the demonstration went into hiding or exile. Many government officials who supported the demonstration were punished. Foreign investment dried up, and the economy ran into the ground.

In 1992, in an attempt to alleviate the fear among Chinese and foreign investors caused by the crackdown and save the economy, Deng Xiaoping conducted his famous "Southern Tour" from Beijing to the southern city of Shenzhen and openly called for continuing economic reform and opening up further. His call restored some confidence of both potential investors and Chinese people in the

Chinese government and gave the economy a much-needed boost. A new round of economic development started. By now, the CCP had reconfirmed its focus on economic development instead of waging political movements that had been the main task of the party for decades. Deng advised his comrades to continue this trend and lay low: put aside issues with neighboring countries, do not confront the United States, and just focus on developing China's economy. He reportedly used a Chinese idiom to express his strategy, "*taoguang yanghui*" (China National Radio, 2014), which Chinese official media translates as "hide one's ambitions and disguise its claws"[7] (*China Daily*, 2010). Essentially, hide China's capabilities and bide its time. The implication here is to dominate the world once the party-state is ready, and it certainly served the party-state very nicely, as will be discussed later in this book.

Doubling down on its strategy to develop the economy, the party-state set GDP growth as its main measure to gauge governmental performance at both the central (national) and local levels. Nationally, the party-state would decree a certain percentage number for GDP growth as the goal every year.[8] If that number for a given year was 8 percent, it would be known as "*bao-ba*," where "*bao*" means to guarantee or to ensure and "*ba*" means eight. GDP growth target numbers for 2010, 2015, and 2019 are 8 percent, 7 percent, and 6 percent, respectively (Bai, 2019). The CCP's use of such centralized economic goals stands in sharp contrast with that of democracies.

In democratic countries, citizens use their votes to evaluate the overall performance of the government and its officials. The criteria are flexible depending on the voters' priorities at the time, be they social welfare, environmental preservation, economic growth, or others. However, in China, free voting is not an option, and people

---

[7] Or "hiding one's ambitions and disguising one's claws."

[8] The Chinese government did not set a GDP growth goal in 2020 due to the Covid-19 pandemic (*Xinhua*, 2020). Commentary: Why Does China not Set Specific Economic Growth Target? *Xinhuanet*, May 22 (www.xinhuanet.com/english/2020-05/22/c_ 139079493.htm): Accessed November 16, 2020.

do not have effective means to evaluate governmental performance. The only entity that can do so is the party-state itself. During the Mao era, the party-state evaluated cadres' performance by how loyal they were to Mao. In comparison, using GDP growth as a key measure is, borrowing from Mao, a "great leap forward." It is more objective and beneficial to social welfare, assuming that the population as a whole benefits from economic growth.

Corresponding to the shift in priorities, the CCP's personnel policy – promotion and demotion of local officials – has become closely linked with the economic performance of the region under the official in question. Essentially, the party-state treats local officials as CEOs of companies (Walder, 1995), and rewards or punishes them based on the profitability of the company (i.e., the growth of local GDP).

With such a high-powered incentive, local officials have engaged in fiercely competitive games for promotion, or the "promotion tournament," as it is termed in China (Zhou, 2007). They use any means at their disposal to boost GDP growth of their regions (Luo, She, and Chen, 2015; Park, Li, and Zhang, 2015). They build anything and everything – as long as it can enlarge GDP: manufacturing plants, shopping malls, apartment buildings, highways, and government offices so massive that Washington's Capitol Hill pales in comparison (Park et al., 2015). Under the promotion tournament model and aided by the low rights advantage, China's GDP has been increasing rapidly. From 1992 to 2019, China's GDP grew thirty-three times, from US$427 billion to US$14.3 trillion (current US$, unadjusted for purchasing power parity), averaging to about 13 percent annually. In comparison, the world's GDP grew 3.4 times in the same period, from US$25.5 trillion to US$87.7 trillion, with an average annual growth rate of 4.6 percent (World Bank, 2020b). Based on purchasing power parity, China's GDP reached US$23 trillion in 2019, surpassing that of the United States (which was US$21 trillion in 2019) to become the largest economy in the world (CIA, 2020a) (see Figure 2.5).

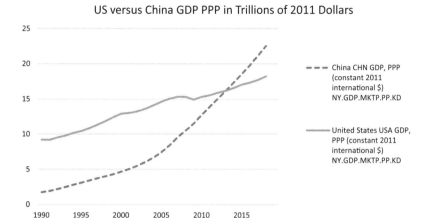

FIGURE 2.5 GDP, United States and China, 1990–2018.
Source: Li and Farrell (2020c) and World Bank (2019b)

But using GDP as the main objective[9] to measure officials' performance has its built-in problems. First, it encourages local officials to pursue projects that may have little value to society (i.e., not improving social welfare). As long as it can add to the gross product statistics, they will want to do it. If the project happens to serve a social need and/or be useful, that would be a nice side-effect. As a result, the promotion tournament wastes substantial resources. Expensive high-speed railways are constructed for remote destinations with few riders, high-rise apartment buildings are built in unpopulous cities, and newly developed shopping malls remain empty. Cities cursed with such wasteful construction have earned the name "ghost towns" (Fong, 2018).

Second, this developmental model relies heavily on capital investment and debt-financing. These numerous projects generate little revenue and profit and, unsurprisingly, cannot repay their debts. In order to keep the GDP growing, local governments need to borrow more and more, thus feeding into an inefficient and unsustainable

[9] The CCP still uses other criteria to measure officials' performance, such as loyalty to the party's leadership and social stability.

cycle. The incumbent party secretary of a region tends to borrow liberally to fund projects and build their achievements. By the time the debts need to be paid, they have already been promoted, only to leave a pile of debt for their successors.

Third, the tournament encourages local officials to cook the books (Li, Selover, and Stein, 2011). Overreporting GDP growth has become a common practice at all levels of government. The close tie between GDP growth statistics and promotions has prompted the people to joke that "officials produce numbers, and numbers produce officials" ("官出数字,数字出官"). The problem of overreporting is so bad that even the central government does not rely on the statistics provided by local governments for its decision-making. For example, China's Premier Li Keqiang reportedly does not believe the accuracy of Chinese GDP statistics. According to a March 15, 2007, declassified US diplomatic cable (released by Wikileaks), Li, who was the party secretary of Liaoning Province at the time, told the then-US ambassador to China, Clark Randt, that Chinese GDP figures were "manmade" and therefore unreliable: "for reference only" (Minter, 2014).

Fourth, to encourage investment by private businesses, the party-state must provide very strong incentives, such as offering tax breaks, providing low-cost land, and suppressing workers' wages and welfare. All these policies favor capital at the expense of workers and taxpayers; thus contributing to China's widening inequality.

2.5   WHY THE MIDDLE CLASS IN CHINA APPEARS TO NOT WANT DEMOCRACY

Indeed, as the engagement supporters from the democracies, such as former US President Bill Clinton, have hoped (see Chapter 1 for the engagement approach and Clinton's remark), China has produced not only rapid economic growth but also a huge middle class in a relatively short period of time. However, what they failed to anticipate is that, unlike their counterparts in Europe's history, the newly emerged middle class in China has been unable to push the country to democratize. Why did the Chinese middle class fail to do so? What makes them different from their European counterparts? To answer these questions, we need to briefly review the literature on the role of the middle class in democracy and democratization.[10]

A well-established theory on the role of the middle class in democracy is built on the relationship between economic modernization and political democratization. It argues that as the economy develops and modernizes, people's living standard improves. Increased income opens the door to more educational opportunities, social mobility, and freedom, and encourages people to assert themselves in social and political matters. In short, it promotes democratization (Dahl, 1971; Huntington, 1991; Lipset, 1959). The theory continues to argue that people in the middle of the socioeconomic hierarchy with a comfortable, bourgeois lifestyle and modest assets have greater incentives to push for democratization than those above and below. The lower class simply does not have adequate economic means, education levels, or enough free time to participate in public affairs and push for democratization. On the other side of the spectrum, the upper class has ample economic resources and connections to authorities that grant them more privileges and protections. The middle class occupies an interesting intermediate space: They fear that an undemocratic government and the upper class may encroach on the property rights they do have, and that is what has pushed them to play the most important role in democratization in Europe. As political scientist Barrington Moore puts it succinctly, "No bourgeois, no democracy" (Moore, 1966).

What kind of people are in the middle class in today's China, and how do they differ from their counterparts in Europe from a few hundred years ago?

---

[10] The literature reviewed here is primarily about Europe's historical experience. Political scientists have found that the role of the middle class in democracy and democratization in the contemporary developing countries is different from that of the early-industrialized countries in Europe (see J. Chen, 2013. *A Middle Class without Democracy: Economic Growth and the Prospects for Democratization in China*. New York: Oxford University Press, for a review).

Many methods exist to define China's middle class, and each gives its own flavor and numbers (Chen, 2013; Zhu and Liu, 2020). However, the variations in definition and the estimated size do not affect our analysis of how the party-state creates and controls the middle class.

According to political scientists, the middle class consists of people who possess a set of socioeconomic characteristics that qualitatively distinguish them from the upper and lower classes. More specifically, these socioeconomic characteristics can be analyzed from the following three dimensions: (1) means of production (e.g., do they own businesses?); (2) position in authority structure (do they manage people?); and (3) possession of skills and expertise (are they professionals?) (Wright, 1997). Based on this definition, Jie Chen (2013) developed an occupation-based, qualitative measurement to identify the members of the middle class in China, which consists of the following three groups:

(1) Managers. These are managers of any type of organization, including state-owned, collectively owned, or privately owned enterprises. The privately owned enterprises can be further divided into Chinese owned, foreign owned, or jointly owned by both entities.
(2) Professionals. Broadly defined, this group includes people with specialized skills that require higher education, including programmers, doctors, lawyers, academics, engineers, artists, and other types of specialists.
(3) White-collar office workers. This group consists of people who are staff members in party and government agencies, and office workers and staff members in all types of enterprises and nonprofit organizations.

The Chinese government defines the middle class as people with annual income ranging from 60,000 to 500,000 yuan (US$7,250 to US$62,500) (China Power Team, 2020). A typical economic profile of the middle class is that the person lives in a city, holds a job in one of the above occupations, owns or is in the process of buying an apartment, has or can afford to have a car, and takes vacation trip(s) every year (Chen, 2013; Zhu and Liu, 2020).

In Chen's 2008 survey in China, 24.4 percent of respondents belonged to the middle class. In a 2020 study on the middle class by

CITIC Securities (one of the largest financial companies in China), the authors put the estimate of China's middle class at 20–30 percent of the population, or 280–420 million people (Zhu and Liu, 2020). Some even estimated that 707 million Chinese are in the middle class (50.8 percent of the population) (China Power Team, 2020).

What is the political attitude of the middle class in China? Do they support democracy? Chen's work may give us some clues. As all survey researchers in China know, interviewing people about their political attitude is risky – for both the interviewer and the interviewee. If the questions are deemed sensitive or subversive by the CCP, the interview will be stopped, at best, or, at worst, the people involved may be detained or even expelled from the country (see (Tempest, 1995; Yu, 2013) for examples). As Chen explained in his survey research, his questions were worded in a way to reduce as much risk as possible and ensure the safety of his interviewees.

Chen's survey gives us a very grim picture of the middle class's attitude toward democracy. He found an overwhelming majority of the middle-class people surveyed (76–77 percent) were against demonstrations and forming organizations outside of the party-state. He also found that 75 percent agreed that "government leaders are like the head of a family; I should always follow their decisions and I don't need to participate in government decision making." Similarly, 72 percent believed that "measures to promote political reform should be initiated by the party and government, not by ordinary people like me." Perhaps most telling, the majority of those surveyed (70–75 percent) felt that democracy means elections of government officials *within*, not outside, the CCP. Chen concluded that the middle class in China,

> shuns political liberties such as the freedom to demonstrate and form organizations. They are neither interested in democratic institutions, such as the fully competitive election of leaders without restriction on political parties, nor enthusiastic about participating in government affairs and politics ... the new middle

class in China *now* is unlikely to serve as an agent or supporter of
fundamental political change toward democracy

(Chen, 2013, p. 90)

Is it possible that these interviewees did not reveal their true attitude
toward democracy? Certainly. Expressing one's true attitude is very
dangerous in China. There are cases in which people privately com-
municated their support for democracy to their friends and were
punished by the government. For example, Chen Shouli, a 41-year-
old construction supervisor, made a joke in a chat group about a
rumored love triangle involving a celebrity and a high-level CCP
official in 2017. Four days later, he was jailed by the police for five
days (Dou, 2017). Thus, what people might say is one thing, but what
they believe is another. There is ample evidence that the middle class
has become increasingly aware and critical of the party-state's behavior: runaway corruption, poor quality and unequal opportunity in
education, restrictions on living in cities, and lack of financial freedom (Chen, 2013; Wong, 2013). Furthermore, a large number of
middle class adults continually flock to the United States to give birth
to their children, who will then be entitled to US citizenship
(MacLeod, 2015). They gain foreign residences and end up investing
in democracies overseas (Nesheim, 2019).

But what makes China's middle class so different from their
European counterparts?

In Europe, England was at the vanguard of democratization. In
pre-modern England, there were relatively strong checks on the monarch by the contractual relationship that was established between the
monarch and other classes, including the merchant class. Other forces
that countered the king's discretion include an assertive parliament
and a relatively independent judiciary (Acemoglu, Johnson, and
Robinson, 2005; Kiser and Barzel, 1991; Moore, 1966). These checks
limited the monarch's power mainly to taxation; they could not
confiscate people's properties at will. This made the merchants and
bourgeoisie relatively more independent of the monarch. Merchants,
shop owners, and international traders by and large obtained their

wealth not because of, but rather in spite of, the monarch. Thus when they pushed for democratic change, not only were they willing to publicly demand participation in politics but they also had the *resources* to do so (Acemoglu et al., 2005; Kiser and Barzel, 1991). The bourgeoisie's financial independence from the crown was the economic foundation for their ability to push for political democracy (Acemoglu et al., 2005; Kiser and Barzel, 1991; Moore, 1966).

In contrast, today's China grants no one, including not just the middle class but also the upper class and the ultra-rich, independence from the CCP. Ren Zhiqiang, a successful real estate developer, was handed an eighteen-year prison term for implicitly criticizing the CCP's general secretary Xi Jinping in 2020 (Buckley, 2020). Jack Ma, the founder of Alibaba, also faced punishment for his actions. He called for more financial reforms a few days before the planned initial public offering (IPO) of Ant Group's stocks, in which he has controlling shares. His remarks were viewed as a criticism of the Chinese financial regulators, so right before the planned IPO date, "Xi Jinping personally scuttled" what would have been "the world's biggest IPO" (Yang and Wei, 2020).

The dependence of China's middle class on the CCP is accomplished by the party-state's "carrot and stick" strategy, which consists of both positive and negative enforcement. The party-state has made itself the only gatekeeper and sole benefactor – and disciplinarian – through whom people in China may achieve (or lose) middle-class status.

First, the party-state is China's largest employer. As of 2018, 173 million people were employed in nonprivate organizations, including government agencies, agencies relying on government funding, state-owned and collectively owned firms, and firms in which the state had invested (National Bureau of Statistics of China, 2019, Table 4-5). Of that total, about 7.2 million are party-state officials and staff, and an estimated 50 million are paid from the government budget (China Economic Weekly, 2016). The organizational structure of the party-state is extensive and complicated. In the hierarchy of the Chinese government system, there is one central government at the top, 30 provinces and equivalents, 333 district level cities, 2,851 counties and equivalents, and 39,945 town and village level units (National Bureau of Statistics of China, 2019, Table 1-1). A county-level government has more than 140 agencies, ranging from party committees, all sorts of bureaus such as an "old cadre administration bureau" (maintaining the perks and privileges of retired officials), and many associations such as an "overseas friendship connection association" (recruiting overseas Chinese to work for China) (Baidu, 2010). Such a vast web of government agencies has a huge demand for workers, creating the bulk of China's rapidly expanding middle class. Take my own class at Peking University as an example (major in economics, 1978–1982): our class had eighty graduates, and *all* were assigned a government job except those who went abroad. Since then, less than half have left their government jobs, and the majority are either still employed by the government or retired from government jobs.

Second, the party-state controls large resources. Directly, the Chinese government controls about 56 percent of GDP through taxes, fees, and state-owned firms (Li and Alon, 2020). It uses these resources, its power, regulations, and policies to provide economic opportunities to people and organizations who hold ties to CCP officials or strongly support the party-state. Shen Jilan (申纪兰) (1929–2020) and her husband, who were both ordinary farmers in Northern China, joined the CCP when they were young. She was later awarded the title of "model worker" by the party, and was made a "People's Representative" (who has the privilege to participate in the People's Congress and vote on issues) by the party from 1954 to 2020 for thirteen consecutive terms (five years per term) and had always voted to support all of the CCP's proposals, thus earning the nickname "automatic voting machine." Because of her loyalty to the party, the party has given her and her family many resources and opportunities. In 1985, the party gave her a hard-to-get license to produce the special metal ferrosilicon. In 1993, a party leader visited her and gave her village 3 million yuan (US$430,000) to build a water supply system. Shen also owned two companies, one of which had an initial investment of 50 million yuan (US$7.1 million). Her children have done well also. Her son is a mayoral rank[11] cadre in the government, and her daughter is a colonel in the People's Liberation Army (Li, 2014).

In terms of negative enforcement, first, the party-state can easily discipline, fire, or incarcerate any state employees deemed disloyal to the party. Bi Fujian, a star anchor at CCTV (China Central Television), China's largest official TV station, was dismissed for singing a parody song at a private dinner making fun of late CCP leader Mao Zedong (BBC, 2015a). Cai Xia, a retired professor at the Central Party School, criticized Xi Jinping and the CCP in a private conversation in 2020. When the CCP learned of this, it expelled her from the party, cancelled her retirement pension and benefits, and confiscated her bank accounts (Yew, 2020).

Second, the party-state can easily take over or close any organization or business if the owner or the organization criticizes the party-state. For example, in 2019 the Chinese government shut down the Unirule Institute of Economics in Beijing for promoting economic liberalization and democracy in China (Wong, 2019).

Third, the party-state can easily force a private firm to punish or fire an employee whom they view as subversive or troublesome. A friend of mine who worked at a private IT firm in China forwarded a WeChat message from one chat group to another on June 4, 2019, to commemorate the anniversary of the 1989 Tiananmen Crackdown. Days later, he was summoned to the police station to be warned and censured. But that was not all: The police further ordered his employer to fire him, and he lost his job.

Fourth, the party-state can easily make life difficult for the family of a dissident. They have ordered landlords not to rent to the

---

[11] The ranks of the Chinese government are, from high to low, national, provincial, mayoral, county, town, and village. Mayoral rank is considered fairly high.

family and schools not to admit their children. Li Heping, a human rights lawyer in China, was jailed in 2015 for defending victims of government human rights violations. The government also ordered the elementary school to reject his 6-year-old daughter. Yuan Shanshan, the wife of imprisoned human rights lawyer Xie Yanyi, and their three children were evicted from their home and have been repeatedly rejected by landlords, all because of police interference (Wang, 2016).

The party is especially vigilant about any inkling of organized opposition, especially since this is how the CCP itself defeated the incumbent Nationalist Party, for the CCP had a better organization. During the Cultural Revolution, many young fans of Mao organized "Mao Zedong Thought study groups" and were thrown in jail, precisely because they *organized* (Yang, 1988). In today's China, organized oppositions (which are very rare) and their leaders are severely punished by the party. In 1998, a group of Chinese democrats – including Wang Youcai, Xu Wenli, Wu Yilong, Zhu Yufu, and others – formed the China Democracy Party. They were all arrested, tried, convicted, and sentenced to long prison terms (Baidu, undated-a; Canada, 2020). Essentially, China under the CCP has "little room for dissent." If you criticize the party, "their [the party's] goal is to make you feel helpless" (Wong, 2020).

The partnership of these positive and negative incentives works so effectively that even individuals with large economic resources realize very clearly how risky it is to demand democracy from the party-state. Whatever they have will quickly be taken away if they criticize the party.

Due to a weak, party-dependent middle class and no formidable opposition, democratization has been elusive in China. Indices developed by international research organizations that monitor and measure the development of democracy, political and economic freedoms, and free press continue to echo this sentiment.

According to "Freedom in the World 2020" by Freedom House, China's Global Freedom Score is 10 out of 100, with Finland (100) and

South Sudan (−2) having the highest and the lowest scores, respectively. China is categorized as "Not Free" out of three categories: "Free," "Partly Free," and "Not Free." China's Internet Freedom Score is 10 out of 100, the lowest in the world (Iceland has the highest score of 95) (Freedom House, 2020).

According to the Heritage Foundation, China is in the "Mostly Unfree" group and is ranked 103rd out of 180 countries, with an Economic Freedom Score of 59.5 (100 = most free, 0 = most unfree) (Heritage Foundation, 2020).

China's press freedom rank is among the lowest and deteriorating: It ranked 173rd and 177th out of 180 countries in 2013 and 2019, respectively, according to Reporters without Borders. China's Press Freedom Score is 78.5, very close to the worst score of 85.8 of North Korea (the best score is 7.9 of Norway (Reporters without Borders, 2020).

2.6   SUMMARY

This chapter explained how the CCP is organized and controls the political system, forming a unique party-state that rules China. It further revealed how such a system of total control creates a low human rights environment that enables the party-state to achieve its objectives with few costs and little resistance. In the past four decades, China has achieved rapid economic growth, creating a large middle class in the process. However, because of its total dependence on the CCP for lives, work, and wealth, the newly emerged middle class is in no position to demand political changes or push for democratization in China.

3   China's Legal System Is Not about the Rule of Law

The Advantages and Limits of the Relation-Based System

China has laws, but no rule of law.

Mo Shaoping[1] (BBC, 2015b)

3.1   INTRODUCTION: CHINA'S LACK OF THE RULE LAW

Professor Jerome Cohen, a founder and pioneer of Chinese legal studies in the West, wrote about his impression of China's legal education after his first trip to China in 1972: "The first thing to learn about legal education in China is that there isn't any." China's constitution, he continued, was mostly "an unenforceable collection of political slogans and principles" (Kruger, 2009). Almost half a century later, China's legal education has greatly changed: numerous law schools have mushroomed in China. However, Professor Cohen's description of China's constitution remains true. Furthermore, as the well-known Chinese lawyer Mo Shaoping and legal experts in the democracies have pointed out, China does not have the rule of law (Alon and Li, 2019; BBC, 2015b; U.S. Department of Justice, 2019a).

According to the Rule of Law Index developed by the World Justice Project, China's score is 0.48 (0 = worst, 1 = best), which ranks China 88th out of 128 countries. Between the lowest score of

---

[1] According to the BBC, "Mo Shaoping is, perhaps, China's most famous defence lawyer who still walks free. Many of his colleagues have been arrested and disbarred but he continues to represent dissidents and artists whose work are deemed too critical" (*BBC*, 2015b). Chinese lawyer Mo Shaoping on his career, justice, and democracy. *BBC*, June 4 (www.bbc.com/news/av/world-asia-33002876): Accessed November 23, 2020.

Venezuela (0.27) and the highest score of Denmark (.90), China is closer to the low end. China's score is below the global average of 0.56 and the average of East Asia and Pacific region (0.60). And the trend of change is not promising: From 2017 to 2020, China's score declined from 0.50 (2017–2018) to 0.49 (2019), and then to 0.48 (2020) (World Justice Project, 2020).

The Worldwide Governance Indicators (WGI) developed by Kaufmann show similar patterns and trends (see Figure 3.1). In the past two decades, improvement in China's rule of law inched upward at about 0.5 points per year, from 34 to 45, which is still below the middle point. Compared to the OECD (Organization for Economic Cooperation and Development) countries, China is substantially behind in rule of law and other governance indicators (Kaufmann, Kraay, and Mastruzzi, 2020).

But the absence or low level of the rule of law in China does not mean that the country is in chaos; China uses a system to keep society and the economy in order that is different from the rule of law. In this chapter, we discuss China's legal system and governance from the cultural, economic, and political perspectives.

3.2 TWO CONTRASTING LEGAL CULTURES: A HISTORICAL PERSPECTIVE

China's legal culture, which has been heavily influenced by many dynasties under the emperor's absolute power, is quite the opposite of the rule of law culture that originated in Europe.[2] The essence of the rule of law is fairness and impartiality, typified by the statue of the Goddess of Justice, who is blindfolded and holding up a scale (Figure 3.2). The ideal of this tradition is that we want the judge to have no preconceived views about the people to be judged, and he/she should not be influenced by the appearance of the parties in front of

---

[2] This section is based on S. Li, 2009. *Managing International Business in Relation-Based versus Rule-Based Countries.* New York: Business Expert Press.

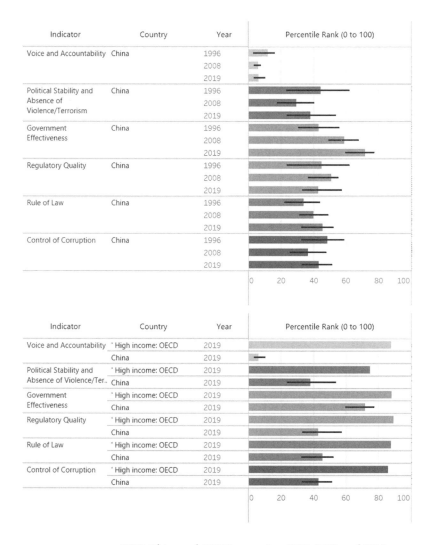

FIGURE 3.1 WGI, China and OECD countries, 1996, 2008, and 2019.
(a) Upper panel: China, 1996, 2008, and 2019.
(b) Lower panel: China vs. OECD countries, 2019.
Source: Kaufmann et al. (2020)

them. The judge presiding over a trial should act more like a referee in sports, whose main objective is to make sure that the two adversaries – the plaintiff and defendant – are treated equally and fairly. Both have a fair chance to present their arguments.

FIGURE 3.2 Bao Gong and Goddess of Justice.
(a) Upper panel: Bao Gong in Chinese opera with a third eye.
(b) Lower panel: Goddess of Justice.
Source: Author

In Chinese history, the dynasties assumed a paternalistic role teaching and disciplining their subjects. Contrary to the rule of law tradition that judges should be blind to the parties' characteristics and only weigh facts, the authoritarian legal culture emphasized that the mission of the judge was not only to take a position in the disputed case but also to accurately unveil the truth and catch the perpetrator. While an exact counterpart of the Goddess of Justice does not exist in Chinese culture, there is a legendary judge by the name of Bao Gong, who has the superpower to read peoples' minds and see past events so that he has never made a single mistake in ruling. In fact, he is so smart in solving cases and is so concerned in protecting the poor, powerless people, that the Chinese have lauded him with the name Bao Qingtian (Bao the Blue Sky). But the most interesting feature of Bao Gong is that, in sharp contrast to the blindfolded Goddess of Justice, the legend has it that Bao Gong has three eyes – the third eye in the middle of his forehead – to help him see through people (see Figure 3.2)!

Thus, the main function of the legal system throughout Chinese history is to identify and punish the bad elements in society at any cost. The judge's role is to assist the state in carrying out its political agenda by legalizing state policies and volitions. In a court, especially a criminal court, the judge takes an active, inquisitive role to interrogate the accused, making the judge almost like a prosecutor. This tradition in the legal literature is known as "inquisitorial," in comparison to the rule-of-law tradition (especially the English common law tradition), which is known as "adversarial" (World Law Direct, 2008). The adversarial court lets the two opposing parties try their best to present their evidence and logical arguments, and a rigorous cross examination tends to result in more thoroughly uncovering the facts about the case and thus having a fairer trial. This is especially true in a juried trial, which is not used in authoritarian countries such as China. On the other hand, the inquisitorial approach may raise the chance of a forced confession and a higher conviction rate in trials (Insideprison.com, 2006).

As a result of the long paternalistic tradition and the strong belief that the authorities carry the mandate of the heavens and should be obeyed, ordinary Chinese people tend to believe the laws are made with good intentions, but the government fails to follow them from time to time. Thus, it can frequently be heard in China that people are calling on the government to follow the true spirit of the law. However, the government not following the law is not the cause, but rather the result, of a deeper problem in China's legal system. Hoping for a Bao Gong in today's China is neither realistic nor effective: Judges who independently follow the laws in both word and spirit are virtually unheard of in China, as the country's lack of open, impartial, and uncorrupt courts has its roots in the economic and political system.

3.3   HOW THE STAGE OF ECONOMIC DEVELOPMENT SHAPES THE GOVERNANCE ENVIRONMENT

This section first introduces a comparative framework known as "rule-based versus relation-based governance" from the economic perspective, and then shows that China relies on the relation-based way to govern socioeconomic activities.[3]

First, we need to introduce two key concepts for the discussion of the alternative system to the rule of law that China uses to maintain order and govern social and economic exchanges. The first concept is governance and the second is the governance environment.

Governance is defined as a mechanism people use to protect their interest in social and economic exchanges. For example, in a society with a fair, open, and effective legal system, people would resort to the courts or public arbitrations for a ruling if disputes arise. On the other hand, when the law is biased and judges are corrupt, then people may not choose the public rule as their means of settling disputes. Instead, they may look for a private way to solve it, which may include mediation or even extralegal means such as violence (e.g., kidnapping). As I will show next, *what governance mechanism people or firms choose in a society is not entirely up to the individual*

---

[3] This section is based on S. Li, (2009). *Managing International Business in Relation-based versus Rule-based Countries.* New York: Business Expert Press.

or firm; it is primarily determined by the dominant governance environment of the society in which they live or conduct business.

Governance environment refers to the set of political, legal, and social institutions that collectively facilitates or constrains the choice of governance mechanism the individual or firm has in a society. Scholars of social sciences have now come to a consensus that, broadly speaking, all societies can be grouped into two major camps in terms of governance environment: those that have good *public ordering*, or rule of law, and those that do not have good public ordering (Dixit, 2004b). While readers from the West are familiar with the first type, they are unfamiliar with the latter, for some obvious reasons, which I will discuss in more detail in this section.

What do people rely on to protect their property rights and other interests in economic exchanges if the public laws are no good? If the public ordering (i.e., public laws and government enforcement) is ineffective, the society must rely on some sort of *private ordering* in order to make certain (minimally) necessary economic activities feasible. But private ordering can have many forms. Some may be conducive to business and others may be hostile or even dangerous to conducting business. For instance, ordering can be based on a dictatorship imposed by a military strongman who monopolizes all business opportunities. Ordering can also be in a state of complete anarchy, in which bandits roam and rob people and make business activities based on free and voluntary exchange virtually impossible.

Ordering can also be based on an extensive informal social network among businesses maintained by tradition or private enforcement, which may function effectively and efficiently under certain conditions. It is this type of particular private ordering that has drawn increasing attention from social scientists. Among the efforts at studying private ordering, a novel approach is to compare the two major types of governance system from the perspective of economic development stage and cost-benefit tradeoff, which my coauthors and I call "rule-based versus relation-based governance" (Li, 1999b; Li, Park, and Li, 2004).

3.3.1 Rule-Based and Relation-Based Governance Systems

We began by examining the governance environment at the societal level from political, legal, economic, and social perspectives, and identified two contrasting orderings, public versus private, in terms of how people protect their property rights and contracts. In this section, we further develop the two orderings into two governance systems: rule-based versus relation-based.

In most developed societies, we observe that firms and individuals primarily rely on public rules – laws and government regulations – to resolve disputes and enforce rights and contracts. We call this reliance on public ordering a *rule-based governance system*. A rule-based governance environment must satisfy the following conditions: the public rules governing economic exchanges (such as laws, state policies, and regulations) are fairly made; the rule-making, rule-adjudication, and rule-enforcement are separate; rule-enforcement is fair and efficient; and public information infrastructure (such as accounting, auditing, and financial rating) is highly reliable and accurate. That the public information must be of high quality and trustworthy is vital for a rule-based economy to function smoothly and efficiently. Firms and people must be able to rely on publicly available information such as financial analyses and auditing reports in order to conduct business and make decisions, saving the cost of privately collecting information and investigating its quality for every potential business transaction. An important feature of relying on public information is that the *information must be explicit and verifiable by a third party*, otherwise it cannot be admitted in court if disputes arise. The court can only enforce the agreements between parties that are publicly (third-party) verifiable; any implicit agreements made privately between them that cannot be verified by the court are not admissible to the court and thus cannot be enforced. As a result, business agreements in a rule-based society are usually formal and clearly written in explicit language. Because of these conditions, citizens and organizations predominantly rely on public ordering in governing transactions.

These features imply that rule-based societies tend to be mature democracies. For instance, for the laws and rules to be fair, a society must ensure fair participation of all interest groups in law making, which requires a representative democracy. For legal interpretation to be impartial, judges must be independent of political influence, which implies checks and balances between different branches of the government, and for the enforcement to be impartial and efficient, the executive branch has to be answerable to the constituents and be checked by the legislative and judiciary branches. This is why mature democracies share many commonalities, while nondemocracies may take many forms, ranging from monarchy to military rule to communist rule to civil war and anarchy. Rule-based societies tend to have similar rules, yet non–rule-based societies may take different forms of private enforcement mechanisms to govern transactions (e.g., community enforcement, private network enforcement, kinship enforcement, or mafia-dominated enforcement). In other words, while rule-based societies converge to the profile described here (e.g., highly rule-based societies are all mature democracies), societies that lack a rule-based governance environment vary widely, ranging from warring states in complete chaos to tightly controlled societies under highly efficient totalitarian rules.

We observe that a specific group of non–rule-based societies that rely on private ordering (e.g., the East Asian societies in their early stages of development and China today) are quite effective and efficient at governing the social exchanges that have been experiencing rapid economic growth. In addition to the absence of fair and efficient public rules because of the lack of any of the aforementioned conditions necessary for a rule-based governance system, these societies have the following in common: They all have a governance environment based on private enforcement that can effectively and efficiently regulate markets and resolve disputes. This is what we call a *relation-based governance system*.

A relation-based society has the following characteristics: public rules (laws, government policies, and government regulations) are less fair because they are usually biased in favor of certain privileged groups (due to the lack of checks and balances); the executive branch of the government usually overshadows the legislative and judiciary branches and is likely to be controlled by a dictatorial ruling elite; courts and judges are controlled by the ruler(s); government operations are secretive and public information and press are controlled and censored by the government; industries and markets tend to be controlled by a small number of insiders (e.g., people who have connections with the ruler) and are closed to outsiders; officials and business insiders are usually locked in a corruption–bribery relationship; and the informal network among the insiders in an industry is so closely knit and powerful that if one of the insiders is said to have broken the (unwritten) norms of the trade, the word of mouth by other insiders will effectively put him out of business.

For example, in China, people form close-knit private groups known as "circles" to improve their opportunities and protect their interests (Baike, undated). Examples of these groups include classmates' groups, groups based on geographic locations/origins – such as Taizhou Bang (merchants from Taizhou, Zhejiang, who help each other (Sina.com, 2007)) – or groups based on parents' occupation, such as the princelings (Bo, 2015).

3.3.2 How Do People Govern Transactions in a Relation-Based Society?

Unlike a rule-based society, where public information is credible and heavily relied on by individuals and businesses (making the protection of business transactions by public ordering feasible and efficient), *public information in a relation-based society is usually untrustworthy.* As a result, people and firms rely on private information to govern their transactions. There are several reasons why public information is not trusted. First, the government controls public information and the media in order to support its rule and agenda. For instance, China – a relation-based society – tightly controls the media and decides what news can be published (Kalathil and Boas, 2003).

The party-state even doctors news stories and times news releases in order to reinforce its rule. News of major scientific discoveries is often saved and released on major political holidays (e.g., the National Day, the Communist Party's birthday). This practice of manipulating public information at the national level by the government does not help business firms to report accurate information. My coauthors and I have undertaken several studies on information manipulation by firms in relation-based societies such as China, some of the results of which will be shown later in this chapter (Li et al., 2011; Li, Park, and Bao, 2014).

Another reason why public information is rarely useful as a means for firms to govern their transactions is the nature of these transactions. When the scale of the economy is small, and business-people predominately deal with people they know, they rely on private information between the transacting parties, and they do not want to make their information available to a third party because the private business relationship is their most important asset. It is a small wonder that successful businesspeople in relation-based societies such as China tend to keep a low profile and avoid the media (Li et al., 2011; Wu, 2008).

Such private relationships and information are usually local and implicit, and the agreement (e.g., a handshake or a pat on the shoulder) is most often informal and cannot be verified by a third party such as a judge in a court. These practices, as discussed earlier, are the opposite of rule-based governance, and as a result, businesspeople must rely on private means to protect their transaction. Specifically, firms in relation-based societies rely on three private monitoring mechanisms to govern their rights in transactions: *ex ante* monitoring capability, *interim* (also known as *ex nunc*) monitoring capability, and *ex post* monitoring capability.

Ex ante means "before the event" and is used in economic analysis to forecast the results of a particular action. Private ex ante monitoring capability refers to the effort invested by a transaction party before a business deal is made. In the absence of public information and enforcement, a firm must privately investigate its prospective transaction partner in terms of his or her track record and reputation. If the prospect has cheated, do not deal with him. If the prospective partner does not have a stable pool of business partners or clients, it implies that he may have a bad reputation and is avoided by other insiders. Such a prospect should be ruled out.

Interim monitoring is the ability of one party to obtain ongoing business and operational information about the other party, specifically whether the other party is on track with a project's schedule or whether the other party has any financial trouble or disputes. In a relation-based society, such information is not publicly available through credit investigating agencies. This is why news of the financial insolvency of a firm in a relation-based society tends to cause large-scale panic. As a result of the lack of reliable public financial data, people do not know whether other firms may also be involved with the insolvent firm and are thus adversely affected. As a result, people stop lending to or withdraw deposits from firms likely to be involved with the insolvent firm (a snowball effect). Therefore, one must invest in the capability of obtaining private and reliable information.

The third monitoring mechanism, private ex post capability, *is the most important of the three*. Ex post, Latin for "after the fact," is used here to refer to the ability to remedy or deter cheating or other opportunistic behaviors by the other party, in the absence of resorting to public regulators such as the courts (which tend to be corrupt, unfair, and inefficient in relation-based societies). In a relation-based society it is not uncommon for a promisee to resort to kidnapping in order to force a promisor to fulfill a promissory obligation (which may be an implicit, oral promise). For relation-based governance to work efficiently, private ex post monitoring must be effective and efficient. A *New York Times* report on informal, relation-based lending in China vividly describes such ex post monitoring (Bradsher, 2004):

> Borrowers default on nearly half the loans issued by the state-owned banks, but seldom do so here on money that is usually

borrowed from relatives, neighbors or people in the same industry. Residents insist that the risk of ostracism for failing to repay a loan is penalty enough to ensure repayment of most loans ... [As one lender puts it], "If it weren't a good friend, I wouldn't lend the money ... " Violence is extremely rare, but the threat of it does exist as the ultimate guarantor that people make every effort to repay debts. "Someone can hire a killer who will chase you down, beat you up and maybe even kill you."

3.3.3 The Costs and Benefits of a Relation-Based Governance System

Since we observe that all advanced countries rely on public rules for governance, we may be tempted to rush to the conclusion that relation-based governance is categorically inefficient and thus detrimental to economic development. However, such a conclusion is premature. Relation-based governance systems are not all inefficient and thus hinder economic growth. Under certain conditions, relation-based governance can be quite effective and efficient due to its differing cost structure.

A well-functioning rule-based system is not free of cost to build and use. Imagine, for instance, public ordering in the United States, one of the most advanced rule-based countries, and the infrastructure it must have in order for public ordering to function effectively and efficiently. In general, public ordering needs the establishment of a three-branch government. First of all, the country must build a legislative body, which in the United States means establishing and organizing the House and the Senate in Congress, the election system in all fifty states to select all the senators and representatives, and the infrastructure that supports the operations of legislation in Congress. Second, the country must build a court system ranging from the Supreme Court to local courts that are autonomous and well-funded. This infrastructure compels the society to invest in an education system that can train a sufficiently large number of judges who are professional, ethical, impartial, and well-paid. The society must also invest in training an army of lawyers and other legal workers with high professional and ethical standards. Last but not least, public ordering requires a credible and powerful law enforcement branch – the executive branch of the government, including a police force that must be well-trained, adequately paid, and thus uncorrupted.

Simply put, *a well-functioning rule-based system requires a large investment in legal infrastructure that is costly and takes a long time to build.* From a cost accounting perspective, such an investment at the national level can be viewed as a fixed cost that does not vary regardless of how many people use it. Once the legal infrastructure is built and functioning, *the incremental cost of drafting and enforcing one more contract is relatively low.* In other words, whether the legal system enforces one contract or one million contracts, the fixed, upfront investment in the legal infrastructure is the same (and sunk in the sense that it cannot be recovered), and the marginal cost (the incremental cost of enforcing an additional contract) is minimal.

In contrast, in a relation-based society, *business can thrive with minimal social order.* As long as crimes such as robberies are not out of control, business can be conducted and governed by well-functioning social-industrial networks maintained by private players (individuals or firms). Well-connected and wealthy people are not particularly concerned about the unreliable police, which is common in relation-based societies, as they take the law into their own hands. In China, the private bodyguard industry has grown rapidly. A coal mining executive in Shandong explained why he used private bodyguards: "When you run into trouble, you can't just dial 110," the executive said, referring to the Chinese police hot line. "They could be off eating lunch, and who knows when they would arrive" (Feng, 2013).

Another interesting difference in contract fulfillment and enforcement between the two systems is that, unlike public enforcement of contracts, which relies on third-party verifiable information that may be only part (the written part) of the general agreement between two parties, private enforcement is based on private information, which may not need to be verified by a third party. In this sense, private enforcement can be more complete than public enforcement, and even include implicit agreements based on mutual understanding, the spirit of cooperation, or past practices.

In general, compared to the cost structure of the rule-based system, the relation-based governance system incurs few fixed costs (since it does not rely on a nationwide legal infrastructure). But the marginal (incremental) cost of privately enforcing contracts increases as the scale and scope of one's business expands. For example, if someone only does business with his/her siblings, the marginal cost of the three types of monitoring (ex ante, interim, and ex post) is low, because he/she knows their reputation, their ability to deliver, and where their assets are (in case he/she needs to seize them). But when his/her business grows and he/she runs out of family members, he/she may have to deal with people he/she does not know as well, such as neighbors or distant relatives, and his/her marginal cost of monitoring increases. In general, the marginal (incremental) cost of establishing new relationships rises because cultivating new relationships becomes more and more expensive and time-consuming when one's private network expands from family members to strangers. For this reason, in a relation-based society people first do business with family members and then with friends and people they know. They try to avoid dealing with strangers because it takes a long time to develop close relationships, and the costs of private monitoring and enforcement are high (Figure 3.3).

Therefore, when the scale and scope of the economy are small, relation-based governance may be effective and efficient, as the society avoids costly investment in developing and maintaining the legal infrastructure. In the early stage of China's economic development, markets were fragmented and localized, and people and firms were constrained to small markets near their home. Entrepreneurs were

FIGURE 3.3 Relation-based hiring preference.
Source: Author

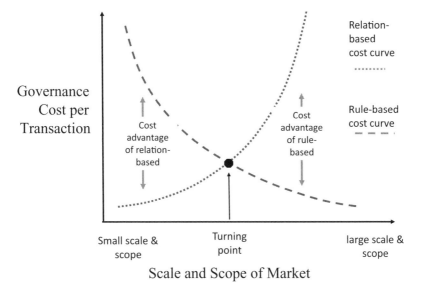

Governance Cost per Transaction

Relation-based cost curve

Rule-based cost curve

Cost advantage of relation-based

Cost advantage of rule-based

Small scale & scope

Turning point

large scale & scope

Scale and Scope of Market

FIGURE 3.4 Cost and benefit of rule-based and relation-based governance. *Source*: Author

confined locally and were content to work with family members, friends, and people in closely knit circles. As illustrated in Figure 3.4, when the market is small, the average governance cost is lower in relation-based societies, giving them a comparative advantage during the take-off stage of their economy.

However, when an economy expands from local to national and international scope, relation-based governance becomes inefficient. The average cost of finding and establishing new relationships rises and thus the average cost of governance surpasses that of rule-based economies, as illustrated at the turning point in Figure 3.4. At this point, a relation-based society begins to lose its comparative advantage in governance costs compared to a rule-based society. It faces pressure to evolve into a rule-based governance environment. A postponement of the transition caused by resistance from people who are deeply entrenched and vested in the existing relational network hinders a country's economic development. This point will be further elaborated later.

The cost–benefit perspective of relation-based governance provides an explanation of China's high economic growth that has been missed: China has extensive informal social networks that enable it to rely on the relation-based system to govern economic activities. This system has helped China to save the huge fixed cost of building an effective public governance system. In other words, China did not have to wait until it could build a vast, expensive legal infrastructure for its economy to take off. Relation-based countries in general have relied on private governance mechanisms maintained and enforced by family members, friends, cronies, and related people in high places (possibly through bribery) to protect their business interests and operations. If we expand our explanation beyond China to include East Asia, where countries have traditionally relied on relation-based governance, the so-called East Asian economic miracle has been achieved with the help of the relation-based governance system (Li, 1999b; Li et al., 2004).

Furthermore, we can now see that the Chinese rely heavily on *guanxi* (Chinese for connection and relation) in business activities not only because of their cultural heritage but also, and more importantly, because the public rules are not effective and efficient in providing fair protection for their property rights and interests. Relying on the relation-based way to conduct business activities is not merely a cultural phenomenon; it is fundamentally determined by the stage of political and economic development in a society. Relying on private relations to settle business disputes is not unique to China or East Asian societies. Historically, feudal Europe and the United States were primarily relation-based societies (Li, 1999b, 2002b). Contemporarily, many developing and transition economies such as Azerbaijan, Bahrain, Egypt, Pakistan, and Qatar are relation-based even though they do not have the Chinese or East Asian cultural heritage (Li, 2019b). Table 3.1 highlights the main contrasting features of the two systems we have discussed so far.

Table 3.1. *Differences between relation-based and rule-based governance*

Relation-based governance	Rule-based governance
Relying on private and local information	Relying on public information
Complete enforcement possible	Enforcing a subset of observable agreements
Implicit and non-verifiable agreements	Explicit and third-party verifiable agreements
Requiring minimum social order	Requiring well-developed legal infrastructure
Low fixed costs to set up the system	High fixed costs to set up the system
High and increasing marginal costs to maintain	Low and decreasing marginal costs to maintain
Effective in small and emerging economies	Effective in large and advanced economies

Source: Li et al. (2004)

3.3.4   Caution: Rule-Based versus Relation-Based Are Not Black and White

It should be noted that all human societies, including relation-based ones, have various degrees of formal rules. When we say a country is relation-based, it does not mean that this country has no formal laws. Even the most lawless country must have a set of published legal codes of some sort. But the state may not follow the laws and the ruler may simply ignore them. What distinguishes relation-based societies from rule-based ones is not who has the most comprehensive written laws; it is that people in relation-based societies tend to *circumvent* formal rules because the rules and their enforcement tend to be unfair, particularistic (depending on who has better relationships with people in power), and corrupt.

Another caveat is the distinction between relation-based governance systems and relational business practice. By our definition, relying on a relation-based governance system means using private measures to fulfill the social function of protecting property rights, such as enforcing contracts, which is usually done by the government in societies where public ordering functions well. Thus, strictly speaking, relying on relation-based governance is to ignore the public law at best or violate it at worst, even though the law itself may be unfair or inefficient. In other words, resorting to the relation-based governance system implies that one must break an existing law in some way.

Relational business means conducting business though private relationships, such as knowing one's customers in person and matching individual customers' needs with a service uniquely tailored for the customer. It does not necessarily mean to circumvent the law. Thus, the relation-based governance system, which is the main focus of this chapter, is different from relational business (such as relational marketing).

3.3.5   The Difficulties of Protecting Investment When Public Information Is Untrustworthy

While it is well known that accurate financial information is vital for making investment decisions (such as purchasing shares of a company), what is less known is how people protect their investment when publicly disclosed information is not trustworthy, which is an important fact in relation-based societies such as China. In this section, we will discuss the pitfalls of investing in China.

A key concept we need to understand first is earnings management, which is a managerial accounting practice that manipulates earnings information by making it appear either higher or lower on the books. A firm's income fluctuates from time to time. The manager of a firm may want to smooth the earnings report over time by using certain accounting measures. For example, if the manager wants to make earnings look high, he/she can keep uncollectable losses as accounts receivable for a longer period than usual. On the other hand, if the manager wants to hide profits for "rainy days" or other purposes, then he/she may set aside a greater amount of reserve for uncollectable accounts. In addition to these practices, which may still be within the legal limit, the manager may also use outright illegal means to manipulate the accounting information, in the same way that managers of the now defunct Enron and WorldCom did to mislead their investors.

Indeed, the incentives for earnings management exist for firms in both rule-based and relation-based economies (Li et al., 2011). However, the practice is more prevalent among firms in relation-based countries. One of the reasons for this disparity is government policy in relation-based societies. As explained earlier, a relation-based political regime is usually authoritarian (or totalitarian), which needs to control information for its absolute rule. Information control and manipulation by the Chinese government is a common practice. For example, for abnormal deaths – such as deaths resulting from famine, political campaigns, and diseases (such as the Covid-19 outbreak) – the common practice of the Chinese government is to keep the totals secret or manipulate the numbers (Alon, Farrell, and Li, 2020b). As I reported in Chapter 2, even China's Premier did not believe in the economic data reported by local governments. The "officials make numbers, and numbers make officials" phenomenon (see Chapter 2) can be termed "information management" at the government level to parallel "earnings manipulation" at the firm level.

As a result of public information management by the government, people in China have not had much faith in official news or statistics. Public information in general is less trustworthy in relation-based societies, and people living in these societies are always seeking reliable information from informal channels, such as rumors and hearsay.

3.3.6 *Information Management by Firms in China*

In an environment where the government manipulates public information, there is very little reason why firms should not do the same to their advantage, so they mimic what the government does and manipulate their operating information. According to our interviews with accountants in China, it is common for firms to manipulate their earnings reports.

Private firms tend to lower earnings to avoid taxes. Studies show that tax evasion by firms in China is widespread. Large losses tend to trigger auditing by the tax authorities, so firms that manipulate earnings in order to avoid taxes only show a small loss.

Managers of state-owned firms report more earnings to get promoted or simply to keep their jobs. In their study of executive compensation and firm performance in China, economists Kato and Long found that "Chinese executives [of state-owned firms] are penalized for making negative profits" (Kato and Long, 2006). But they also found that the executives are not further rewarded for profits that are much greater than zero. Their study confirms the existence of a very strong incentive for Chinese state firm executives to engage in earnings management to bring the profit rate into positive territory. But there is also no further incentive to push profits higher.

These two tendencies suggest that firms in China tend to manipulate their profit rate to close to zero. To verify this, my colleagues and I did a simple statistical analysis (Li et al., 2011): We examined the relationship between cash flow (as measured by the amount of cash a firm has) and reported profit (as measured by return on assets of a firm, or ROA) in all manufacturing firms in China by their profit level to assess the degree to which they misreport profits. ROA is *reported* and thus is more prone to manipulation; on the other hand, cash flow must have actual cash in the bank to back it up and therefore is harder to fake. If the firms accurately reported their ROA, we would observe a one-to-one match: the amount of cash flow and the amount of profit should be the same. Statistically, the correlation between the two would be very high – close to one. Graphically, if we scatter-plot the ROAs and cash flows of all firms, we should see that the ROA and cash flow fall near the 45-degree line.

As a benchmark we compared the Chinese data with US data. Figure 3.5 shows the visual pattern of the comparison of ROA versus cash flow for our sample firms in China and listed US firms. As can be

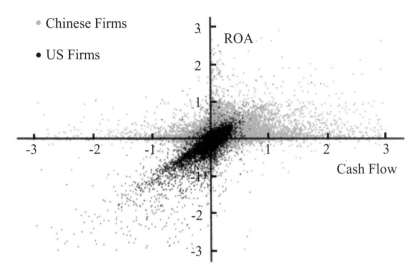

FIGURE 3.5 Return on assets (ROA) vs. cash flow, Chinese and US firms. *Source*: Li et al. (2011)

seen from the figure, the distribution of US firms (black dots) falls near the 45-degree line, whereas the distribution of firms in China (gray dots) shows that ROA clusters around zero (mostly above zero) irrespective of the value of cash flow. In other words, there is little correlation between the ROA and cash flow for firms in China. This provides strong evidence that firms in China manipulate their profits to near and slightly above zero.

While the purpose of earnings management in China may be tax evasion or promotion seeking, a serious unintended consequence results. Outsiders cannot rely on a firm's financial report to accurately evaluate the firm, which means that outsiders may not be willing to invest in the firm. This deterrent explains why relation-based firms tend to rely on internal and informal financing. Or, if outsiders are willing to invest in a firm, such as by purchasing its stocks, the unreliable information released by insiders – the firm's managers – may adversely and illegally affect the investors' interests.

There have been numerous reports about listed companies in and from China misleading investors through earnings management and outright lies (Rapoport, 2020). A well-known case is a listed company named Tiange Technology, whose products included freshwater snapping turtles, a delicacy in China. In the late 1990s and early 2000s, Tiange was found to have issued misleading information. When insiders wanted to purchase its stocks, the management would issue negative news such as "hails and tornadoes killed turtles" or "nearby peasants stole turtles." And after the insiders' purchase at the lowered price, turtles would have miraculously swum back (Yang, 2002)! In 2020, the US-listed Chinese company Lukin Coffee was found to have fabricated about 2.2 billion yuan (US$310 million) in sales in 2019 (Tan, 2020).

Unlike direct investment, in which the investor is also the insider who manages their finances and operations, indirect (portfolio) investment relies entirely on information that is publicly released by the insiders. So if the insiders cheat, the investors are like sitting ducks.

Similarly, in relation-based societies, formal credit risk management does not work efficiently and banks often incur high losses from bad loans because of the difficulty of obtaining accurate credit information from borrowers. For example, as the *New York Times* story quoted earlier shows, in China, nearly 50 percent of formal bank loans to small borrowers cannot be collected, whereas informal loans arranged privately using the aforementioned monitoring mechanisms (ex ante, interim, and ex post) seldom go bad (Bradsher, 2004).

The implications of our discussion on information and investment in relation-based societies such as China are that first, investors must be aware of the distinction between rule-based and relation-based societies, because it plays a key role in determining how they can effectively protect their investment. Second, as a result of the low quality of public financial information, the risk of investing in the public financial market, such as the stock market, is higher. Following the same logic, because firms' accounting information is less reliable (as reflected in the high level of earnings management in Chinese firms), outside investors are reluctant to invest in relation-based firms. These facts suggest that the capital market is limited mostly to relational investment, and the cost of capital in the public capital market is higher in a relation-based economy to compensate for the higher risks resulting from inaccurate public information.

The complexity of property rights differs from industry to industry. In general, the property rights structure is relatively simple in manufacturing industries, such as the shoe and garment industries, where the quality and quantity of the products are easy to verify and thus workers and manufacturers can be paid on a regular basis. Logically, the protection of property rights and investments in those industries is relatively straightforward. This to a large extent explains why China has become the world's largest manufacturing base. On the other hand, in the financial industry, the property rights structure can be very complex, such as in the initial public offering of stocks (IPO), options, and other complex financial deals. For those products and services, property rights protection is complicated and requires strong legal protection, which is better in rule-based societies. Thus, in general, for investors who are evaluating different industries in which to invest in a relation-based market, if everything else is equal, the investors should favor industries that have simpler property rights structures.

3.3.7   Relying on Relationships Can Be a Double-Edged Sword

It is vital for a foreign player entering into a relation-based market such as China to invest in establishing reliable relationships in the local market. In doing so, the foreign player should be aware of two caveats. First, using relations to circumvent formal rules may be illegal, even in a relation-based society. Second, when the foreign player uses relations to gain advantage in the local market, its partners and competitors also use relations to try to outcompete it. And local partners or competitors may have stronger relationships within the power circle. In the early 1990s, McDonald's obtained a prime location in Beijing through *guanxi*, only to find that a Hong Kong businessman, Li Ka-shing, who had a stronger *guanxi* had McDonalds' evicted for Li Ka-shing's real estate development project (*The Economist*, 1994).

3.3.8 Do Not Take Written Laws at Face Value

A common mistake made by foreign investors is that they see that China has passed many new laws and therefore it must be safe for investment. However, the risk of investing in China is not because China does not have laws or rules; it is because the laws and rules are not impartially and fairly enforced. Commenting on our framework of rule-based versus relation-based governance, *The Economist* magazine warned foreign investors about the danger of investing in China:

> Beware, foreigner, beware ... They see the introduction of new rules that protect investment. Insiders see a state of flux created by changing relations among market participants. Outsiders see an opportunity to invest. Insiders see an opportunity to loot. This may help explain, say Messrs Li [Shuhe Li and Shaomin Li], why you are finding it so tough to do business in China right now.
>
> *(The Economist, 2000)*

After our discussion of China's relation-based governance and on the need for a relation-based society to make the transition to rule-based governance when its economy expands globally, a logical and important question is whether China is ready to make the transition.

3.4 THE PROSPECT FOR CHINA TO TRANSITION FROM RELATION-BASED TO RULE-BASED GOVERNANCE

Will China stay as a relation-based society or will it become a rule-based society?[4] These are no small questions and I do not expect I can definitively answer them. However, I will present two opposing views and my analysis.

---

[4] This section is based on S. Li, (2013). China's (Painful) Transition from Relation-Based to Rule-Based Governance: When and How, Not If and Why. *Corporate Governance: An International Review*, 21(6), 567–576.

3.4.1 Arguments Why China Will Not Transition to Rule-Based Governance

The arguments why China will not transition from relation-based governance to rule-based governance are to a great extent derived from the view that China is unique and has its own model of development that is different from the West, which has been a main school of thought in the debate regarding the "Chinese model" versus the "Western model," a hotly contested topic in social sciences since the beginning of China's reform in the 1970s (the two views were discussed in Chapters 1 and 2 from the political and economic perspectives). Scholars who believe that China cannot adopt the Western style of public rules such as democracy and rule of law mainly argue from two perspectives.

The first, and foremost, is the cultural argument, which primarily argues that as a result of the Chinese cultural heritage that emphasizes informal social networks of reciprocity and mutual obligations, the impersonal rule-based system is not congruent with Chinese society, and thus China will not transition from a relation-based to rule-based society (see Lau and Young, 2013; Dirlik, 2012; Wang and Zheng, 2012 for reviews on the cultural view). Another dimension of the cultural view is concerned with the political culture of contemporary China, which is a mix of Marxism and traditional Chinese values. This unique ideological environment makes the transition toward the Western political and economic system risky because it will threaten one-party rule (Lau and Young, 2013; Lin, 2011). This brings us to the second most common argument about why China cannot transition to a rule-based society: the argument based on political (in)convenience, which I call the "entrenchment" argument.

The entrenchment argument believes that the intertwining between the politically and economically vested interests held by the powerful elites in China is so well entrenched that they have greatly benefited from the system and created an insurmountable resistance to any effort to move away from it (see a similar argument from Lin, 2011).

3.4.2   Arguments Why China Will Transition to Rule-Based Governance

In this section, I will argue from logical, theoretical, and empirical grounds why China should make the transition from relation-based to rule-based governance.[5]

The Logical Argument

The logical argument is not difficult to make: It is based on the different cost structures of the two governance systems. As I explained earlier in this chapter, in order for the rule-based system to function effectively and efficiently, it must have a well-established legal infrastructure and an efficient public information infrastructure. Establishing these systems is costly; however, the costs are fixed in the sense that once the systems are well in place, the incremental cost of enforcing one more transaction is minimal. Thus, a rule-based system inherently favors economies that have large scale and scope.

The opposite is true for the relation-based system: It has few fixed costs. Firms and people take enforcement into their own hands by resorting to their private relations. Whether the police and the courts are well funded is not as important as in a rule-based society. Since most successful firms tend to be well protected by their private networks and connections, they only need minimal public order to conduct normal business. And they only deal with people they know well – to keep their governance costs low.

But when their businesses expand beyond their local regions to national and international levels, cultivating and relying on personal connections to do business will become impractical: The cost of getting to know strangers well and making sure they can establish an effective *ex post* monitoring mechanism to deter opportunistic behavior will become prohibitive.

---

[5] In Part III of this book I will show that under certain international conditions, China will make the transition to rule-based governance.

So the logical conclusion is that *as the scale and scope of an economy grows bigger and bigger, relation-based governance will lose its cost advantage and must transition to rule-based governance in order to expand and stay competitive* (see the turning point in Figure 3.4).

Four decades ago, when China began its economic reform, effective public rules to govern economic transactions were virtually non-existent, and people relied on private relations to protect their business activities. China's economy took off without a sound legal system. In the past three decades, China has greatly benefited from relation-based governance by avoiding the establishment of costly legal and public information infrastructures, both of which are necessary building blocks for a well-functioning rule-based system. During this time, the Chinese economy has been rapidly expanding from local to global markets. While empirical studies are needed to estimate where China is along the cost curve of relation-based governance (Figure 3.4), one thing is certain: As the Chinese economy grows in scale and scope, it has to make the transition to move away from its relation-based governance and to establish a more rule-based governance.

From the social justice theory perspective (Rawls, 1971), the transition is also inevitable. Using one's well-established relations to obtain public goods and protection is a privilege, which means that only a few powerful and well-connected people can enjoy it and the rest of population do not have it. Thus, a relation-based system favors a small exclusive class of people who are well connected and well-endowed in a society because of their family background or other private connections, while the majority are disadvantaged in obtaining public goods (including public protection), not because of their abilities to compete for these public goods, but because of their lack of a well-connected private network or certain family background. Thus a relation-based system denies social justice and is not equitable. If we believe that the worldwide long-term trend of social development is toward social justice and equal opportunity, then China must change toward a rule-based system.

Can the two systems coexist as dominant modes of governance in a society? Can China establish a rule-based system as a dominant mode of governance while keeping its relation-based system as another dominant mode of governance? In other words, can the two dominant modes function in parallel in the long run (achieving equilibrium)? The logical answer is no. Using private relations to obtain public goods that one otherwise cannot get implies circumventing (violating) the public rules. If such a mode of governance is dominant, then people will eventually try to avoid public rules, rendering them ineffective and causing a relapse back to the relation-based system. On the other hand, if most people have faith in and rely on the public rules, organizations or individuals circumventing it systematically will be caught and punished (Platteau, 1994). The relation-based way will be discouraged and eventually reduced to a residual mode of governance. So, the two systems cannot be dominant simultaneously.[6]

The Problem with the Cultural Argument

One way to test the cultural argument against China's possible transition to a rule-based system is to find societies with cultures similar to China's and examine their governance systems. Cases that come to mind immediately are Hong Kong and Taiwan, where the Chinese culture is dominant. While Hong Kong had been ruled by the British for about a hundred years until 1997, the British cultural influence had been limited to the ruling elites and the small expatriate population. The majority of Hong Kong residents are Chinese who have kept a strong traditional Chinese culture. Based on the Hofstede cultural dimensions, Hong Kong's culture is remarkably similar to China's (Figure 3.6).

Historically, Taiwan had been part of China until 1949, when the CCP overtook China by defeating the ruling Chinese Nationalist

---

[6] Having said this, I recognize that existing governance environments are not pure: There is no perfectly rule-based system, nor is there a wholly relation-based system without any public ordering.

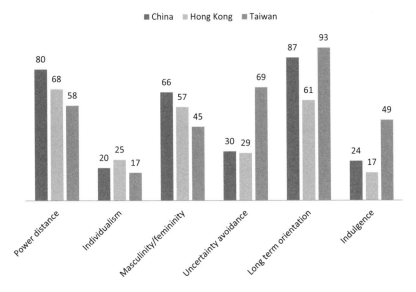

FIGURE 3.6 Hofstede culture dimensions, China, Hong Kong, and Taiwan. *Source*: Author completed based on data from Hofstede Insights (2021)

Party, which then fled to Taiwan. Taiwan's culture is inherited from China, and Taiwan has preserved the traditional Chinese culture better than China because it has not suffered a communist revolution that destroyed traditional culture. A comparison of the Hofstede cultural dimensions between Taiwan and China shows similarities in several key dimensions (Figure 3.6).

However, the governance systems of the three societies show large gaps. I will use two sets of governance measures to examine the gaps. The first is the Governance Environment Index (GEI) developed by Wu and Li (Li, 2019) and based on five governance dimensions: (1) political rights; (2) rule of law; (3) level of public trust; (4) free flow of information; and (5) quality of accounting standards. The first two dimensions measure the development and enforcement of public rules, the third and fourth measure the quality of public information, and the fifth captures the business practice that facilitates the

Table 3.2. *Governance Environment Index (GEI) and Worldwide Governance Indicators (WGI), China, Hong Kong, and Taiwan*

	GEI (highest = 6.03, lowest = −6.50)	WGI (percentile rank)
China	−3.31	50.0
Hong Kong	1.55	85.3
Taiwan	1.89	79.9

Source: Compiled by author based on data from Li (2019b) and World Bank (2015)

rule-based system. Based on the GEI ranging from 6.03 (most rule-based: Sweden) to −6.50 (least rule-based: Libya), Taiwan was the most rule-based among the three (GEI = 1.89); Hong Kong is in the middle with a GEI of 1.55; and China has the lowest GEI of −3.31, ranked fiftieth out of the fifty-six countries for which we had data.

I also use the Worldwide Governance Indicators (WGI) as an alternative measure to examine the differences in governance among the three societies. Hong Kong and Taiwan are highly rule-based with percentile ranks of 85.3 and 79.9, respectively, and China is the least rule-based with a percentile rank of 38.5, below the world average of 50 (Kaufmann et al., 2020) (see Table 3.2).

These comparisons show that although Hong Kong and Taiwan have similar cultures to China, their governance systems are substantially more rule-based. Therefore, the argument that China will not transition to a rule-based system because of its Chinese culture does not hold.

The Need for China to Make the Transition

The need for China to make the transition has been increasingly recognized by both scholars of political economy and policymakers. In 2012, Zhuo Xiaochuan, the then governor of China's central policy bank, the People's Bank of China, harshly criticized the relation-based system and openly called for reforms to establish a rule-based system.

He said in high-profile interviews that "real and fundamental financial reform must be guided by legal rules and regulations, not by the discretion of individuals." He openly mentioned that the "higher-ups" (the central government) are the ones creating "resistance to and interference with the reform" (Backchina.com, 2012).

Zhou's candid comments are highly unusual in a relation-based society such as China, in which officials keep low profiles and avoid making any public comments that may have any substance. The nature of relation-based governance requires keeping vital information for decision-making secretive, and punishing any insiders (officials) who violate this unwritten but closely followed rule. Perhaps no one knows this rule better than Jiang Zemin, the retired Communist Party chief and president of China. In a Hong Kong news conference, he did not reply much at first to reporters' questions, but then lost control and revealed the secret: "Keep silent and make money!" ("Meng sheng fa da cai." (Xiao, 2003)). The fact that Zhou was willing to openly criticize the relation-based system of his higher-ups showed not only the urgent need for reform toward rule-based governance but also the weakening ability of the relation-based way to punish insiders like him who broke silence.[7]

Zhiwu Chen, a former Yale University scholar of China's reform, criticized China's current industrial policy that governs the entry of an industry as "based on one's connections, not capabilities." He pointed out that China's economy will not be able to sustain further growth without reforming this relation-based method (Chen, 2012). Moreover, Weiying Zhang, an economist at Peking University, recently stated the need for China to establish a true free market based on fair public rules. Interestingly, he is very skeptical of the so-called China model, characterized by a powerful state and a few big firms with special privileges. He also argued that the idea of

---

[7] As I will show in Part II of this book, such a critical comment on party policies is no longer possible under the party leadership of Xi Jinping, which indicates the country moving further away from adopting more rule-based measures.

establishing a free market based on fair public rules is not inherently "Western" and can find its roots in the Chinese tradition (Zhang, 2012, 2019). Yasheng Huang, an MIT scholar of China's reform, argued that the lack of rule of law actually hurts privileged individuals in China, including the most powerful officials. When they lose in power struggles, they will be unfairly treated, jailed, or even executed (Huang, 2012). The secretive governance system that these powerful individuals have helped create often devours its creators. A good example is the case of Gu Kailai, a once powerful lawyer, successful businesswoman, and wife of Bo Xilai, a former top communist party official in China. Gu was a beneficiary and ardent supporter of China's relation-based system. She wrote articles and books in praise of the Chinese legal system that can swiftly deal with the bad elements of society. Now she herself is labeled as a bad element and has received a life sentence with a well-orchestrated showcase trial (FlorCruz, 2012). Legal scholar Yu Jianrong at the Chinese Academy of Social Sciences, the top official policy research and think tank in China, argued that China has come to a crossroads where it must establish the rule of law and get rid of the economic system that is based on private connections benefiting few at the expense of the vast, unprivileged population; otherwise China may fall into political chaos and trigger a revolution (Yu, 2012). Minxin Pei, a Claremont McKenna College scholar of China's reform, built a case for China's need for the transition using evidence from other countries and domestic pressure (Pei, 2012). Pei argued that China's authoritarian government, whose officials are the main beneficiaries of the relation-based system, may not survive for much longer based on worldwide statistics indicating that most authoritarian regimes must change when income per capita reaches a middle-income range. Pei also pointed out that for every seven college graduates, only one is lucky enough to be admitted to the CCP, a necessary membership leading to an exclusive club that enjoys the benefits of the relation-based system. These facts, Pei argued, will result in political instability and mounting pressure for the transition to a more open, fair, and rule-based system. In 2012, more than seventy scholars signed an open letter calling for reform. Specifically, they called for the government to obey the constitution, implement democratic voting, respect the freedom of expression, deepen economic reform, establish judiciary independence, and make the constitution effective (Gongshiwang, 2012).

3.4.3   Empirical Evidence of China's Transition (or Lack Thereof)

Qualitative Evidence

As we discussed in Chapters 1 and 2, in the late 1970s, the Chinese government started economic reform that aimed at introducing market forces; establishing new economic laws and regulations that aimed to more clearly demarcate and protect property rights; and gradually divesting the government from businesses. All these efforts were meant to shift China away from the old relation-based method of governing economic activities and to establish more effective public rules. In this sense, economic reform is an attempt to transition from a relation-based system to a rule-based system. In the late 1990s, the government called for banking reforms to base bank financing more on the market rather than relations to disfavor state-owned and well-connected firms. The government also announced its intention to clean up smuggling, which is essentially relation-based trading in which well-connected firms can import without paying tariffs, and to wean government organizations away from conducting business, thus reducing the opportunities for officials and their relatives to enter restricted and lucrative industries (Hofman and Wu, 2009).

Further evidence of the transition comes from China's attempt to adopt international standards governing trade and finance. In 2001, China entered the World Trade Organization. Six years later, China made an effort to converge to the International Financial Report Standard, or IFRS. Based on our Governance Environment Index, the quality of accounting is an important part of rule-based governance (Li, 2009). The fact that China has (at least partially) adopted IFRS, which provides more stringent standards and open criteria for the public to access and evaluate firms' financial information – a vital element of a rule-based system – shows the Chinese government efforts to become a member of the international, more rule-based community. Research shows that investors in the Chinese stock market have increasingly relied on publicly released financial information after China's convergence toward IFRS (Qu, Fong, and Oliver, 2012).

Another powerful driving force that has contributed to the transition in China is the Internet. Relation-based governance and the Internet clash head-on in the following three dimensions (Li, 2009). First, relation-based governance is highly centralized in an organization or society. The boss has absolute power. The Internet is a network of interconnected computers without a center. It is decentralized and democratic. Second, relation-based governance is characterized by compartmentalization in which each private network or circle has its own secret ways of communicating, whereas the Internet promotes open and universal protocols and interconnectivity. Third, a relation-based system relies on secrecy and control of information; the Internet, on the other hand, promotes the free flow of information.

In China, there have been many cases in which corrupt officials were exposed by "netizens." Theoretically, the Internet will help public information to disseminate more efficiently, which will therefore improve the efficiency of rule-based governance. On the contrary, given the secretive nature of information in a relation-based system, the use of the Internet as a tool for greater transparency is limited. In other words, the Internet will make the gap in scale-based governance efficiency between relation-based and rule-based systems larger, putting more pressure on the relation-based system to transform into a rule-based system (Li, 2009).

Quantitative Evidence
Quantitative measures regarding how China has evolved in terms of its governance system over time are difficult to obtain. One way to

gauge the progress is to look at the economic governance-related indices developed by international rating agencies. I examine two such indices that measure governance-related indicators over time. The first is the Economic Freedom Index (EFI) published by Fraser Institute (Fraser Institute, 2020). The index "measures the degree to which the policies and institutions of countries are supportive of economic freedom" (Gwartney and Lawson, 2012). It is based on forty-two variables designed to measure the degree of economic freedom in five broad areas: (1) size of government, (2) legal system and property rights, (3) sound money, (4) freedom to trade internationally, and (5) regulation. As can be seen, three areas (2, 4, and 5) are pertinent to a sound rule-based governance system, and I therefore use it as a proxy to examine China's transition toward a rule-based system. In 1980, China's EFI was 3.91. By 2018, it was much higher: 6.21 (Table 3.3) (Note: the EFI has a range from 1 (least free) to 10 (most free)).

On the other hand, the more recent years saw deterioration in some measures, especially in the dimension of legal system and property rights. As can be seen from Table 3.3, of the seven measures of legal system and property rights, four declined and one was unchanged.

We can also revisit the Worldwide Governance Indicators (Figure 3.1 (a)) to assess whether China has moved toward rule-based governance. A comparison of China's WGI between 1996 and 2019 shows mixed results: Government Effectiveness showed the largest improvement; while Political Stability, Rule of Law, and Control of Corruption improved modestly. From 2014 to 2019, corruption has worsened. Voice and Accountability has been very low all along with little improvement. Regulatory Quality has gradually deteriorated over the years.

Summarizing the observations from the two indices, we can see that in a nearly forty-year span since China started economic reform, its economic institutions have moved substantially toward becoming more rule-based (as seen in the change of EFIs from 1980 to 2018).

Table 3.3. *Legal system and property rights index and components (partial), China, 1980–2018*

Ranting items/ year (1 = least free, 10 = most free)	1980	1990	2000	2010	2018	Change from 2010 to 2018
Summary Ratings	3.91	3.69	5.52	6.04	6.21	Increase
1. Size of Government	3.65	3.48	3.44	4.64	4.85	Increase
2. Legal System & Property Rights	3.67	4.79	4.90	5.42	4.93	Decrease
A. Judicial independence	2.84	3.12	2.98	3.53	3.75	Increase
B. Impartial courts	4.52	4.52	4.18	4.59	4.62	Increase
C. Protection of property rights	3.75	4.04	3.74	5.64	5.07	Decrease
D. Military interference in rule of law and politics	6.67	3.33	3.33	5.00	5.00	None
E. Integrity of the legal system	4.39	4.40	5.88	5.34	4.98	Decrease
F. Legal enforcement of contracts	4.25	5.87	5.74	5.87	4.75	Decrease

Source: Compiled by author based on data from Kaufmann et al. (2020)

However, we also notice that in recent years, the move toward a more rule-based system has not only slowed down, but has retreated in several dimensions. These apparent declines run counter to my argument that China is moving toward more rule-based governance. If this is true, what is the reason?

In both the EFIs and WGIs, the indicators that have been retreating from becoming more rule-based are voice and accountability, constraints on government, legal system and property rights, and control of corruption. All these are related to the increase in the size and power of the government. Since 1980, the size of government has become larger and larger (Table 3.3).

A clearer picture of China's transition (or lack thereof) is emerging: While China has made great strides toward instituting more public rules, the government has become bigger and more powerful due to the lack of accountability and rule of law, which in turn fuels corruption. It seems that the source of this lack of progress toward more rule-based governance is the government itself.

The Evolving Role of the State

In the early 1980s when the CCP initiated the economic reform, privatization and reducing government involvement in economic activity were key objectives. As a result of the reform, more economic and commercial laws were established; state policies and regulations became more rule-based; citizens and private firms gained greater freedom and opportunities to conduct business and pursue profits; and property rights became more secure (Hofman and Wu, 2009). In the late 1980s, a big wave of government employees quit their secure jobs to "jump into the (commercial) sea" (xiahai下海) to become entrepreneurs (Baidu Baike, 2012). This trend continued well into the 1990s, during which several developments occurred that may have helped reverse this trend. The first was the reconsolidation of government power after the 1989 crackdown on the pro-democracy movement, which made the CCP realize that it could not afford to open the door for power sharing or any political loosening up, because that would lead to the demise of one-party rule (see Chapters 1 and 2). The total collapse of communist regimes in the former Soviet Union and other Eastern European states further reconfirmed this belief among the leaders of the CCP. Second, in order to revitalize the economy, the CCP began a large-scale privatization to sell off most small- and medium-sized state-owned enterprises to people who were party officials or had good connections with the party. Typically, the buyers would bribe the officials in charge of the sale, and the latter would hand over the state-owned enterprise at a fire sale price. In the process, the newly made entrepreneurs and government officials became rich. Third, the productivity and efficiency gains from the privatization wave, along with the low rights advantage (see Chapter 2), have propelled the Chinese economy to enjoy a high growth rate. This in turn enabled the officials to extract more rent from the economy without encountering too much resentment from the population, as the trickle down of the high economic growth also improved the lot of the common people, although at a slower rate than their counterparts in the government.

As the economy grew rapidly, the government's revenue became bigger, and the officials became more powerful. According to Zhiwu Chen's calculations, from 1995 to 2007, the Chinese government's revenue increased 470 percent, a much higher percentage than the income growth of citizens, which were merely 60 percent and 20 percent for the urban and rural population, respectively (cited from Huang, 2012). The leaders of the CCP, while enjoying the lion's share of the economic growth, increasingly realized the benefit of monopoly and became determined to keep their firm control over the whole country without any sign of willingness to share power. In addition to enforcing the party's dictatorship, the government began to re-enter into the economy as a major player (US–China Economic and Security Commission, 2017). The high-paying jobs with many privileges in the state sector have made them the most preferred jobs for college graduates (Wu, 2016), which is a remarkable reversal of the "jumping into the sea" in the late 1980s and early 1990s (see Chapter 2). In 2006, the government announced that the state must maintain "absolute control" over industries that are important for national security, as most of them are highly lucrative, such as petroleum, telecom, and banking. The government established the State-owned Assets Supervision and Administration Commission (SASAC) to oversee the 121 largest non-financial companies owned by the central government, most of which enjoy a monopoly status and arbitrarily high profits (Xinhuashe (New

China News Agency), 2006). Many of the largest state-owned firms are controlled by the children and relatives of senior party officials, or the "princelings." According to a Bloomberg report, twenty-six princelings of eight revolutionary leaders who were comrades of Mao (known as "the eight immortals") control vast amounts of state assets. Moreover, all these princelings are connected through marriage. While the total amount under their control is difficult to know, Bloomberg estimated that three of the princelings controled about US$1.6 trillion in 2011 (Bloomberg, 2012).

3.4.4 It's the Political System, Stupid

The most fundamental resistant force against the transition from relation-based to rule-based governance is not the culture; it is the party-state and its well-entrenched officials. In this regard I partially agree with the entrenchment argument. While the conventional entrenchment argument focuses on the business community's deeply entrenched business network, I emphasize the deeply entrenched party-state officials. There is no doubt that political changes are much needed in China in order for it to move toward more rule-based governance.

While democracy and rule-based governance are separate phenomena (e.g., Hong Kong does not have a mature democracy but has a high degree of rule-based governance[8]), they are closely correlated and overlap through a common denominator: both the rule-based system and mature democracy require strong rule of law. In this sense, calling for political reform or democratization is almost equivalent to calling for the transition to rule-based governance.

The Chinese culture is not the main barrier for embracing rule-based governance. Citing the Chinese culture as the main reason that China cannot adopt rule-based governance is similar to using Chinese

---

[8] Hong Kong's rule-based governance has been reduced since the Chinese government implemented the National Security Law in 2020.

culture (or East Asian/Confucius culture) as an excuse for East Asian countries not adopting democracy, which has been falsified by the fact that many East Asian countries have become mature democracies (e.g., Japan, Taiwan, and South Korea).

The issues facing China's transition from relation-based to rule-based governance are not if and why, but *how* can China start political changes to move away from one-party rule, and *when* will such changes be carried out? Until recently, the debate on how and when had been focused on the political camps within the party-state, such as the liberal-leaning camp ("right," or reformists) that supports political reforms and the more conservative camp ("left") that opposes political reforms within the CCP (Jones and Lim, 2013; Li, 1999a; Nathan and Shi, 1996) (see also Chapters 1 and 2). Back then, the "how" question was what steps the reformists in the party would take to move toward rule-based governance, and the "when" question was about when the reformists would gain an upper hand in the power struggle within the party (Jones and Lim, 2013).

In 2012 when I studied the "how" and "when" questions, I reviewed how some leading scholars of China's reform viewed the emergence of the transition (Li, 2013b). The ones I reviewed all believed that political reform and change would occur soon. Minxin Pei argued that China's economic development had reached the threshold for democratization. He also believed this based on the fact that no modern dictatorship had survived more than seventy years, and the dictatorship of the CCP since 1949 was close to this time limit (Pei, 2012). Yasheng Huang used the personal security of the top leaders in China to argue that they should embrace the rule of law, for without it even the most powerful men in China might be persecuted if they lost a political fight (Huang, 2012). In other words, if the top CCP leaders realized that the benefit of having a better rule of law (providing personal security) outweighed the cost (losing the privilege to collect economic rents), they would push for instituting the rule of law and even democracy. Zhiwu Chen argued that if China did not start a real political reform soon to put some checks on the power of the government and stop the ever-expanding government revenue, social instability might become uncontrollable (Chen, 2012).

Indeed, as the scholars cited discussed, I believed that failure to complete the transition would reduce economic efficiency and worsen the conditions of the people who do not have access to private relationships with the powerful group in China. The Chinese government officials needed to realize the inevitability of the transition and the dire consequences of not completing it, and they needed to take the initiative to pursue the transition peacefully. For businesses, they needed to realize that the relation-based system may be in decline and be prepared to embrace the rule-based method.

Almost a decade later, with the benefit of hindsight, we now know that the party-state appears to be well entrenched in power and has no intention of starting political reform or embracing rule-based governance. What did we miss?

I believe that what we overlooked a decade ago is that China's success in globalization not only alleviated the social issues in China (see Chapter 2), but also has increasingly pushed the left and right in the party to merge into one force with one goal: to defend the benefit that China has gained from global trade and to achieve global dominance. There are no visible camps of left and right, nor are there ideological or policy debates in the party regarding whether China should embrace more rule-based measures. To address the how and when questions, we must consider the role of other countries, especially the democratic countries, in China's possible transition to rule-based governance. This will be discussed in Part III of this book.

3.5 SUMMARY

This chapter discussed China's legal system and governance environment. In terms of its legal system, China is weak when it comes to developing a rule-based governance structure in which the laws are independently and impartially enforced. I reviewed what hinders China's legal development from cultural, economic, and political perspectives. My central argument is that in the absence of a rule-based system, China has been relying on a relation-based system in which transactions and disputes are governed by private relationships. Understanding relation-based governance is key for foreign investors to protect their interests. I also discussed under what conditions the relation-based system can be efficient, and whether it will be replaced by the rule-based system in China.

4 Mao plus Deng

A Highly Aggressive and Productive Culture

If we learn anything from the history of economic development, it is that culture makes all the difference.

David Landes (1998)

4.1 A TALE OF TWO HIGH SCHOOLS

In my international business classes, I use the cases of two high schools to give my American students a sense of what they will face in global competition, and how culture plays an important role in it. The two schools are located on the opposite sides of the world in almost every sense: the United States and China.

4.1.1 Maury High in the United States

I live in Norfolk, an old, mid-sized city (population 244,000) in Southern Virginia with a lower income level and higher concentration of minorities than its neighbors. One of Norfolk's five public high schools is Matthew F. Maury High School.[1] It is the best in Norfolk and ranked 3,139 out of 24,000 nationwide, approaching the 90th percentile. However, its academic performance is not high by any standard: Maury students' Proficient in Reading score is 87 percent (Virginia's state average is 90 percent), their Proficient in Mathematics score is 73 percent (Virginia's state average is 80 percent), and their College Readiness Index is 49.9/100 (U.S. News & World Report, 2020). Overall, Maury High's academic performance leaves much to be desired.

---

[1] The information about Maury High School is partly based on interviews and school visits by the author (2005–2012).

However, a visit to the school may surprise you in a positive way. The school has a good infrastructure: An indoor swimming pool, a nice library, and an up-to-date computer lab. Teachers are dedicated, with advanced degrees from esteemed universities such as Duke University and the University of Virginia. Admiring Maury's magnificent Greek-style building, I was imagining what it would be like if we could airlift the whole school and put it in China – it would probably be a great school with high academic performance.

But why does a school with a good infrastructure and high quality, dedicated teachers fail to achieve higher academic performance in Norfolk? It is the desire to learn, the motivation to succeed academically that is missing among most students, many of whom are from broken families with one or both parents absent, or with parents who simply do not care about education. For example, it is not uncommon for Maury students to hang out late at night: In 2009, its football team captain was gunned down on the street around 1 a.m. after returning from a party (Wittmeyer and Wilson, 2009).

The small number of students from families that do value education excel at Maury. Maury teachers are thrilled by their achievement. For example, the physics teacher would use his own funds to award a US$100 scholarship to everyone who gets the top possible Advanced Placement test score in his class. Every year Maury will send a few students to some of the best universities: Harvard, Princeton, Yale, or MIT.

What sets the failing and the successful students apart in Maury, aside from the different intellectual abilities, is not the quality of the infrastructure or the quality and dedication of the teachers, but the culture of the students and their families that propels students to either value their education or forgo it.

4.1.2 Maotanchang Middle School in China

Some 7,600 miles (12,231 kilometers) away from Norfolk, there is another school, Maotanchang Middle School, located in its namesake, Maotanchang, a small town in Anhui Province, a less developed area of China, with a local population of

22,000.[2] Maotanchang, which was an obscure town about two decades ago, is now well known for its unique industry: the production of students with a high *Gaokao* score by Maotanchang Middle School, which is essentially an intensive "cram school" (guancha.cn, 2015; zh.wikipedia.org, 2020a).

The *Gaokao*, a high-level examination, can be thought of as the Chinese equivalent of the SAT. It is offered only once a year, in early June, and is the sole criterion to determine which college one can attend. Every year about 10 million college-bound high school graduates take the *Gaokao* on the same day throughout China. Given the large number of *Gaokao* takers, their chance of getting into a top school is very slim.

The reason the *Gaokao* is the sole determinant of college admission is that in a society with little public trust and high-level corruption and fraud, the *Gaokao* is the most fair and objective criterion for college admission. In China, where brand name and educational achievement are greatly emphasized, having a college degree from a prestigious university is necessary to be admitted into the professional and elite class. Thus, Chinese parents and children take the *Gaokao* very seriously. In order to achieve a high *Gaokao* score, parents send their children to cram schools. The Maotanchang cram school is not only one of the best but is also widely viewed as providing students of the lower class with average or lower academic records a much-needed chance to realize their dream (zh.wikipedia.org, 2020a). It attracts tens of thousands of students, who, along with their parents or grandparents, are willing to pay high tuition and living expenses to study there just for a chance to obtain a good *Gaokao* score and thus get into a decent university (People.cn, 2015b).

At the Maotanchang cram school, everything revolves around one and only one goal: helping the students score high on the *Gaokao*.

---

[2] In China's education system, middle schools include both middle (grades 7–9) and high schools (grades 10–12). This section used some material from my book: S. Li, 2016. *East Asian Business in the New World: Helping Old Economies Revitalize*. New York: Elsevier.

Students spend 17 hours every day studying, from 6:00 a.m. to 10:50 p.m. They crowd in about 40 classrooms with about 150 students in each. Many of them are accompanied by their parents or grandparents, who pay high rents to stay in small, partitioned rooms nearby and cook meals for them. To avoid the wait and lunch crowd, parents or grandparents bring lunch to students, who often eat quickly on the street and then go back to studying. In order to create a quiet environment to enable the students to study and rest well, the township government makes a great effort to keep noise down. Students do not walk, they run. They run to eat, run to buy daily necessities, and run to the bathroom.

The pressure to do well is high, and not everyone can take it. In late December 2015, just before the New Year, an eleventh grade male student jumped from the fifth floor of the school building and died. Before that, he called his father and said that he was tired of studying (guancha.cn, 2015).

In late May every year, as the *Gaokao* nears, preparation for the tests intensifies: students pay tribute to the "hall of fame" in the school with names of former students who scored high on the *Gaokao*; they release hot air lanterns into the sky for good luck; parents go to temples to burn incense and offer prayers. When the *Gaokao* comes, which usually lasts about three days, it is the moment of truth: Maotanchang sends more than 100 buses to transport test takers to the exams. Over 10,000 people – their parents and media from all over the world – gather there to see them off. Even the order of the buses has to be auspicious: Female students first, since the sound of "male" (nan) in Chinese is the same as "difficult" and thus a bad omen. The first bus driver should be born in the year of the horse according to the Chinese zodiac; an animal symbolizing speed and success (Jiang, 2014, Jun 5) (see Figure 4.1).

Maury High School and Maotanchang Middle School stand in stark contrast in several ways. At Maury, students' activities and lives are diverse: Some do sports, others do arts and music, and academic study is one of these activities. Many students do not plan to go to college. In Maotanchang, students breathe to do one activity: study,

FIGURE 4.1 Parents see students off for annual college entrance examination (*Gaokao*), Maotanchang (2018).
Source: Getty Images

and for one goal – getting into a university. All these factors point to one key difference: *culture*.

My question to my students is: Assuming that globalization will enable people from different countries to compete for jobs, are you ready to compete with the students from Maotanchang, or from China in general, who are more rigorously trained, but more importantly, are disciplined and have a hardworking culture?

4.2   CULTURE AND PRODUCTIVITY

4.2.1   *Culture Matters*

Why do economies grow differently despite having similar economic institutions such as market access for jobs and products?[3] For

---

[3] This section is based on S. Li, S. H. Park, and D. Selover (2017), The Cultural Dividend: A Hidden Source of Economic Growth in Emerging Countries. *Cross Cultural & Strategic Management*, 24(4), 590–616. http://dx.doi.org/10.1108/CCSM-08-2016-0149.

emerging countries such as China, one of the most important goals is improving economic growth. In order to boost economic growth, analysts and policymakers of emerging countries have been focusing on political and economic systems and policies. Needless to say, this vast effort by political economists and policy analysts has not been able to provide satisfactory explanations for why some economies grow faster than others despite having similar or even less efficient political and economic institutions.

Take China for example. Compared with countries with similar levels of institutional quality and income, China greatly outperformed its peers in productivity gains by as much as five times (17.8 percent versus 3.5 percent) in the decade from 2001 to 2011, the early stage of China's economic development (Table 4.1). In this regard, China's much higher performance relative to its peers is a puzzle. And the puzzle points to a deficiency in the study of economic development. In the quest to understand the determinants of economic performance, one factor has been conspicuously missing: culture.

What exactly is culture? There are many different definitions of culture, but most of them agree on the essential points. The Merriam-Webster dictionary defines culture as "the integrated pattern of human knowledge, belief, and behavior that depends upon the capacity for learning and transmitting knowledge to succeeding generations" (Merriam-Webster, undated). The American Heritage New Dictionary of Cultural Literacy defines culture as "the sum of attitudes, customs, and beliefs that distinguishes one group of people from another. Culture is transmitted, through language, material objects, rituals, institutions, and art, from one generation to the next" (cited from Li et al., 2017b). Hofstede, Hofstede, and Minkov (2010) bring a digital insight, describing culture as, "the collective programming of the mind that distinguishes the members of one group or category of people from another." These definitions have three characteristics more or less in common: (1) the idea of culture is broad and includes knowledge, beliefs, customs, attitudes, and behavior, (2) different groups or societies may have different cultures, and (3) culture

Table 4.1. *Productivity gains, institutional quality, and income level of low-income countries and China, 2001–2011*

Country/region	Income per capita	Annual labor productivity gain (2001–2011)	Institutional quality (Economic Freedom Index)	Change in institutional quality (Economic Freedom Index)
Group 1 (countries with per capita income US$750–$1,250) (excluding China) (n = 11)	$935	3.5%	5.40	0.39
China	$1,000	17.8%	5.28	0.39

Source: Li, Park, and Selover (2017b)

is passed on from generation to generation. Summarizing this, my coauthors and I define culture as the set of beliefs, values, social norms, and attitudes that shape people's behavior in a given group of human beings and are transmitted from one generation to the next (Li et al., 2017b). This section addresses the following question: What is the relationship between culture and labor productivity growth?

To continue with the case of China, it has had a high economic growth rate of approximately 10 percent annually for about thirty years, creating an economic miracle that few would deny. However, as to what factors caused such a miracle, there is little consensus. The dominant view is that the economic institutional change that began after Mao's death in 1976 was the main cause of the phenomenal economic performance of China (see Chapter 2). While it is true that the economic reform played an instrumental role in China's economic growth, we must recognize that economic institutional quality alone cannot explain the high economic performance of China. As Table 4.1 shows, China's economic institutional quality is similar to that of its peers (i.e., countries with a similar income level), and its change in institutional quality is also similar to that of its peers; however, its productivity gain is substantially higher than those of its peers.

In fact, China's economic institutions have some features that are not very conducive to growth: It has a huge public employee population supported by taxpayers, and these employees do not exhibit a high level of efficiency; state-owned enterprises account for a large share of the economy and enjoy government protection; property rights protection is weak, and the restrictions on private firms are many. How could China achieve great economic growth given such an institutional environment?

One factor that may help explain the economic miracle, but which has been missing in most academic research on this topic, is culture (see China Watch, 2008; Mao and Su, 2012). These observations have motivated my coauthors and I to examine the relationship between culture and labor productivity, which is the fundamental source of economic growth (Li et al., 2017b). As the comparison of Maury High School and Maotanchang Middle School shows, the presence or absence of a culture that values education and hard work sets them apart.

4.2.2 What Do We Know about Culture and Economic Performance?

There is a rich literature on the evolution of scholars' thinking on culture and economic performance. In this subsection I provide a detailed review of the literature to facilitate readers such as researchers who want to delve deeper into how the issue has evolved. Other readers can skip this and go to Section 4.3 on how culture affects productivity.

Researchers have been concerned with culture and economies for well over a century. Even casual observers of culture have long felt that culture has important implications for economic behavior and economic outcomes. In the nineteenth century, Western adventurers to Africa and Asia felt that they could explain the differences between Europe and Africa by reference to culture. Anthropologists have thus been concerned with culture for a long time.[4] Sociologists, such as Max Weber (1958 (1904–1905)), have attempted to explain the economic development in northern Europe as partly due to the "Protestant ethic," encouraging people to work hard, build enterprises, engage in commerce, be self-reliant, be frugal, and accumulate capital for investment in enterprise. Anthropologist Oscar Lewis (1959) attempted to explain the modern incidence and persistence of poverty through the concept of "a culture of poverty," an idea that became the subject of much controversy. Political scientists, such as Almond and Verba (1965), employed the concept of culture, attempting to explain political outcomes by the reference to political cultures.

However, unlike the anthropologists and sociologists, modern economists have been reluctant to accept the concept of culture as a driver in explaining economic growth and development. This has come about for several reasons. First, culture is a multi-dimensional concept that seemed too broad, too imprecise, and too amorphous to be used in economic research. Second, historically, early economists would often ascribe phenomena that they could not explain as resulting from culture. Thus, the concept gradually came to represent an admission of ignorance. Third, economists focus on the central organizing principle of the rational agent, the idea that economic actors form their behavior by optimizing profits and utility subject to resource and income constraints. They focus on the concept of rationality to the almost complete rejection of the idea of culture, an anthropological concept that developed later than economics. Culture

---

[4] Interested readers may read Franz Boas (see F. Boas, 1963 (1911). *The Mind of Primitive Man*. New York: Collier Books, B. Malinowski, 1922. *Argonauts of the Western Pacific*. London: Routledge and Kegan Paul, and Ruth Benedict, 1961. *Patterns of Culture*. Boston: Houghton Mifflin.

is a concept that seems to undercut the idea of rationality, at least partially (although it need not do so). For these reasons, economists today are reluctant to use the concept of culture in their theories and economic models.

More experts on culture, such as Hofstede et al. (2010) and Tromenaars and Hampden-Turner (2012), often describe culture as like a "layered onion." The deepest, most immutable characteristics of culture, such as the basic assumptions and deepest values, lie at the center of the onion, covered by a layer of social norms and values, and that layer in turn is covered by the most overt and most changeable characteristics of culture (including symbols, artifacts, and attitudes). While it is often difficult to measure the deepest values and basic assumptions of a culture, it is much easier to examine social norms and attitudes.

For society, a very important part of culture, especially as it pertains to economics, is the idea of social norms, that is, "shared understandings about actions that are obligatory, permitted, or forbidden in society" (Ostrom, 2000). Ostrom describes how social norms might have evolved in human societies because the survival of human groups depended on those groups being able to efficiently solve "day-to-day collective action problems." "Those of our ancestors who solved these problems most effectively ... had a selective advantage over those who did not." Thus, we see a natural selection not only of individuals with beneficial characteristics but also a natural selection and evolution of the social norms that enable societies to survive.

Douglass North (1990, 1991) emphasizes the role of institutions in determining the advance of economic development. However, it should be noted that North's definition of institutions includes much of what we might properly consider part of culture. For example, "Institutions are the humanly devised constraints that structure political, economic and social interaction. They consist of both *informal constraints (sanctions, taboos, customs, traditions, and codes of conduct)*, [emphasis by author] and formal rules (constitutions, laws, property rights)." Thus North (1991) considers culture to be an important part of the institutions on which he expounds. North (1990, 1991) points out that even though strong formal institutions (such as the US Constitution) might be transferred from one society to another, the results might be radically different. What explains the difference? North (1990) suggests that it is the informal constraints in society, such as culture.

Kuran (2009) finds that within civilizations there are complementarities between culture and material life that make it difficult to transfer institutions from one society to another. This is why it is difficult to successfully establish political and economic reforms. It will also make it difficult to empirically establish the connection between culture and economic performance.

Adkisson (2014) gives a concise survey of the literature regarding the relationship of culture to the economy. Many people have pointed out that before we can quantify and test the relationship between the economy and culture, we first need a way of quantifying and measuring culture. Several researchers have attempted to quantify culture and to decompose it into constituent parts. One of the most successful and influential of these researchers has been Geert Hofstede. Hofstede (2001) initially decomposed culture into four dimensions, but the framework has subsequently been expanded into six constituent dimensions: (1) Power distance, a concept that measures the extent to which less powerful members of society accept an unequal distribution of power. (2) Uncertainty avoidance, which gives a measure of societal tolerance for uncertainty and ambiguity. (3) Individualism versus collectivism, which gives a measure of the extent that individuals are integrated into groups. (4) Masculinity versus femininity, which measures the value that society places on competitiveness, assertiveness, ambition, and power versus relationships and the quality of life. (5) Long-term orientation versus short-term orientation, which measures the value that society places on sacrificing the present for a better tomorrow in contrast to a short-run approach to life. (6) Indulgence versus restraint, which measures society's propensity for free gratification and an enjoyment of life versus restraints on gratification and a need to be regulated by social norms.

In an expansion of Hofstede's model of culture, Hofstede, Hofstede, and Minkov (2010) view culture as the "software of the mind," a mental programming that enables individuals to be able to form a mental framework and use that framework to be able to communicate and interact with other individuals around them. This view emphasizes the importance of culture for the interaction of individuals within society.

Trompenaars and Hampden-Turner (2012), among others, offer an alternative decomposition of culture. However, because Hofstede has developed a plausible and useful dimensional framework, and has made relative measurements of these dimensions for most of the nations of the world, many researchers have begun using Hofstede's dimensional breakdown. The present research uses Hofstede's cultural dimensional framework to study the potential effect of culture on labor productivity.

Many researchers have attempted to link the relationship of national cultures to national economic performance. David Landes (2006) wrote an economic history treatise describing the economic development of the world's great civilizations and why some succeeded and some failed. His bottom line is that economic development often comes down to a question of culture, and that some cultural characteristics promote economic development and some discourage development. In a potentially important economic theoretical model of culture, Bisin and Verdier (2001) examined the effects of cultural transmission on social preferences.

A number of researchers have approached the question of the effect of culture on growth directly, by estimating economic growth equations and including cultural variables as explanatory variables. These include Franke, Hofstede, and Bond (1991), who use correlations and regressions to analyze the effects of culture directly on economic growth. They find that growth is aided by "Confucian dynamism," including thrift, perseverance, and hierarchical organization. Swank (1996) investigates the effect of culture on economic growth and finds that although culture is not dominant, it probably has some impact on economic growth. Granato, Inglehart, and Leblang (1996) test whether or not cultural factors affect economic development and find that cultural factors have significant and important effects on economic growth. Johnson and Lenartowicz (1998) investigate the relationship between culture, economic freedom, and economic growth. They find a strong positive correlation between economic freedom and economic growth and conclude that economic freedom appears to be the missing link between culture and economic growth. Beugelsdijk (2007) finds that within Europe, entrepreneurial culture has statistically significant positive effects on economic growth.

The problem with growth equations is that there are many different factors that can cause or inhibit growth, and consequently this approach is very susceptible to omitted variables bias. Moreover, most of the growth equations estimated here use overly simplified equations. Another problem with this approach is that culture does not directly have an effect on macroeconomic growth. Culture instead operates through various behavioral mechanisms, which in turn have an effect on economic growth. The mechanisms through which cultural variables might have an effect on economic growth are multi-faceted and often indirect. For that reason, it is probably a better strategy to estimate models in which culture has direct effects on different growth factors, and those factors in turn have an effect on growth. Examples of these types of studies might be the effect of culture on saving behavior, work-effort behavior, labor productivity, and risk-taking behavior, to mention just a few.

4.2.3 How Culture Affects Productivity

Here we focus on how culture affects productivity gains. We draw on theories from social science to build our case with a focus on emerging economies while searching for clues to boost economic development. Based on our qualitative studies and literature review, we propose the following explanation for how culture affects labor productivity, integrating economic, political, and social cultures.

Cultural characteristics have an effect on society's demand for goods and on society's productivity in producing those goods. For example, social norms or values on hard work, on independence, on self-reliance, on thrift, on investment, on commerce, on delayed gratification, on time, on education, on quality of workmanship, on willingness to face risk, on trust, on honesty, on openness to new ideas, on creativity, and on willingness to break with the past are all values that would help a person become a more productive worker. In contrast, stronger values placed on socializing, adhering to old customs, and paying over-deference to seniors might lead to slower productivity growth.

In recent times, socioeconomic conditions have changed faster than culture, so that culture is always in the mode of evolving to help improve the prospects of its individuals. Now in the early twenty-first century, we are seeing that individuals from the Confucian cultures – China, Korea, and Japan – tend to succeed and produce even more wealth for their economies (under the right formal economic institutions). Confucian values, such as values on education, thrift, and on hard work, may have certain advantages for economic growth. Baumann and Winzar (2017) explain how Confucian values may promote a work ethic beneficial for economic growth. However, other Confucian values, such as respect for elders, may have disadvantages for economic progress, scientific discovery, technical innovation, and creativity by placing overly restrictive definitions on the relations between people and over-deference to older generations.

What are the mechanisms by which culture can have effects on labor productivity? There are several different potential mechanisms. People who can exercise more self-restraint and who are more long-term oriented tend to invest more time in education and training. Consequently, they exhibit greater improvement in their labor productivity. A cultural propensity for learning and education can help create a more educated, more scientifically oriented workforce that can forge technological progress. Some cultures are more fastidious and emphasize attention to detail, a characteristic helpful in scientific discovery and mass production. Some cultures pay more attention to conformity and authority. This may promote progress in mass production, but may inhibit progress in scientific discovery and creativity. People who are less risk averse are more likely to start new enterprises. Countries in which individuals save more will have more funds available for investment in new plant and equipment. With more capital equipment, such societies can increase their labor productivity, thus leading to increased economic growth, greater wealth, and a higher standard of living. People who are more patient tend to become better workers and produce higher quality products. They are more likely to invest in human capital development and education. They are also less likely to engage in disruptive economic activity, such as labor union strikes and political movements.

4.2.4 Our Postulations

Our main argument is that culture is an important factor affecting labor productivity, and therefore economic performance. Specifically, we have the following arguments.

First, a person's desire to work hard is shaped by a desire to improve their economic welfare. According to Maslow's (1954) hierarchy of needs theory, the poorer people perceive themselves to be, the stronger the desire to earn money by working hard. This attitude is also closely linked to attitudes toward inequality and redistribution. People who hold a hardworking attitude tend to believe they will do better than the average population, and they are thus more tolerant toward the inequality that results from competition. They tend to dislike high taxes (Weil, 2013), and they tend to plan for the long term because they believe they can receive greater economic reward by sacrificing immediate consumption (see Hofstede et al., 2010). *Therefore, we expect that all these economic-related attitudes affect labor productivity gains.*

Second, politically, people who hold a hardworking attitude tend to be more conservative (or more traditional) in the sense that they are more willing to follow authority and forego freedom (see Przeworski, Alvarez, Cheibub, and Limongi, 2000). More specifically, they tend to maintain greater power distance (Hofstede, 2021), rely on government as opposed to valuing autonomy, and demonstrate more conformity and less tolerance of different attitudes. *Based on this reasoning, we expect that these political attitudes lead to less conflict and thus exert a significant effect on labor productivity gains.*

Third, socially, people's attitudes toward work are passed on from generation to generation, and family is one of the most important channels through which this culture is learned. There is a rich literature in sociology showing that people growing up in broken families tend to perform more poorly in work and study (see Foran, Beach, Slep, Heyman, and Wamboldt, 2013; Macionis, 2001; Popenoe, 1993). Drawing on this, we argue that people who support traditional family values tend to have higher productivity. Using the same logic but from a different perspective, Baumann, Hamin, and Yang (2016) emphasize the role of education in the development of the work ethic. From a generational transfer and thus a family perspective, when the children grow up and become adults, they modify their attitudes and behavior (and hence their culture) to conform to the changing economic conditions and to maximize their well-being, and then in turn pass on the new, modified culture to their children. In each generation the change in attitude and behavior is not very great because it is socially costly to change attitudes and behavior. Culture thus cascades down from generation to generation, being modified with each new generation according to the evolving economic and social environment. Two-parent households make the cultural transmission stronger, while broken households weaken the transmission. *Summarizing this, we expect that attitudes toward the family affect gains in labor productivity.*

In Section 4.4, I will present the empirical evidence for these postulations.

4.3 A PERFECT CULTURAL STORM FOR CHINA'S RISE

Based on historical, political, economic, and legal reasons, I argue that from Mao's death in 1976 to today, China has had an exceptionally strong pro-economic growth culture. Historically, the Confucian culture of frugality, hard work, and respecting the family is conducive to economic productivity. Of course, the Confucian culture had existed in China for about two thousand years, and for many long periods in history, China did not have high economic growth. As we will show later, any productive culture must be accompanied by pro-growth political and economic institutions.

Politically, the authoritarian political system has shaped a population that is relatively more obedient and deferent to authority – traits that contribute to efficiency for low-skilled work such as manufacturing or customer service.

Economically, decades of poverty under Mao's rule left a horrible memory of absolute poverty and made people extremely motivated to work hard to make money. The economic deprivation under Mao can be reflected in the saying regarding the "three most desirable jobs" during that era: "Stethoscope, steering wheel, and sales," because medical products and services, transportation, and virtually all goods were in extreme shortage (Xinxianren, 2015).

Legally, the weak rule of law and lack of a legal tradition nurtured a relation-based culture that encourages people to circumvent the law and get things done using private connections (see Chapter 3). All these cultural traits have been invigorated by the CCP's pro-growth policy, such as allowing private ownership and free markets in nonstrategic industries and agriculture. This combination and timing have created the strongest wealth acquisition culture in China since the founding of the PRC in 1949.

In this perfect cultural storm, two values stand out and have played key roles in shaping Chinese work ethics. The first is the lawlessness taught by Mao Zedong (1893–1976), who founded the PRC in 1949 and ruled it with a lawless style. The second is "getting rich is glorious," promoted by Deng Xiaoping (1904–1997) (see Chapter 2), who was the de facto leader of China after Mao's death until his death in 1997.

4.3.1 Mao's Call to Be Lawless

Mao's China can be characterized as a proletariat society ruled by extreme radical communism. Being rich was shameful. The less property one had, the more glorious one became. Private property was not respected or protected. The ideology of anti-wealth and anti-property ownership can be clearly seen in the four versions of China's constitution that the CCP has written since it took power in 1949.

From the 1950s to Mao's death in 1976, in addition to staging numerous political purges (see Chapter 2), economically, the CCP confiscated private properties without due process. Business owners were forced to turn their assets over to the state. According to Chinese government figures, for example, in 1952, private businesses still accounted for 55 percent of China's industrial output; by 1962, that number had dropped to zero. In 1958, Mao staged the "Great Leap Forward," causing one of the biggest famines in history – some 30–40 million Chinese died of starvation. During the peak of the Cultural Revolution, from the 1960s to the 1970s, not only were private properties taken by the state, but state properties were openly robbed by the revolutionary masses as well. The history of the communist revolution in China is a history of repudiating property ownership. Usurping properties from the propertied class is a glorious act. When people had no private property, they lost their sense of the sacred, inviolable nature of ownership, one of the most important heritages of civilization. In all civilized societies throughout history, violations of private property rights, such as stealing and robbery, have been viewed universally as crime. However, when private properties were wiped out in the name of revolution and "social justice," this was no longer true, particularly when it came to public properties, because they did not belong to a specific person or persons but to a vague, abstract notion of "the whole people." The argument was that because every citizen was one of "the whole people," everyone had a claim to the property. Thus, it was perfectly moral for citizens to help themselves to public assets. The net result was a lack of respect for property rights.

Mao was famous for ignoring the legal rules he set up (Li and Yeh, 2008). In 1970, Mao told American journalist Edgar Snow,[5] "I am hairless and lawless! Just like 'a monk carrying an umbrella'"[6] (Chinanews.com, 2008). As Geremie Barmé explained about Mao's monk expression here, "Mao was in effect saying that he, or rather the revolutionary enterprise he led, was beyond restraint" (Barmé, 2018).

Mao's radical communism had left an indelible imprint on the culture of contemporary China, not only for common people but also for business leaders. A study my coauthor and I conducted (Li and Yeh, 2008) shows that Mao's tactics in political struggles, military strategies, and his doctrine that the end justifies the means are widely followed by business executives in China. We interviewed fifteen Chinese CEOs, and fourteen of them told us they often turned to Mao's teachings for management ideas.

A tactic Mao used was keeping the country in a state of chaotic flux and playing one group against another. To make a change in the political landscape, Mao would orchestrate a movement that sucked in the entire population, such as the campaign against Liu Shaoqi (the number two leader in the CCP) and his allies, then resort to a mixture of agitation, networking, and rallying to mobilize people at the grass roots to denounce certain cadres, or senior officials. Most of the cadres

---

[5] Snow was the first western journalist who extensively covered Mao and the CCP and introduced them to the world in the 1930s. His best-known book is *Red Star over China* (Random House, 1939).

[6] "A monk carrying an umbrella" is a Chinese allegorical humor (*xiehou yu*). It means the subject is like a monk who is 'hairless' (*wufa/fa* 无发（法）: a pun for lawless) and that since he is carrying an umbrella there was no sky above him (*wutian*无天: a pun for following no pre-ordained principle), G. R. Barmé, 2018. For Truly Great Men, Look to This Age Alone: Was Mao Zedong a New Emperor? *China Heritage*, Jan 27 (http://chinaheritage.net/journal/for-truly-great-men-look-to-this-age-alone/): Accessed November 29, 2020.

would be forced out of their jobs, and Mao would rehabilitate a few. Deng Xiaoping was denounced in this manner, rehabilitated, and denounced again.

In our study we found several Chinese chief executives who employ a business version of that tactic: They cement their authority by keeping even senior managers in a constant state of uncertainty, sometimes mobilizing lower-level employees to criticize and pressure mid- and upper-level executives.

A call center company we studied offers an example. Rather than directly fire some of her middle managers, the CEO mobilized lower-level employees to defy them, leaving them with no choice but to resign (the CEOs we spoke to did not want their names used). In another instance, a former general manager of a call center told us she had to quit after her subordinates were directly mobilized by the parent company's CEO to circumvent her orders and pressure her to resign.

Many high-profile Chinese business leaders are Mao's admirers and have used his strategies and tactics in their operations (Wu, 2006). Next are some examples.

Zong Qinghou is the founder and former CEO of Wahaha, the French-Chinese beverage joint venture. He claimed that "I learned from Chairman Mao on how to manage my company" (Wu, 2006). Around 2006–2007, Zong circumvented the formal organizational procedures during a dispute and mobilized Wahaha employees to publicly denounce the French management (Li and Yeh, 2008).

Shi Yuzhu, who is well known for the dramatic rise and fall of his company named "Giants," has extensively studied Mao's military thoughts and has applied them in his business operations. His company organization mimics Mao's military hierarchy and structure, and he used Mao's people's war strategy and mass mobilization for his marketing campaigns (Wu, 2006).

Huawei's CEO Ren Zhengfei proudly said, "my teacher is Chairman Mao." Ren especially admires Mao's military strategy and tactics: mass mobilization, the use of criticism and self-criticism (see

Chapter 2), and keeping the company in a state of chaotic flux (Laomao, 2019). His recent statement that, in the face of sanctions by the democracies, Huawei must "kill to open a bloody road forward" was a common revolutionary slogan in Mao's era (Xu, 2020).

As will be shown in Part III of this book, Mao's thought is the theoretical foundation for the aggressive strategies and tactics that CCP uses in international affairs (such as the "wolf warrior" tactics, see Wikipedia, 2020i).

4.3.2   Deng's Call to Get Rich

Beginning in 1978, post-Mao China began its economic reforms (see Chapter 2). Deng Xiaoping was a pragmatic man with a vision of making China prosperous. One of his most famous sayings was a reversal of Mao's policy: "getting rich is glorious." The Chinese people took him seriously. They began to get rich. But neither Deng nor his successors realized – or perhaps they conveniently ignored – that to emulate the success of the advanced economies, China needed to restore the institutions of property rights, including formal institutions (laws) to protect them and informal institutions (culture) to respect them.

Thus, the combination of Mao Zedong's legacy of no respect for property rights and lawlessness and Deng Xiaoping's slogan "getting rich is glorious" implies that people can get rich by any means – no matter whether the rights of the state, foreign investors, or private businesses are violated in the process. Thus, we observe simultaneously the booming of money-making activities and the looting of properties in China.

4.3.3   Consequences of the Mao-plus-Deng Culture

In China, depending on the types of ownership, such as state-owned, foreign-owned, or privately owned, there are different ways of viewing property rights violations.

For state-owned properties, the prevalent view is that stealing them is not as bad as stealing from private owners, because state properties belong to no one and are wasted by the bureaucrats anyway. A common view is that for state properties, "if you do not steal it, someone else will" (Nanhaiwang, 2008; Sohu.com, 2020b). The large scope and persistent loss of state assets in China is a good example (Baidu Baike, 2015). In China, "state asset loss" is a special term that refers to the losses of state assets by the investors or managers who, intentionally or not, make mistakes or violate laws and regulations. Most of these losses end up as private gains for the people in charge. Since the government keeps state asset loss statistics secret, we do not have the complete picture of their extent. One article reports that from 2012 to 2017, the Central Commission for Discipline Inspection (Zhong Ji Wei, see Chapter 2) disciplined several dozens of state asset managers who stole 800 million yuan (US$123 million) (Wu, 2019). An article by MBA Lib compiled some data on state asset losses. These included a 1992 underreporting of 31 billion yuan (US$4.8) by state-foreign joint ventures. Additionally, funds stashed away for discretionary use are estimated to be 14.8 billion yuan (US$2.3 billion), and the government improperly took 110 billion (US$16.9 billion) from state-owned firms (MBA Lib, circa 2006). According to Ernst & Young, by the end of 2001 China's bad loans had reached US$480 billion (equivalent to about 40 percent of China's GNP). Since then the Chinese government has made great effort to crack down on relation-based loans, with little effect: in 2020, Chinese banks disposed of 3 billion yuan (US$465) in nonperforming loans (Trivedi, 2021). Money from state banks is up for grabs. Whoever has power and connections will get it. In fact, banks in China give loans to related parties, such as senior bank officers and major shareholders, who never repay them. This is a primary concern about opening the banking sector to private investment in China: The major shareholders of these banks would simply "borrow" the money of depositors and never repay it.

For a different political reason, but stemming from the same genre of lack of respect for property rights, the rights of foreign investors are also violated. According to communist doctrine, foreign investment exploits the indigenous people. Therefore, violating the property rights of foreign investors is not only justified but also popular among citizens, given that the act is viewed as "usurping foreign capitalists." For example, there are many reports that foreign companies' intellectual properties were illegally taken by Chinese partners and the state is not only reluctant to stop such theft, but in some cases helps the perpetrators, such as the case of DuPont in China. When DuPont Co.'s Shanghai office reported suspected intellectual property rights (IPR) violation by its Chinese partner to the Chinese authorities, the Chinese police raided DuPont's office, demanded passwords, printed documents, seized computers, and intimidated DuPont employees. Instead of helping DuPont to protect its property, the state used "an array of levers to pry away American intellectual property" (Wei and Davis, 2018). Foreign companies are also targets of selective enforcement of laws and regulations. Walmart has been a frequent target for fines and censures. For example, from 2006 to 2011, the Chinese government took twenty actions against Walmart (Sina.com, 2011). In 2014, Shanghai Husi Food, a subsidiary of US food supplier OSI Group, was raided and several executives were arrested and subsequently imprisoned by Chinese authorities for violating food safety. The evidence against them was merely an anonymous video clip showing that a piece of meat was dropped on the floor. OSI and some Chinese employees of Husi believed that it was unfairly targeted and unfairly treated by the Chinese government (Guancha.cn, 2014; Jourdan, 2015).

A personal story also illustrates this vividly. A friend of mine, a Chinese American, is a partner in a US-based investment fund. In the early 2000s, he went to China to oversee the operation of a joint venture that his fund invested in with a local Chinese firm. During a meeting with the executives of the Chinese firm, the two sides disagreed on a major issue. One of the Chinese then pulled my friend out of the meeting and said, "Don't protect the interests of these American capitalists, we can make a deal under the table." My friend was outraged. But for the Chinese, there was nothing wrong with the proposition.

Recently, there have been a growing number of cases in which the state has forcibly taken over or confiscated private businesses. Two of the most highly visible cases are the insurance giant Anbang Insurance Group (estimated assets: 1.97 trillion yuan (US$318 billion)) that was taken over from the main shareholder Wu Xiaohui, who was sentenced to eighteen years in prison and fined 10.5 billion yuan (US$1.7 billion) in 2018 (BBC, 2018b), and the Tomorrow Group (estimated assets: more than 1 trillion yuan (US$15 billion)) that was taken over from its controlling shareholder Xiao Jianhua, who "was snatched from a Hong Kong luxury hotel and disappeared into Chinese custody" in 2017 (Stevenson, 2020).

The lack of property protection also leads to capital flight. Most of China's nouveaux riche and the middle class feel insecure about their assets. Evidence of this can be seen in the trend common among them to move a substantial portion of their assets overseas. Beijing does not release numbers on capital flight. A commonly used method to indirectly estimate the amount of capital flight is to examine the item known as "errors and losses" in the official international revenue and expenditure statistics. From 2011 to 2017, the cumulated amount of "errors and losses" was US$1.3 trillion (Yu, 2017).

Perhaps the most damaging and life-threatening product of the Mao-plus-Deng culture is the thriving counterfeit goods industry in China. Following this "anything goes" culture, businesses cut corners and produce fake products. An online joke about this declared

> The Chinese have greatly enriched their knowledge of chemistry in recent years, not through national science education, but by eating food with added chemicals such as melamine (in dairy products), paraffin wax (in rice), dichlorvos (in ham), malachite green and formaldehyde (in seafood), copper sulfate (in mushroom), clenbuterol (in pork), methanol (in alcohol), Sudan red I (in duck eggs) . . .
>
> *(Lattemann, Fetscherin, Alon, Li, and Schneider, 2009)*

Although most of these terms are alien to people outside of China, the world has certainly learned the word "melamine" from

China, which is a high-nitrogen chemical that many Chinese firms add to animal feeds and human foods – such as poor-quality milk products to boost the protein levels in lab tests – that also cause kidney failure and death. By 2008, more than 51,900 children had been hospitalized and six had died from kidney failure. In 2007, many dogs and cats in the United States died because of melamine added to their food. Worldwide, numerous products in many countries have been contaminated with melamine originating in China (World Health Organization, 2008). According to the Chinese government, over 40 percent of goods sold online in China are counterfeit (Reuters, 2015).

In sum, the combination of lack of respect for and protection of property rights and the drive to get rich by any means has undermined the confidence of investors and consumers – both domestic and foreign. It will hinder China's economic development in the long run.

4.4 KEY CULTURAL FACTORS THAT IMPROVE PRODUCTIVITY

Recent developments in collecting cultural-related data across countries have made empirically studying the relationship between culture and productivity more feasible.[7] My coauthors and I conducted a statistical analysis on how culture affects productivity based on our postulations (see Li et al., 2017b, and Section 4.2). The data and findings of that study are reported next.

4.4.1 The Data

We examined over one hundred possible explanatory variables using data from reliable sources such as the World Bank, the World Value Survey, and the Conference Board to identify the cultural variables that would affect labor productivity. After a preliminary screening, we

---

[7] This section is based on S. Li et al. (2017), The Cultural Dividend: A Hidden Source of Economic Growth in Emerging Countries. *Cross Cultural & Strategic Management*, 24(4), 590–616. http://dx.doi.org/10.1108/CCSM-08-2016-0149.

narrowed down the list to a smaller number of cultural characteristics and studied their effects on the growth of labor productivity.

The main variable of interest and the dependent variable (the variable that we believe is affected by culture) is the growth of labor productivity, computed between 2001 and 2011 from the national labor productivity in GDP per hour as collected from the Conference Board Total Economy Database (see Table 4.A in Appendix).

The main independent variables of interest (the variables that we believe affect productivity) are the cultural variables, including the Hofstede cultural dimensions of "Long-term Orientation" (LTO), "Uncertainty Avoidance Index" (UAI), and the "Power Distance Index" (PDI). One of our innovations is to use Hofstede's cultural variables to explain gains in labor productivity. Other cultural attitudinal variables include "attitudes toward income inequality," "attitudes toward taxes," "tolerance and respect for others," "perceptions of freedom and autonomy," "attitudes toward government regulation," and "attitudes toward single parent families." These variables come from the World Value Survey (see Table 4.A).

The control variables (other variables that we are not interested but may also affect productivity) are per capita gross national income, people's perceptions of their financial situation, the change in the rate of literacy, and the change in the economic freedom index (see Table 4.A).

4.4.2 The Findings

After extensive analysis of the data, we have the following findings.

Economic-Related Attitudes

We used three indicators to measure the association of productivity gains and economic-related attitudes across countries.

People's satisfaction with their own financial situation. The first indicator is based on the World Value Survey (2012) (WVS) question, "How satisfied are you with the financial situation of your household?" This is a subjective question about one's self-perception, with

"1" being "dissatisfied" and "10" being "satisfied," respectively. As can be seen, people in countries with high productivity growth (the HP group) have substantially lower levels of satisfaction toward their own financial situation. An analysis of variance indicates a statistically significant difference (p = 5.9%) in the levels of satisfaction between the groups, with the high productivity growth countries being less satisfied. The post hoc difference between the low (L) and the high (H) productivity gain countries is statistically significant at the p = 5% level. This supports Maslow's (1954) hierarchy of needs theory.

Long-term orientation. The second indicator we use is Hofstede's "long-term orientation" (LTO), which measures people's propensity to seek quick results or future rewards. A culture of long-term orientation has "a strong propensity to save and invest, thriftiness, and perseverance in achieving results" (Hofstede, 2021). We find that the aggregate attitudes of countries with high productivity gains are more long-term oriented. There is a positive relationship between long-term orientation and productivity gains.

Uncertainty avoidance index. The third is Hofstede's "uncertainty avoidance index" (UAI), which measures to what extent the members of a society accept uncertainty and ambiguity. Cultures with a strong UAI index "maintain rigid codes of belief and behavior and are intolerant of unorthodox behavior and ideas" (Hofstede, 2021). In other words, they tend to avoid risk-taking. We find that people in countries with higher productivity gain are more risk-taking. There is thus a negative relationship between uncertainty avoidance and productivity growth.

In sum, we observe that countries in which people are unsatisfied with their financial situation, plan longer-term, and are more risk-taking tend to have greater productivity growth. China belongs to this group.

Attitude toward income inequality. In a WVS question, people were asked to choose between a number close to 1 if they agreed that "incomes should be made more equal" and a number close to 10 if they agreed that "we need larger income differences as incentives for individual effort." More people in the groups with higher productivity gains (Mid-productivity gain and High productivity gain) are in favor of having larger income differences as incentives for individual effort. As expected, there appears to be a positive relationship between views on income inequality and productivity growth. This relationship holds in China. A 2012 survey by Globescan asked people in twenty-three countries whether they agree that "most rich people in my country deserve their wealth." A high percentage of "agree" can be interpreted as high tolerance of income inequality. The percentage of "agree" for China is 52 percent, which is high and ranked fifth (Australia has the highest percentage: 61 percent and Greece the lowest: 9 percent) (GlobeScan, 2012). A 2019 report on attitudes to wealth by the law firm Withersworldwide observed that "In China, the inequality gap doesn't anger people as much as inspire them to join the millions of others around them they see pulling themselves up into a burgeoning middle class" (Withersworldwide, 2019, p. 6).

Attitude toward taxes. When it comes to taxation, the survey respondents from the high productivity-gain countries dislike taxes more than their counterparts in the low productivity-growth countries. This is revealed by examining two WVS questions: The first asks people to choose between "a society with extensive social welfare, but high taxes" and "a society where taxes are low and individuals take responsibility for themselves." The other asks people whether "cheating on taxes if you have a chance" is "never justified" or "always justified." The results show that, people from low productivity-gain countries replied more positively toward higher taxes and higher social welfare, and China does not belong to this group.

Summarizing all of this, we find that the social attitudes of high productivity-gain countries (1) prefer self-reliance and tolerate income differences, and (2) do not favor high taxes.

4.4.3   Effects of Attitudes toward Authority and Freedom

There have been a vast number of studies on how people's attitudes toward authority and autonomy affect their work efficiency. We use several cultural variables to examine this relationship.

Power distance. Hofstede's "power distance index" (PDI) measures "the degree to which the less powerful members of a society accept and expect that power is distributed unequally."

> People in societies exhibiting a large degree of power distance accept a hierarchical order in which everybody has a place and which needs no further justification. In societies with low power distance, people strive to equalize the distribution of power and demand justification for inequalities of power.
>
> *(Hofstede, 2021)*

We found that people in countries with high productivity gains have substantially higher power distance, a positive relationship.

Tolerance and respect for others. This is measured by a WVS question that asks people whether they encourage children at home to learn "tolerance and respect for other people." The percentage of people who answered yes is lower in countries with higher productivity gains, and we found a negative relationship.

Freedom and autonomy. To gauge people's perceptions of their freedom and control over their lives, we used a WVS question that asked respondents "to indicate how much freedom of choice and control you feel you have over the way your life turns out," and to choose between "none at all" and "a great deal" of control. Interestingly, people in countries with higher productivity gains felt they had less freedom of choice and control, a negative relationship between perception of control and productivity growth. There is a statistically significant difference (at a 2 percent level) between the low (L) and high (H) productivity-gain countries.

Government regulation vs. people being responsible for their own actions. This WVS variable can be used to measure people's attitudes toward the role of government. In this sense, it can be part of economic culture as well. The question asks the respondent's preference between "a society that assures safety and stability through appropriate regulations" and "a deregulated society where people are responsible for their own actions." A low value indicates a preference for more regulation, and a high value indicates a preference for low regulation. People in high productivity-gain countries prefer strong government regulation to individual self-responsibility.

In sum, the culture of the high productivity-gain countries tends to be more authoritarian and less free in orientation, and people in high productivity-gain countries tend to prefer more government regulation as opposed to individuals taking responsibility for their own actions. They tend to feel that they have less control over their lives, and they tend to be less tolerant and have less respect for others. China belongs to this group.

4.4.4   Effects of Family-Related Culture

The family – the most basic element in a society and the primary organization in which a person is brought up and socialized – plays the most important role in forming the norms and values to which a person adheres. It is the most important vehicle through which culture is passed from generation to generation. When the family is broken, it will adversely affect children's learning of the established culture of a society. We examined the relationship between people's attitudes and behavior toward family and productivity growth, using the following variables.

View of happy family: Both parents present. One WVS question asks whether the respondent "tend[s] to agree" with the idea that "a child needs a home with both a father and a mother to grow up happily." Respondents from higher productivity-gain countries show a higher percentage of agreement with this statement.

View of single mothers. To the WVS statement that asks is it OK if "a woman wants to have a child as a single parent but she does not want to have a stable relationship with a man," respondents from higher productivity-gain countries responded with a much lower percentage of approval for single parent households.

Marital status/divorce rate. Based on the WVS data, respondents from higher productivity-gain countries have a lower divorce/separation rate. This is a measure of behavior, which confirms the attitude of the respondents toward the family and marriage.

Summing up these findings, we can see that the higher productivity-growth countries, including China, tend to prefer stronger family values and have more intact families.

4.4.5   Caveat: Economic Institutional Change Is Still Important

According to North (1990), the fundamental reason for a country's poverty is in its economic institutions. Thus, for underdeveloped, low-income countries to boost their economic growth, first and foremost, they must start economic reforms to establish the building blocks of a market economy, including a system of property rights, a free-market exchange system, incentive systems, and a sound legal system that protects property rights and economic transactions. In this regard, we can say with firm conviction that without such economic institutional change, poor countries cannot achieve high productivity growth no matter how conducive their cultures are to productivity gains. Our study on the importance of the role of culture on productivity gains does not negate the importance of economic institutional change in instigating productivity growth.

4.5   SUMMARY

This chapter discussed how culture affects economic development. Based on historical, political, and economic reasons, I argued that China today has a strongly pro-economic growth culture. Historically, the Confucian culture of frugality, hard work, and respecting the family is conducive to economic productivity. Politically, the authoritarian political system has shaped a population that is relatively more obedient and deferent to authority – traits that contribute to efficiency for low-skilled work such as manufacturing. Economically, decades of poverty under Mao's rule made people extremely motivated to work hard to make money. All these cultural traits contributed to China's high economic growth.

I also drew attention to the fact that Mao had left an indelible imprint on today's business leaders in China, a unique and important phenomenon that the international business community should be aware of. Finally, I showed that the "Mao plus Deng" effect – Mao's lawlessness and Deng's call to get rich – is the root cause of property rights violations and especially the persistent problems of product safety and counterfeit goods in China.

4.6 APPENDIX

Table 4.A. *Data Sources*

Variables	Description	Source
Country names and code		World Bank Data.worldbank.org; In Excel file: "productivity culture wealth data Jason and yi"
Labor productivity	"LP-person GK" for the LP data, 2001 and 2011 Labor productivity is GDP per hour.	The Conference Board Total Economy Database™ Output, Labor, and Labor Productivity Country Details, 1950–2011 January 2012 www.conference-board .org/data/ economydatabase/ In Excel file: "productivity culture wealth data Jason and yi"
Hofstede culture dimensions	(1) Individualism vs. collectivism; (2) Uncertainty avoidance; (3) power distance; (4) masculinity vs. femininity; and (5) long-term orientation	http://geert-hofstede .com/argentina.html In Excel file: "productivity culture wealth data Jason and yi"

Table 4.A. (*cont.*)

Variables	Description	Source
GNI pc USD	GNI per capita, Atlas method (current US$), 2001	World Bank http://data.worldbank .org/indicator/NY.GNP .PCAP.CD?page=2 In Excel file: "productivity culture wealth data Jason and yi"
Wealth tolerance score, 2008 and 2012	"Do you think most rich people in your country deserve their wealth?"	Globescan www.globescan.com/ commentary-and-analysis/press-releases/ press-releases-2012/84-press-releases-2012/220-public-remains-concerned-over-wealth-inequalities-global-poll .html In Excel file: "productivity culture wealth data Jason and yi"
Culture, growth, and economic freedom indicators	Data from Williamson and Mathers (2011).	Williamson, C. R. and Mathers, R. L. (2011). Economic Freedom, Culture, and Growth. *Public Choice*, 148(3–4), 313–335. doi: 10.1007/ s11127-010-9656-z In Excel file: "productivity culture wealth data Jason and yi"
Variables from World Development Indicators	Adolescent fertility rate (births per 1,000 women ages 15–19), 2001 Total fertility rate, 2000 Literacy rate, 2000 Tax rate, 2000	World Bank http://data.worldbank .org/indicator/SP.ADO .TFRT/countries?page=2 In Excel file: "productivity culture

Table 4.A. (*cont.*)

Variables	Description	Source
	GNI per capita, 2001 Repeaters, elementary school, 2000 Social transfers, 2000	wealth data Jason and yi″
Emerging market index	EME = 1 if a country is an Advanced Stage EME, or EME = 2 if a country is an Intermediate Stage EME, or EME = 3 if a country is an Early Stage EME, or EME = 4 if a country is dormant, or EME = 0 if a country is not on the following list.	SKOLKOVO Business School – Ernst & Young Institute for Emerging Market Studies (IEMS) www.skolkovo.ru/ public/media/ documents/research/ IEMS_research_2012-08_ eng.pdf In Excel file: "productivity culture wealth data Jason and yi″
WVS variables	Trust, respect, self-control, obedience, attitudes toward divorce, single mother, happy family, social welfare, tax, poverty, etc.	World Value Surveys, 2012
Divorce rate	Divorce rate	UN Demographic Yearbook
Economic Freedom Index	Economic freedom, judicial independence, impartial court	Economic Freedom of the World (Fraser)
Political Right Index	Political rights, civil liberties	Freedom in the World Survey, Freedom House 2001
Rule of Law Index	Rule of Law Index	Economic Freedom of the World (Gwartney et al. 2002)

Source: Li, Park, and Selover (2017b)

PART II **The Rise of China, Inc.**

5   The Emergence of China, Inc.

> Our advantages include ... treating the entire nation as a chessboard,[1] mobilizing every sector, and concentrating resources to do something big.

(Chinese Communist Party, 2019)

5.1   THE CCP'S INCREASING CONTROL

After a brief period of thawing and liberalization from the late 1970s, the old guard in the party led by Deng Xiaoping quickly began to fear that if the liberalization continued, the party would lose power (see Chapters 1 and 2). So, in 1979, Deng Xiaoping laid out "four cardinal principles": upholding the socialist path, upholding proletarian dictatorship, upholding the leadership of the CCP, and upholding Mao Zedong Thought and Marxism-Leninism. "The core of the four principles," according to Deng, "is the party's leadership" (Central Commison for Disciplinary Inspection, 2018).

After the 1989 Tiananmen Crackdown (see Chapter 2), the era of Jiang Zemin (CCP general secretary, 1989–2002) focused on economic recovery and development, and Hu Jintao's term (CCP general secretary, 2002–2012) enjoyed a high economic growth rate but at the same time was infected by rampant corruption. The second half of Hu's era also saw increasing control by the party-state, the so-called *guojin mintui* (国进民退, the state advances, the private sector

---

[1] "Treating the entire nation as a chessboard" in Chinese is "全国一盘棋" (*quanguo yipanqi*). This is a metaphor meaning that all individuals and organizations in China must follow the party's order and coordination to achieve the goals set by the party.

retreats) (Baidu, undated-c). Since Xi Jinping became the general secretary in 2012, the state's advance has gone further (Voice of America, 2019).

If during Deng's time the CCP leadership reinforced its grab on power out of necessity – for fear of losing control – later on successive CCP leaderships increasingly realized that they should grab more and more power for their own control and benefit. In fact, the best strategy was to increase their control over all aspects of society as much as possible. As a result, China has turned into one giant corporation run by the CCP (Li and Farrell, 2020c). In this chapter, I will show how China, Inc., is built.

5.1.1 The System of Mobilizing the Entire Country as a Whole

In recent years, the CCP has been promoting what it calls "*juguo tizhi*" (举国体制), which means "the system of mobilizing the entire country as a whole." Xi Jinping calls for "maximizing the advantage of our system of mobilizing the entire country as a whole" (Beijing Daily, 2019).

According to experts in China, the system is to

> mobilize the country's manpower, material inputs, capital for national interests and to realize the nation's highest goals. It is to conquer the world's cutting-edge basic sciences or technologies, or to accomplish key national projects or systems. The system of mobilization is the advantage of socialism that enables us do something big.
>
> *(Beijing Daily, 2019)*

The mobilization system has the following features: first, it is under the absolute leadership of the party; second, it focuses on new technologies and industries deemed strategic by the party; and third, it is linked to globalization and the international markets (Beijing Daily, 2019).

5.2 THE FIRM FROM A COMPARATIVE PERSPECTIVE

Before delving into China, Inc., I need to provide some background on a number of key concepts such as the firm (or hierarchy), business unit, market, and society, and the relationship between them.

5.2.1 Firm versus Business Unit/Department

A firm (or a company) is a for-profit business organization, such as a corporation, that produces and sells products or services in a market (Kenton, 2020). A firm is an independent entity and usually has a single owner or multiple owners. The owner of the firm usually enjoys the property rights of the firm, including its tangible and intangible (intellectual) assets. The owners' full property rights have four dimensions: the right to use the firm (or its assets), the right to earn income from the firm, the right to transfer the firm to others (e.g., sell or destroy it), and the right to enforce their ownership (Dixit, 2004; Econ Journal Watch, 2011).

The owner of the firm can also hire others to work for the firm, and the employees of the firm must follow the orders of the owner and forego certain rights (or follow the restrictions imposed by the owner), such as not sleeping on the job or criticizing the firm or disclosing the trade secrets of the firm.[2]

In comparison, a business unit or a department of the firm is not independent; it belongs to and is therefore part of the firm. Unlike the owner of the firm, the director of the business unit or a department of a firm – such as the general manager of a keyboard production unit of a computer firm, or the general manager of the meat department of a supermarket – does not have the full property rights of the business unit or the department they operate. The head of a business unit or department may be able to hire others to work for their unit, but they must be authorized by the owner to do so.

---

[2] In a society under the rule of law, firms cannot impose any rules that violate the law.

5.2.2   *Country versus Firm*

Originating from the Western countries, economic and management researchers have largely focused on firm behavior under the assumption that the macro institutional setting is a free market in which the firm's assets and autonomy are protected by the rule of law (Dixit, 2004, p. 2).

In this setting, the government's power over the firm, such as the firm's operations and personnel, is rather limited (recall the rule-based governance in Chapter 3). For example, the US president cannot tell Amazon to fire an employee because they have criticized the president. Likewise, the US government cannot prohibit any firms – including firms from China – from doing business in the United States or confiscate their assets without due legal process.

Employees of a firm and residents of a country (citizen and noncitizens residing in the country) have different rights. Residents may have diverse views about the country. As a resident of a rule-of-law country, they enjoy extended rights and may push the country to change according to their views through legal and civil channels. For example, they can publicly disagree or even ridicule the leader of the country, demonstrate against the government, or leave the country, or rather, *not* leave the country even if the leader of the country hates them. These entitlements include many rights that residents may not even be aware of, for these rights are so basic and natural. For example, residents may choose where to live in the country. They can freely invest anywhere in the world, or convert their assets such as cash in the form of the country's currency to any foreign currency. In sum, these rights are basically entitlements, a default option, born with or automatically given to citizens and legal residents.

In contrast, as an employee of a firm, their rights are more restricted. An employee is expected to work hard to help the firm make money. They should refrain from openly criticizing the leader of the firm. If an employee does not get along with or objects to the decisions of the management or the owner, the latter can fire them.

Of course, the employee has the option to quit (even this may not be free, depending on the terms of employment), but if they choose to stay, they must obey the restrictions imposed by the firm. If the firm offers housing to its employees, the employees must follow the terms of the firm. If the firm wants them to leave the company housing, they must oblige. Employees cannot freely invest in the firm: the owner must approve it; employees cannot freely sell the firm's assets or convert allowances such as meal coupons the firm gives them to cash in the market. In sum, the employees are not born with or entitled to these rights; they are granted by the firm and the firm has great discretion to decide whether to terminate all their rights or even fire them.

5.2.3 Market versus Hierarchy (Firm)

The market versus the hierarchy is a classic debate in organizational economics relating to the theory of the firm, which asks the questions of why do firms exist, and why does a firm perform certain tasks within the firm and farm out other tasks (Coase, 1937)? The hierarchy means to complete tasks within the firm, or to rely on the corporate hierarchy, and the market means for a firm to use other firms or contractors to do a job (relying on the market). For example, should a media firm, such as a newspaper or a book publishing house, print its own newspapers or books (the hierarchy) or ask an outside printing firm to print them (the market)? The answer, in a nutshell, is that the firm should choose the option that has the lowest transaction cost.

A newspaper company prints newspapers every day. If it uses a contractor to print its newspaper, the contractor may be busy and fail to print the newspaper on time. So, it is more efficient to own its own press (the hierarchy). A book publishing house, on the other hand, does not need to print books daily and can do them in batches. So, it does not have to own a press, which can be costly when the book publishing house does not have enough books to print on a daily basis.

Table 5.1. *Market versus hierarchy*

	Benefits	Costs
Market	Informational efficiency, High-powered incentives	Transaction costs, Market power
Hierarchy	Authority, Unified ownership, Coordination	Bureaucracy, Agency costs

Source: Made by author based on Collis and Montgomery (1997)

In general, the benefits of keeping a task in house (the hierarchy) are that the firm can effectively order its workers to do things (authority); its unified ownership of all resources within the firm ensures that everyone works for the same goal; and the management of the firm can effectively coordinate all subunits and workers to work on a project. The costs of hierarchy stem from more layers (business units, departments), which incur more bureaucracy and agency costs such as cost overrun and waste (Table 5.1).

The benefits of assigning a task to a vendor or contractor (the market) are informational efficiency (the interaction of supply and demand generates most accurate prices available) and enjoying high-powered incentives (bidders compete for the firm's work). The costs of the market are transaction costs of negotiation, contracting, and enforcement, and that a big vendor may use its market power to take advantage of the buying firm (Collis and Montgomery, 1997) (Table 5.1).

The contrasting characteristics between the key concepts reviewed in this section provide the foundation for the argument that my coauthor, Matt Farrell, and I made when we built our case for how the CCP runs China as a giant firm (Li and Farrell, 2020c). In the remaining chapter, I will present our argument and support it using the contrasting features between market and hierarchy, country and firm, and firm and business unit.

5.3   LIVING AND DOING BUSINESS IN CHINA

To start a business in China, one needs to go through many steps that do not exist in most market economies. [3] First, naming a firm is strictly controlled by the government. Words such as "China," "Chinese," "central," "state," "national," "nationwide," or "international" are controlled by the government and cannot be used in a firm's name without the permission of the central government (Chinese Government, 2017, Chapter 3, Article 19). Second, the address of the business must meet the rules of the government and be approved. "Not all buildings zoned for commercial use can be approved by the state for business registration, first make sure you have a registerable office address," someone who went through the process warned (Ji, 2013). Third, the business must agree to let tax authorities directly take funds from its bank accounts (Ji, 2013).

A businessperson said,

> Privately owned firms are 'rootless trees' because we are not allowed to own the key resources vital for us. We only are allowed to use them. All these resources are controlled by the government at various levels. The government may take them back and kill your business at any time. Its decision is absolute and cannot be challenged by laws.
>
> *(Cai, 2019)*

According to the rules of the CCP, if there are three or more CCP members in an organization such as a business, the organization must establish a party branch office. There are over 90 million party members in China so the chance of having a few of them in a firm is not low. Furthermore, based on the rule that "the party must lead everything in everywhere" (see Chapter 2), the party secretary of the branch office can interfere with or even overrule the business

---

[3] Sections 5.3–5.5 are based on S. Li and M. Farrell (2020). The Emergence of China, Inc.: Behind and beyond the Trade War. *International Journal of Emerging Markets*, in press.

head/owner. A blogger confirmed it, "That is true ... when I quit HP (China), I had to get the approval (to quit) from the party branch office" (Zhihu.com, 2015).

In 2019 the Hangzhou City government announced that they would install one hundred "representatives of governmental affairs" in one hundred important firms such as Alibaba and Zhejiang Geely Holding Group. Similar actions have been taken in other regions (Radio Free Asia, 2019b).

On the flip side, the party-state helps firms in China, including privately owned firms, as if they were its own. For example, Huawei Technologies Co., Ltd., is a privately owned firm that was founded by Ren Zhengfei in 1987. Ren served in the People's Liberation Army as a deputy regimental chief, a position for which only an ardent CCP member is qualified. Ren has kept a close relationship with the party-state. Early on, Huawei used illicit and secret payments to local officials to obtain service contracts and sell equipment (Harwit, 2007). According to a *Wall Street Journal* report, Huawei has received US$75 billion from the Chinese government in the form of grants, credit facilities, tax breaks, and other financial assistance (Yap, 2019). Another example is the Commercial Aircraft Corporation of China Ltd. (COMAC). In addition to financial support, the Chinese government used state intelligence forces to implement cyberattacks on, and to recruit from, foreign companies in order to obtain needed technologies to aid COMAC in its development of a commercial aircraft called the C919. The known victims of the cyberattacks include Ametek, Honeywell, Safran, Capstone, and GE (Hruska, 2019; Kozy, 2019). In 2019, the Chinese government issued tax exemptions for certain IC and software firms, a measure commonly believed to help mainly Huawei and ZTE, since they were under US investigation or sanction (Neihan Shiwusuo, 2019).

As expected, the opportunity to run a business comes with the responsibility to do what the party-state asks the business to do. Here are some examples.

- To help the Nationalist Party (Kuomintang) in Taiwan to win the 2020 election (which they did not), the party-state ordered the major airlines in China to offer half-price tickets to Taiwanese doing business in China so that they could more easily return to Taiwan to vote (Andongni, 2019).
- A study found evidence that Chinese local governments pressured private firms to hire more workers than they needed (Li, Tang, and Zuo, 2017a).
- After months of pro-democracy movement activity in Hong Kong in 2019, Beijing asked large state-owned firms to increase their investment and control in the crisis-hit city (Zhai, 2019).
- When China wanted to improve its relationship with the Czech Republic, shortly before a state visit by Xi Jinping, a privately owned firm in China, CEFC China Energy, "sent a big gift to Prague" by injecting capital into a Czech airline company, a soccer club, and a brewery (Radio Free Asia, 2019a).
- The Chinese government has a policy of "window directing" ("窗口指导" *chuangkou zhidao*) for security trading companies. If the stock market is viewed as too hot by the government, the government will order the trading companies to sell in order to cool the market; if the market is viewed as too depressed, the government will order the trading firms to buy to push it up (Shi, 2019; Ying, 2019; Yu, 2019a).

The government imposes stringent restrictions on the use of Chinese currency and on how much foreign currency people can exchange and send overseas (Yu, 2019b). The limit for each Chinese resident to convert yuan into foreign currency is US$50,000. Transactions of 50,000 yuan (US$7,200) or more and transfers of 200,000 yuan (US$28,800) or more are directly regulated by the central bank. Any private exchange of currencies is a criminal offense (hotbak.net, 2020).

The party-state can require Chinese firms and people to collect intelligence overseas.

According to China's National Intelligence Law, Article 14, "State intelligence work organs, when legally carrying forth intelligence work, may demand that concerned organs, organizations, or citizens provide needed support, assistance, and cooperation" (Girard, 2019).

A senior US official warns that tech companies Alibaba and Tencent, along with Huawei, " … can in some important respects or for some purposes act as arms of the state – or more precisely, the Chinese Communist Party, to which the Chinese state apparatus is itself subordinate" (Li, 2019a).

A former CCP member, commenting on the nature of Huawei, said that while Ren Zhengfei is the largest shareholder (1.1 percent) and CEO, the party secretary is Zhou Daiqi. Based on the principle of "the party leads everything in everywhere,"

> The top leader of Huawei is Zhou, not Ren. Huawei is not an independent, privately owned firm, nor is it a simple state-owned firm … it is a tool of the CCP. The party lets Huawei employees to hold 98.9% shares on paper so that it looks like a privately owned firm. This is to mislead the world … in China, there are no real privately owned firms anymore.
>
> *(Liang, 2019)*

In its plan to develop Xiongan, a city in Hebei Province near Beijing, the Chinese Government decided that there will be no privately owned housing. All dwellings will be owned by the government and will be leased to people who either own businesses or have work contracts. Thirty-one large state-owned firms have pledged to support the government's plan. The government has essentially made Xiongan a "company town" with firms handpicked to relocate there. Chinese people who do not own firms or work there cannot live there (Chinese Economists, 2019).

The CCP, directly or through the Chinese government, disciplines and punishes firms and people politically, financially, and physically. As mentioned in Chapter 2, the CCP's Disciplinary Committee (Zhong Ji Wei) can arrest and imprison people without any legal procedure or restrictions (Zhou and Li, 2018). The official media, People.cn, admits that, while the party maintains an appearance of separation of the party and the government, the party orders the government to discipline employees (People.cn, 2015a). Government employees who criticize the CCP will be terminated (Chinese Government, 2019c).

The Chinese government has established a punishment rule named "Restraining Order on High Level Consumption" and has established a Blacklist of Untrustworthy (people and firms) that are subject to the order. The list for 2018 had 14,210,000 entries (Chinese Government, 2019a). People who are on the list cannot engage in the following: luxury travel (flying, taking business class train or cruise ships, staying in hotels), luxury consumption (buying real estate, taking vacations), and cannot even send children to private schools. Business owners, managers, or other individuals can be listed if they are deemed to have failed in their financial responsibilities or have engaged in other behaviors deemed offensive by the party-state (baike.baidu.com, 2017b). In the "709 Crackdown" (July 9th Crackdown) in 2015, lawyers who helped people on human rights issues were arrested and jailed. Their families were barred from renting homes and their children were barred from attending schools (Amnesty International, 2018). As mentioned in Chapter 2, I learned firsthand from a former executive of a private company that the local CCP office ordered his company to dismiss him in 2019 after he mentioned the Tiananmen massacre of June 4, 1989. Any foreign countries, firms, or individuals that mention words deemed offensive to the party-state may be banned from entering China or doing business there, as shown in the 2019 NBA case in which China blocked its game broadcasting because an NBA employee expressed his support for the democracy movement in Hong Kong (Dreyer, 2019; see Section 7.7 for more details).

Reacting to people who criticized the CCP, Xi Jinping reportedly said that, "No one is allowed to eat from the party's wok and break it" (Sixiang Huoju, 2014). Apparently, Xi and the CCP regard China as their property: Indeed, the party-state owns all the land. Strictly speaking, without their permission, no one can engage in income-generating activities in China.

5.4   MAKING THE COUNTRY A CORPORATION

The data, facts, and information examined so far in this chapter are by no means comprehensive, but by piecing them together, we can see a clear pattern concerning how the party-state manages the entire country as a whole.

5.4.1   The Country Is Like a Firm

As shown in Table 5.1, the firm, or the hierarchy, has three major advantages: authority, unified ownership, and coordination. The party-state has them all. The party-state has absolute authority over the country and its people; its total control over all resources in China is equivalent to a unified ownership, which gives the people and businesses in China a common goal (working for the party-state); and its system of "mobilizing the entire country as a whole to do something big" gives it the ability to coordinate among regions and industries to accomplish projects that have high priorities for the party.

The party-state's power to coordinate can lower the transaction costs of doing business in China, such as providing land at little to no cost for key projects, demolishing buildings for new construction without market rate compensation, and laying off or reassigning workers with little resistance (see Chapter 2 on the low human rights advantage). All these resemble the management of internal departments of a corporation.

The Chinese government treats its currency to some extent like a firm regulating its internally circulated coupons. The cash assets that Chinese people (or foreigners in China) have in the form of Chinese yuan are not free to be converted or transferred without government approval.

Similar to strategic planning for a corporation, the party-state sets a target for China's growth every year (see Chapter 2). In 2019, the target was announced by the government in March in the range of 6–6.5 percent (Chinese Government, 2019b). The government regulates housing prices

(Wang, Qi, and Yang, 2019) and stock market prices. Since the beginning of the economic reform, the government has gradually reshaped its old central planning function into a strategic development function (see Chapter 6). In 1998, the government changed the State Planning Commission, a legacy of the planned economy, to the State Development and Planning Commission. Later, in 2003, the commission was changed again to the State Development and Reform Commission. In the Phase 1 agreement with the United States, the Chinese government agreed to buy US$40 billion a year of US farm products (Associated Press, 2020). The governments of most countries are not in a position to buy huge quantities of farm products – only firms and private agents are. This further shows that the Chinese state acts like the top management team of a corporation, which is the entire country of China.

Organizationally, the leadership of the party-state is the top management team, with the general secretary of the party as the chairman and CEO (See Figure 5.1 for the hierarchy between General Secretary Xi Jinping and his staffs and workers, who dress and act uniformly.); the Politburo is equivalent to the board of directors; the State Development and Reform Commission acts like the corporate strategy department; and the country as a whole is its assets and resources.

5.4.2 Firms Are Like Business Units or Subsidiaries of China, Inc.

In general, owners of firms in China do not have the full property rights that their counterparts in countries of rule of law enjoy. The extent to which firm owners in China have the property rights of their firms varies across different types of ownership. Of course, the owner of the state-owned enterprises (SOEs) is the state; therefore these firms do not have independence. SOEs are the backbone of China, Inc. How much does the state own in assets? The Chinese government has not released clear, understandable information about this. Of course, from the perspective of running China as a corporation, it does not have to release such information that is pertinent to the firm. Another possible reason is that assets under government control are

FIGURE 5.1 Chinese President Xi Jinping (R) talks with workers during his visit to Changchun Railway Vehicles Co., Ltd under CRRC Corporation Limited in Changchun, capital of northeast China's Jilin Province, July 17, 2015.
Credit: Yao Dawei/Xinhua/Alamy Live News

so complicated and extensive that the official statistical office simply cannot count them accurately. According to a CCTV (China Central Television) report, SOEs account for 32 percent of assets in the manufacturing sector, and for 64 percent of firms (note: firms, not assets) in the service sector. The same report also mentioned that the government is pushing for SOEs to attract investment from private and foreign investors to form joint stock companies. Two-thirds of large SOEs that report to the central government have restructured to become joint stock companies, and 49 percent of SOEs that report to local governments have done so. This restructuring effort implies that the government controls more assets than before by controlling these joint stock companies (CCTV.com, 2019).

According to a research note by a World Bank economist, SOEs contributed 23–28 percent of China's GDP in 2017 (Zhang, 2019a). SOEs are like *business units*, as they have virtually no autonomy. State-invested joint stock companies are like subsidiaries of China, Inc., as they have other shareholders and thus more autonomy than SOEs. There are a small number of firms that are classified as "collectively owned." These are the legacy of the planned economy under Mao (Park, Li, and Tse, 2006). These firms have close ties with the government but have more autonomy than SOEs, and thus can also be viewed as *subsidiaries* of China, Inc.

Privately owned firms in China refers to firms owned by private investors who are Chinese nationals. They enjoy greater autonomy than SOEs, collectively owned firms, and other state-invested or state-related firms. However, they are not as independent as their counterparts in a free market based on the rule of law. First, they need permission to operate, and this permission is not automatic, nor is it an entitlement. Any individuals or entities that do not have a good standing with the party-state cannot get a business license. For example, if someone has criticized the party-state, they cannot operate a business in China. Every step or procedure to establish and operate a business requires the party-state's approval and blessing, including naming the new company, as discussed earlier in this section.

A report in Chinese newspaper *The Masses' Daily* (*dazhong ribao*) described the headache of a private firm general manager in choosing to buy equipment. For the equipment, the manager wanted to buy from a domestic maker, while the city government wanted the firm to buy a foreign-made, more expensive version, because then the purchase price could be counted as "foreign investment" to boost the city officials' performance. And the general manager admitted that if they defied the city, the city could make their operation difficult, including by telling banks not to give the firm the loan for the purchase (*The Masses' Daily*, 2001).

Suning Holding Group is a privately invested and owned conglomerate with businesses in the retail, real estate, and finance sectors. In Suning's 30th anniversary celebration in 2020, its CEO Zhang Jindong declared, "Suning always answers the calls of the state policies . . . we serve the state policies . . . When a company is small, it belongs to the individual [owner], when it is big, it belongs to the society, the state" (Radio France Internationale, 2020).

As compared to foreign-owned firms, which will be discussed next, privately owned firms are a closer part of China, Inc., as they can be easily mobilized and coordinated by the CCP to achieve the objectives of China, Inc., such as the case of Huawei, in which Huawei's doing business with Iran is widely viewed as fulfilling the Chinese state's strategy of helping Iran overcome US sanctions. The way in which private firms must closely follow the party-state's orders is to a great extent equivalent to the party-state having some ownership of the firm, which, in most cases, can essentially determine the firm's fate. In this sense, private firms are more like a *joint venture* between the private owners and the party-state, with the latter having a *de facto* controlling right. A good example of a private firm under such control is Ant Group, a financial service provider founded by Jack Ma, the founder of the e-commerce behemoth Alibaba. The group owns China's largest digital payment platform that serves more than one billion users with a total payment volume of 118 trillion yuan (US$17 trillion) in the first half of 2020. The group was scheduled to make an initial public offering (IPO) in November 2020 in the stock exchanges of Shanghai and Hong Kong to raise US$34 billion. Despite its colossal size and dominant market power, the party-state directs and controls it as if the party owned it. In early November, after Jack Ma made some witty but unflattering comments about the state's financial regulations, the party summoned and scolded him, and cancelled the IPO. It is reported that in the meeting with the CCP's officials, Ma told them "You can take any of the platforms Ant has, as long as the country needs it" (Wei, 2020). The party did not take his offer. Based on the China, Inc., perspective, the party does not have to take any of Ant's assets *de jure*, as it is the *de facto* controlling shareholder of all private firms in China.

Foreign-owned firms have greater autonomy but are also subject to more restrictions than privately owned firms. All restrictions on private firms apply to foreign firms. Furthermore, foreign firms are not allowed to operate in internet information services, publishing, printing, and most media businesses (see Chapter 7). They do not receive as much support as Chinese-owned private firms, as the latter is a more obedient instrument for the party-state to use. The greater autonomy of foreign firms is based on their "foreignness" and their ability to get support from their home government and from the international community.

One of the restrictions for foreign-owned firms is that taking the profits or the proceeds of selling the business out of China needs the party-state's approval. And many foreign investors found that they could not get it. For example, in the early 2000s, IDG, a US-based investment fund, could not take the money it earned in China out of the country (Li, 2002a). Around 2017, a private equity fund manager told me that for a long time, they could not take their legitimate income out of China. And then at a meeting he ran into a senior official of the People's Bank of China who was in charge of currency exchange and happened to know the fund manager. After he complained to the official, the official promised to let him take the money out. This fund manager was extremely lucky: out of numerous foreign firms in China, how many could get to know a senior official in China who could help them with their legitimate requests?

For foreign firms, doing business in China is not an entitlement. Not all foreign firms have an equal opportunity to enter China, contrary to what is prescribed by Chinese law. Only those that maintain good relationships with the party-state may get permission to operate in China, and under the terms set by the party-state, which are often not in the purview of the public. In this sense, foreign firms are like *franchisees* of China, Inc.

Figure 5.2 illustrates how the party-state treats firms of different ownership structures in terms of the degree to which the party-state controls and supports them. The degree of control by the party-state is

Organizational Structure of China, Inc.

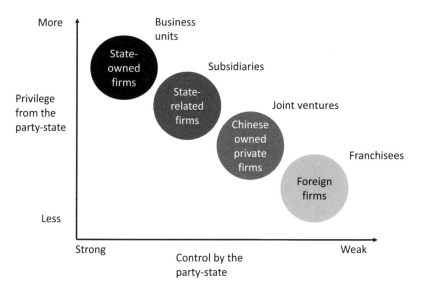

FIGURE 5.2 Organizational elements of China, Inc., and their relationships
with the party-state.
Source: Author

positively associated with the level of privilege granted by the party-
state. At the upper-left corner are state-owned firms, which enjoy the
most privilege and are subject to the most control by the state. These
firms have guaranteed income and the least incentive to work hard.
As the circles move toward the lower right corner, the firms have less
privilege and more autonomy. They do not have the luxury of the
SOEs in terms of market monopoly or protection, and therefore have
the strongest incentive to operate efficiently to be profitable.

The CCP allocates industries among firms of different ownerships based on the risk and profit level and the strategic importance of
the industries. Industries that have high certainty (low risk), high
profit levels, or natural monopoly are kept in-house – they are the
privilege of the departments and subsidiaries of China, Inc. – the state-
owned and state-related firms. They monopolize or dominate the

industries of tobacco, oil and gas, banking, aviation, railroad, and other low risk-high profit or strategically important industries. For private firms owned by Chinese nationals (Chinese privately owned firms), the party-state allows and encourages them to enter industries characterized by a high level of uncertainty and rapid competitive dynamics, and uses them to counter foreign firms and gain global dominance. The party-state uses foreign firms primarily for technology transfer and filling gaps in products and services that domestic firms cannot provide.

Under the party-state support, a number of private firms have grown into large global firms, such as Alibaba (e-commerce), Huawei (communication technology), and Contemporary Amperex Technology (CATL, car battery maker, see Chapter 6). There is evidence that the CCP is increasingly relying on private firms to carry out what used to be considered core tasks of the party, such as internet content monitoring and censoring. Not only does the volume of internet content grow very fast but also the topics, vocabularies, and public attitude change rapidly as well. Because of these features, private firms are more suitable than the party-state or the SOEs to efficiently handle the task of monitoring and censoring internet content for the CCP (Batke and Ohlberg, 2020).

State-owned firms may grow as big as possible, since they are business units of China, Inc., and have the closest relationship with the headquarters – the CCP. Their earnings are 100 percent the party's and therefore their monopoly is not a concern. For example, China Petroleum & Chemical Corp (SNP) and PetroChina Co. (PTR) monopolize China's oil market and are the two largest oil companies in the world. For joint ventures – Chinese-owned private firms – their growth needs to follow the party-state's plan. When the party-state wants them to compete against large foreign rivals, it will support and encourage them to grow big. However, if the party-state feels that they are growing out of control, the party-state may impose more restrictions on them by invoking antimonopoly laws, increase the party-state's "share" of the firm, or completely take them over. And this is what happened to Jack Ma's Ant Group and Alibaba.

In 2020, the party-state began to investigate Ant Group and Alibaba for monopoly. According to Xie Wen, a former Yahoo China president, the reason that the Chinese government actively supported these giant internet firms was to use them to compete against American rivals, which have been banned from the Chinese market. Now the focus of the government has changed. It wants to build the domestic market, and, for that purpose, it now supports small and medium-sized firms. This is why the government now gives a high priority to antimonopoly policies in order to spur competition (Mu, 2020). "At that time people believed that Chinese internet companies were competing against the U.S. firms, and they are China's pride. But now we are switching to internal circulation," Xie commented (Yu and Goh, 2020).

From the China, Inc., perspective, we can see that such a measure makes sense: As the objectives of China, Inc., change, it will redirect its joint ventures – private firms – to fit the new objectives. Alibaba's role in keeping foreign rivals out of China is no longer needed, and the party-state does not want it to be out of control. Furthermore, the party-state has no need to take shares from Ma, because the party-state has the control rights over Alibaba, similar to headquarters' control over one of the company's joint ventures.

5.4.3   Residents Are Like Employees of China, Inc.

Residents in China are not true citizens or residents of a country because they do not have the entitlement to freely choose where they can live. The government controls permits to legally live in a city, known as the "household registration" (hukou). As demonstrated by the cases in Section 5.3, the party-state can order a private firm to fire an employee and order a landlord not to take a tenant. Living and working in China needs to be approved by the party-state. In this sense, residents in China are like employees of China, Inc.; if the

CEO and the management do not like someone, the individual and their family will not be able to live and work in China like a normal resident.

5.4.4 AI, Internet, and Big Data Make China, Inc., More Feasible

Managing China, Inc., with 1.3 billion people efficiently and effectively is not easy for the party-state. Many tasks are still left to the market and society. However, with artificial intelligence, the Internet, big data, and surveillance cameras becoming more and more advanced and available, managing China, Inc., is becoming more and more feasible. China has the most surveillance cameras installed in the world: 349 million as of 2018 (Gan, 2020). The Chinese government has actively promoted mobile payment, which accounted for 83 percent of all payments in 2018 (Statista, 2020). All these activities are under the watchful eyes of the party-state. In China, with the government having everybody's information, if you carry your cell phone with you and expose your face or your walking style, the government will know where you are, whom you are with, what you do or buy, and how much you spend, making managing China, Inc., feasible, effective, and efficient.

5.4.5 Political System versus Organizational Structure of China

Politically, China is a dictatorship; organizationally, it is like a corporation. Not all dictatorships can run their countries like a corporation. North Korea, under the communist dictatorship of Kim Jong-un, runs the country more like a military camp. The key difference between the military camp style organization and the corporation style organization is that the former does not rely on positive economic incentives for people to follow orders; rather, it primarily relies on negative incentives – punishment – to force people to follow orders. The CCP provides strong positive economic incentives. As will be shown, another difference between Kim's Korea and the CCP's China is that the former is closed while the latter is open to global trade (see Chapters 7 and 8).

5.4.6 Flexibility of China Inc.

While organizationally being like a corporation, China is still a country nationalistically and politically. As such, this new type of organization differs from a typical corporation or a democratic, free market country. Compared to corporations in free market economies, China, Inc., has the following distinguishing features.

Unlike workers in normal corporations, who have lives and therefore freedoms outside the corporations, the "workers" of China Inc., live in the corporation, which restricts what they can say or do. Moreover, they are obligated to carry out the headquarters' orders (the state's mission), even when they are outside China. Normal corporations are subject to the rule of law of the host country, which means that the workers may resort to laws outside of their workplace to resolve any issues. In China, Inc., the top management team (the party-state) sets the laws and thus the workers cannot address their grievances against the corporation. Furthermore, "workers" in China, Inc., need permission from the party-state to "quit" (leave). There are many cases in which residents are barred from leaving China, known as biankong (边控, border control, or exit ban), which applies to both Chinese passport holders and foreign passport holders. The Chinese government "has never made the list of biankong public ... Lawyers and analysts estimated that it could reach millions" (Radio Free Asia, 2019c). This measure is extralegal and has been applied so subjectively with the complete discretion of the CCP that it prompted the US State Department to issue a warning to Americans that,

> The PRC government arbitrarily enforces local laws, including by carrying out arbitrary and wrongful detentions and through the use of exit bans on U.S. citizens and citizens of other countries without due process of law ... In most cases, U.S. citizens only become

aware of an exit ban when they attempt to depart the PRC, and there is no reliable mechanism or legal process to find out how long the ban might continue or to contest it in a court of law.

(U.S. State Department, 2020)

On the other hand, the Chinese government can use its huge financial resources, policies, and state intelligence power to support any firms or individuals that the party-state favors.

There are also key aspects that distinguish China, Inc., from other countries. In democratic countries, the government's power is limited as to what it can ask firms or individuals to do. Its executive power to use resources is limited to the budget passed in the congress or parliament. Furthermore, the incumbent political party is always checked and challenged by the opposition party in governing the country or in dealing with a foreign country. In contrast, China, Inc.'s CEO (the CCP leader) can use all available resources from their company (China) to achieve their goals, including ordering any firms or individuals to fulfill tasks the CEO wants to get done. Actually, the head of the party-state is more powerful than a CEO (or top management team) because he/she is bound by no laws, any checks and balances, or competition. As illustrated in Figure 2.3, in mature democracies, all entities are subject to the rule of law, the government is limited, and the existence of people and firms is, to a great extent, independent of the government; whereas in China, the party is omnipresent, and, through the government, rules over everything.

5.5   WHY OTHER COUNTRIES SHOULD CARE ABOUT THE CCP RUNNING CHINA LIKE A CORPORATION

During four decades of trial and error, the CCP has realized that concentrating and centralizing power as well as treating the country like a corporation is more efficient for the party to achieve its goals. The outcome of this process has created a giant entity between a society and a hierarchy that the international community had not anticipated when it supported China's reform and opening up (see Chapter 1).

Hungarian-born communist reform economist and author of the seminal book *Economics of Shortage* Jonas Kornai, who can be viewed as the founding father of the economics of communist reform and who played an instrumental role in China's reform, now calls the reform process that has resulted in today's China "a 'monstrous' turn," and current dictatorial and expanding China a "nightmare," and regrets that he, along with other enthusiastic reform scholars, helped to create it,

> Are not western intellectuals also responsible for this nightmare? We not only watched China's transformation with approval but actively contributed to these changes. We are the modern version of Mary Shelley's *Frankenstein* . . . who brought a dead body to life using . . . electric shock. The resurrected creature became a murderous monster.
>
> *(Kornai, 2019)*

This new form differs from the old communist state, in which people and firms had no access to markets or the outside world, and no incentives to produce. And the new form is also different from countries that have free markets and democracy, and has not been studied by the literature on transition economies.

Firms and citizens in mature democracies enjoy property rights (see the definition in Section 5.2) and human rights, respectively. Human rights (as opposed to property rights) are " . . . inherent to all human beings . . . Human rights include . . . freedom of opinion and expression, the right to work and education, and many more. Everyone is entitled to these rights" (United Nations, 1948). As we have documented in this chapter, firms in China do not have property rights similar to the rights enjoyed by their counterparts in free markets, and people in China do not have human rights similar to the ones enjoyed by their counterparts in democracies.

Working in a corporation is not a right, but a privilege given to a select few. Similarly, for people in China, living, schooling, working, or doing business are not rights, but privileges granted by the party.

In examining China and its firms from the perspective of China, Inc., some puzzling phenomena may begin to make sense. For example,

China has a large number of non-performing loans (see Chapter 3) and numerous business failures, and yet there are few bankruptcies (Wei and Ng, 2019). Of course, if the loans and business failures are "internal" between business units and members of China, Inc., the headquarters (the party-state) must coordinate and rearrange them, with no need to go to court (which, by the way, is just another department of the corporation). Another example is that the United States controls several vital technologies that Huawei relies on. But why is sanctioning Huawei so difficult? From the China, Inc., perspective, Huawei is a prized business unit of the corporation. So, the issues are: First, how much support will the headquarters (the party-state) give to save Huawei? Evidence shows that the party-state strongly supports Huawei and retaliates against any foreign countries that place sanctions on it (Myers and Bradsher, 2020; Yap, 2019). Second, since the headquarters are "all in" to save Huawei, then other countries would have to wage a war against the headquarters – which is the Chinese government, namely China as a whole – in order to sanction Huawei. Obviously, few countries that want to ban Huawei are prepared to go that far.

The flexibility of China, Inc., and its dual functions of corporation and state enable it to unfairly compete with the corporations and the states of other countries. And this is why other countries are concerned about it. US Senator Marco Rubio commented,

> It is a fact that when you're doing business with a Chinese company, you're doing business with the Chinese Communist Party ... When it comes to Chinese firms, our companies aren't competing with private enterprises; they are competing with a large and powerful nation-state.
>
> *(Rubio, 2019)*

5.6 SUMMARY

This chapter elaborated on the emergence of what I call China, Inc. After four decades of learning by trial and error, the CCP has achieved total control over every aspect of society, including all resources, firms, and the population. This, along with its objective of "treating the entire nation as a chessboard," has propelled the CCP to run the country as a corporation. Living, working, and doing business in China are not rights, but privileges granted by the party. To a great degree, state-owned firms are business units, state-related firms are subsidiaries, Chinese-owned private firms are joint ventures, and foreign firms are franchisees of the party-state, with the party leader being the CEO of China, Inc. The interplay between China and other countries is essentially a rivalry between a huge corporation and other states. And the competition between a Chinese firm and a foreign firm can become a match between the Chinese state and the latter. This new perspective will help the international community reexamine global competition. It will also aid researchers to further explore this new phenomenon.

6 China's Industrial Policy as a Corporate Strategy of China, Inc.[1]

> The next fifteen years (1996 to 2010) is an important era ... We must nurture and improve the big enterprises, and let go of small enterprises ... select the good ones, support the strong ones, and close the poor and weak ones ... focus on a group of large enterprises and enterprise groups.
>
> The Chinese Communist Party (Chinese Communist Party, 1995)

In order to fully realize the potential of running the entire country as a corporation, the CCP formulates and implements its industrial policy as a developmental strategy for China, Inc. My coauthor Matt Farrell and I have conducted a study to assess China's industrial policy in relation to China, Inc., and its implications for international business (Li and Farrell, 2020a), and I will share it in this chapter.

6.1 THE HISTORICAL AND INTELLECTUAL ORIGIN OF NATIONALISTIC DEVELOPMENT STRATEGIES

6.1.1 *Learning from Prewar Germany and Japan*

China's industrial policy is heavily influenced by the nationalistic development view held by thinkers of Europe's industrialization era, such as the French political economist Jean-Baptiste Colbert and the German economist Friedrich List (Clairmonte, 1959; Dettmer, 2020; Wen, 2019). Colbert argued for using tariffs and public work projects to develop the domestic economy in the seventeenth century (Chisholm, 1911). Later, List more clearly articulated the nationalistic development strategy (List, 1909 (1841)). Disagreeing with Adam

---

[1] Adopted and extended from S. Li and M. Farrell, 2020a. China's Industrial Policy and Its Implications for International Business. *European Journal of International Management*, in press.

Smith's view that individuals following the invisible hand of the market can create social goods, List believes that only "the power of the State" (List, 1909 (1841), p. 166) is capable of fostering the welfare of all its citizens. He advocates imposing tariffs on imports and maintaining free trade of domestic goods, and argues that only when a nation gains supremacy via protection can it enter free trade with other nations. His idea is known as the "National System" or the National System of Innovation (Freeman, 1995). Interestingly, China calls its system the neo-national system of innovation.

List's thought provided the foundation for National Socialism in Germany (more commonly known as Nazism) (Tribe, 2007). Japan also followed his model (Fallows, 1993), as can be seen in the international economic policy of Meiji Japan (1868–1912) (Linebarger, Chu, and Burks, 1956). This nationalistic strategy helped to propel the two countries into conflict with other nations, leading to the Second World War.

6.1.2   Borrowing from New Trade Theory and Strategic Trade Policy

Contemporary economic thought also provided theoretical foundations for China's industrial policy. In the 1970s, a new trade theory emerged that argues that if economies of scale are important for an industry, then the government of a country should support a domestic firm to obtain the economies of scale by implementing protective measures such as subsidies. The firm may then become the dominant player in the global market and earn an above-average return that can more than offset the subsidy, thereby benefiting the country (Brander and Spencer, 1985). The new trade theory espoused a strategic trade policy that favors government intervention to support domestic firms to gain advantage in the global market (Brander, 1986; Krugman, Obstfeld, and Melitz, 2012).

However, Krugman and colleagues later argued that even if the new trade theory and the corresponding strategic trade policy make logical sense, it is impractical to implement such a policy in reality because (1) it is impossible for a government to accurately calculate the amount of subsidies; (2) domestic politics will make the subsidies be used inefficiently and in the wrong industries or firms; and (3) it will trigger retaliation and trade war from other countries. All these may outweigh the potential gains of strategic trade policies (Krugman, 1987). Furthermore, "strategic policies are beggar-thy-neighbor policies that increase our welfare at other countries' expense ... Few economists would advocate that the United States be the initiator of such policies" (Krugman et al., 2012, p. 277). In conclusion, free trade is still the best practical policy for all countries (Krugman, 1987, 1992). Interestingly, when Krugman et al. specifically warned the United States not to use the strategic trade policy, they failed to consider a major country that was implementing it at large scale with full speed: China.

6.1.3   Evolution of China's Industrial Policy

After the CCP took power in 1949, it nationalized the ownership of all industrial firms, dismantled the market function of supply and demand, and delinked economic reward and efficiency. From the early 1950s to the late 1970s, China's economic policy followed the Soviet model of central planning to set output targets for all industrial materials and products in its five-year plans (see Chapters 2 and 5). These measures took the incentive to produce away from people, and the economy was inefficient and wasteful, causing overproduction of useless outputs and shortages of useful products (Dreyer, 2010; Hill and Hult, 2019; Kornai, 2019; Meisner, 1999).

After the death of Mao Zedong, the CCP changed its stance from state ownership and central planning to a "socialist market economy with Chinese characteristics" (Dreyer, 2010). The CCP began to allow private and foreign ownership to exist and to develop markets for products and services. Its industrial policy evolved from administratively setting output goals to setting developmental priorities and allocating resources to achieve them, while leveraging market forces to improve the efficiency and competitiveness of Chinese firms (see Section 6.1.4 for a more detailed discussion).

Across the past few decades, several studies have examined industrial policies, and China's in particular (see Kenderdine, 2017 for a detailed review). Initially, China's industrial policy goals tended to be industry-specific and largely ineffectual (Eun and Lee, 2002), focusing on rationalizing production but hamstrung by incentive misalignments between local and central governments. In 2003, the Hu-Wen administration began to steer the policies more toward long-term, cross-sectoral goals that were less prone to appropriation by special interest groups (Heilmann and Shih, 2013), bringing about the current state of affairs.

6.1.4 What Scholars Say about China's Industrial Policy

Most studies on China's industrial policy examine it from the traditional economic argument of "market failure," and their main research question is "does industrial policy work?" Unfortunately, the answer to that question is not conclusive, as both successes and failures are found (Dettmer, 2020). Further, we argue that market failures are not necessarily what Chinese industrial policy is attempting to address. According to the White House (2018), the focus of the Chinese government is on obtaining new technologies and intellectual properties from other countries in order to drive future economic growth.

Using China's electricity and telecom industries as examples, Brandt and Rawski documented the Chinese government's great effort in mobilizing resources and addressing its institutional shortcomings, and concluded that the result was "a complex mosaic of success and failure in both technical and commercial dimensions" in the two industries (Brandt and Rawski, 2019, book summary). Ling and Naughton (2016) studied China's techno-industrial policy from the economic development framework. They found a shift in China's policy from market to intervention in 2003, and attributed it to two forces: politically, the interventionists gained the upper hand against market reformers, and economically, conditions and capabilities changed. Rodrik argued that the reason China achieved more success in exporting than other countries with similar levels of development was its government policies (Rodrik, 2006). Liu examined the role of state intervention on sectors with market imperfections, and found that intervention in upstream sectors, which are large in size, tends to produce positive effects for the economy (Liu, 2019). Using shipbuilding as a case, Barwick, Kalouptsidi, and Zahur (2019) show that China's policy support for its shipbuilding industry dramatically increased its capacity and world market share, at the cost of creating more distortions and waste.

Most of these studies agree, either explicitly or implicitly, that without its industrial policy, China's economy would not have grown so fast and become so powerful (Dettmer, 2020; Liu, 2019; Rodrik, 2006). At the same time, most scholars believe the Chinese government cannot always identify the right industries to support and that its "heavy-handed intervention is becoming increasingly ineffective." The implicit conclusion is that "China should shift to more market-oriented policies" (Dettmer, 2020; World Bank, 2019a) and follow the rules based on free trade (Li, Park, and Bao, 2019).

What these studies missed is that correcting market failure may not be the main goal of the industrial policy of China's ruling party, and the "shift to more market-oriented policies" – which may be good for China in developing a market economy – may not be in the best interest of the CCP, as we will show next.

6.2 CHINA'S INDUSTRIAL POLICY AS CORPORATE STRATEGIES

As explained in Chapter 5, under the philosophy of "treating the entire country as a chessboard," and concentrating the entire country's resources to do big things, the CCP runs the country and coordinates its resources like a corporation. Correspondingly, the CCP designs its industrial policy not merely as a guideline with incentives/disincentives in select industries for people and firms to follow, but rather as a mandatory rule to follow in nearly all industries since the party-state controls all the necessary resources for entering and operating businesses, such as land use and financing approvals (Jiang and Li, 2010; U.S. Chamber of Commerce, 2017).

China's industrial policy is formulated based on the party-state's assessment of the economies of China and the world. It identifies industries, products, and technologies to develop. For example, its "List of Currently Important Industries, Products, and Technologies to Be Encouraged by the State (1)" published in 2000 (Chinese Government, 2000) covers 28 industries and 526 products. The measures for the party-state to implement the list include permission to enter, project evaluation and approval, land use approval, bank loan approval, and forced closing (for discouraged industries). Essentially, without "encouragement" by the party-state, no one can operate in an industry (Chinese government, 2005; Jiang and Li, 2010).

6.3 GENERAL GOALS AND MEANS OF CHINA'S INDUSTRIAL POLICY

The general goals of China's industrial policy are to identify industries, products, and technologies to be developed or to be curbed. The ones to be developed tend to be industries that are deemed by the party-state as important, futuristic, and having high technology content. The ones to be curbed tend to be low-tech, polluting, and sunset industries (Jiang and Li, 2010).

The general means to develop key industries include direct subsidies to domestic firms to develop them, protectionism against foreign competition, and supporting domestic firms to compete in the global market. For example, in the "Made In China 2025" plan, the party-state identified ten strategic industries to gain world dominance: next generation information technology, high-end numerical control machinery and robotics, aerospace and aviation equipment, maritime engineering equipment and high-tech maritime vessel manufacturing, advanced rail equipment, energy-saving and new energy vehicles, electrical equipment, new materials, biomedicine and high-performance medical devices, and agricultural machinery and equipment. According to a study, the ten industries account for 40 percent of China's entire industrial value-added manufacturing (U.S. Chamber of Commerce, 2017). Under such a strategy, China attracts foreign firms that innovate more, and Chinese firms go abroad for market and resource access (Blomkvist and Drogendijk, 2016; Li, Huang, Xu, and Yu, 2018).

Next, we have compiled cases of how China developed its dominance in several industries.

6.4 CASES OF CHINA'S INDUSTRIAL POLICY'S IMPLEMENTATION

6.4.1 China's Electric Vehicle (EV) Battery Industry

The Chinese government's strategy on the development of the EV battery industry was taking shape in the early 2010s. In 2013, Beijing implemented a subsidy program to encourage local and foreign auto makers to sell more EVs, making China the largest EV market in the world (International Energy Agency, 2019).

In the early stage of the development of the EV battery industry, the government's strategy was to support domestic firms with a clear emphasis on scale – only firms with a large capacity could operate. In its 2015 directive "Vehicle Power Battery Industry Regulations," the state specified that EV battery producers must meet the annual production threshold of 200-megawatt hours. In the same year, the government also published the directive of "Lithium Ion Battery Industry Regulations" to specify the types of material and technology allowed. The state also published a "Whitelist of EV Battery Firms" (as opposed to a "blacklist"), designating state-supported EV battery producers. From 2015 to 2016, four such lists were published, totaling fifty-seven firms, which were all domestic (Ren, Lian, and Guo, 2019).

For EV makers to receive state subsidies, they have to use batteries made by the whitelisted domestic firms. While automakers can forego the subsidy and use batteries made by foreign firms, "they were warned by Chinese officials to use local batteries or face reprisals in a country where foreign companies face a constant struggle to stay on good terms with the authorities" (Moss, 2019).

To secure raw material supply and reduce costs for the domestic makers, the government also sponsored global acquisitions to lock up much of the raw materials for batteries, such as cobalt in the Democratic Republic of Congo (Moss, 2019).

Under the state policy, local battery producers made a great leap forward. From 2009 to 2018, China's installed EV batteries more than doubled on a yearly basis to 57 gigawatt hours. By 2018, China accounted for about 60 percent of the world market in EV batteries. Contemporary Amperex Technology Ltd (CATL), a little-known Chinese company started in 2011, has taken advantage of the policy to become the world's biggest maker of EV batteries. Speaking about China's protective policy and the rise of CATL, Jiang Lingfeng, a former CATL project manager, commented, "What the government did was a good thing for China." "Without its restrictions, I don't think CATL would ever have been successful" (Moss, 2019), a sentiment with which other analysts concur (Shao, 2019).

Now that Chinese firms are well established in the global market of EV batteries (all top ten suppliers in China are domestic and three of the top five global suppliers are Chinese), the state has changed its policy from protection and emphasizing size to encouraging them to upgrade and compete globally. In 2019, the government abolished its whitelist, reduced subsidies, and encouraged firms to digitize and implement smart production technologies (Ren et al., 2019).

In preparation for the weaning of state subsidies, CATL has begun to set up subsidiaries or branch offices in foreign countries, and has signed partnership agreements with major automakers in the world to lock them in. Several foreign automakers who had complained about being forced to use CATL batteries now view it as an "important and valued partner" and "felt compelled to help make the company successful for the sake of their own reputations" (Moss, 2019; Shao, 2019).

6.4.2 China's Solar Panel Industry

An emerging technology with importance for the future as well as an energy input good, solar power proved a tempting target for China, with its market share in photovoltaic panels erupting from a tiny fraction to well over 50 percent of the global total within a decade (Earth Policy Institute, 2015). In 2010, the state established a powerful organization called the "China Photovoltaic Industry Alliance" to promote and regulate the industry and to use its government-backing and resources to fight against any charges of unfair subsidies and dumping by other countries. In 2012, the Chinese state published its policy to promote the photovoltaic industry through subsidies, price regulation, favorable fiscal policies, support in land use, and infrastructure construction (baike.baidu.com, 2017a).

Given the trifecta of government support, lower labor costs relative to the United States and EU, and the ability to bypass environmental protections entirely, global dominance was relatively easy to achieve (Shubbak, 2019).

Specifically, subsidies took the form of tax breaks, low interest loans, and active recruitment programs for top talent (Shubbak, 2019). Through the Chinese Development Bank, government officials are able to finance pet projects, such as the solar industry, at rates that unsubsidized firms are unable to attain. "Free money is impossible to compete with," lamented one American solar executive (The Guardian, 2011). Subsidies funded over 70 percent of several solar projects, making rooftop solar a commonplace sight in China (Shubbak, 2019). Through the "Thousand Talents" program (see Chapter 7), the CCP was able to recruit over 4,000 scientists from around the globe, and use their knowledge and network connections to advance Chinese solar technology (Ball, Reicher, Sun, and Pollock, 2017).

While the polysilicon required for photovoltaic panel production typically costs US$84,500 per ton in Western economies, Chinese companies can make the same amount for as little as US$21,000 per ton through bypassing the recycling of silicon tetrachloride, a poisonous byproduct of polysilicon production. In one case, a solar panel manufacturer dumped this waste on a field in a neighboring village, poisoning residents and crops. As a result of the state support of this facility, complaints from the villagers were ignored (Cha, 2008). Though China officially imposed regulations to stop these practices in 2011, it is not certain how well these are being enforced, if at all (Mulvaney, 2014).

When international demand faltered, the Chinese government simply propped up the industry through increasing the already-high subsidies. Specifically, the United States and EU responded to China's dumping with a wave of tariffs from 2012 to 2014, as the various policies China used to support its solar industry rendered the West unable to compete. China retaliated by increasing duties on imported polysilicon raw materials, further harming domestic production, which might have collapsed entirely if not for government stimulus (Shubbak, 2019). Predictably, this has resulted in an excess capacity problem. Curtailment rates, a euphemism for the rate of waste, have reached as high as 30 percent in the rural areas where solar is farmed as a result of the difficulty inherent in transferring this energy to more heavily populated areas (Reuters, 2017).

On May 31, 2018, the Chinese government abruptly reduced or even stopped some of the subsidies for the industry. The policy, widely known as the "531 Policy," caused huge shock waves in the industry (Liu, 2018; Solar, 2018). While surprised by the swiftness of its implementation, most Chinese firms had anticipated or even supported the policy, as those who had greatly benefited from the subsidies were now dominant, and ready to compete in the world market.

6.4.3   China's High-Speed Rail Industry

Much like the cases of solar power and electric vehicle batteries, in the high-speed rail industry, China was able to use state policy to mobilize resources in order to move from a position of inferiority to that of a world leader. In this case, this was in terms of both the size of its high-speed rail network and the sophistication of its technology.

Beginning in 2004, the State Council dictated that China would embrace high-speed rail travel and that it would use conventional tracks for this as opposed to mag-lev technologies (*People's Daily*, 2004). This proved problematic as domestically produced high-speed locomotives were considered to be too unreliable to function as regular passenger transportation (Tokyo Shimbun, 2011). To overcome this barrier, the Ministry of Railways opted to solicit bids from foreign manufacturers. The selected firms each had unique strengths. For example, Alstom of France had better control systems, Siemens and Bombardier, both of Germany, had better transmission technology, while a consortium led by Japanese firm Kawasaki offered power dispersion technology that would reduce energy waste (*People's Daily*, 2004).

China followed a multi-pronged strategy to usurp all of these benefits for its own rail companies and in turn use these advantages to dominate the world in the market for high-speed rail travel. First, China made technology transfer mandatory for these firms in order to grant them access to the Chinese market. The foreign companies had to form joint ventures with Chinese locals and adapt their technology to Chinese rail standards (Bombardier, 2010; Kawasaki, 2004; Kwok, 2009). Manufacturing of trains for the new project also went from complete knockdown kits to wholly domestic in a fairly short span of time (Shirouzu, 2010).

Second, these trains, known collectively as the Hexie, were later re-engineered using the acquired know-how to make an even faster series of trains, the Fuxing (Xinhua News Agency, 2017; You, 2017) (see Figure 6.1). While the Hexie type trains had design elements that were protected by foreign patents, the Fuxing type trains are designed and built in China and as such can be exported with no legal issues (Johnson, 2011; Xin, 2011).

Third, China subsidized the industry so heavily that its investment is still far from breaking even in some areas (Luo, 2016). China embraced high-speed rail as a stimulus project during the Great Recession (2007–2009) and poured billions into developing high-speed

FIGURE 6.1 New bullet train "Fuxing" debuts on Beijing–Shanghai route (2017).
Source: Getty Images

rail routes (Bradsher, 2010; Forsythe, 2009; McDonald, 2010), damaging the domestic airline industry in the process (Li, 2011). In early 2011, China's high-speed rail network became the largest in the world (Barrow, 2018).

Finally, China permitted a merger of its two largest rail companies, CSR and China CNR, creating CRRC Corporation Limited. The goal of the merger, expressly stated, was to become more efficient and more competitive worldwide (The Railway Gazette, 2014). The CRRC is a state-owned enterprise that controls over 90 percent of the Chinese market: in common parlance, a monopoly (Gazette, 2015).

In 2013, the Chinese government introduced its new global expansion strategy known as the Belt and Road Initiative to further leverage and to fully utilize its high-speed rail capabilities (see Chapter 7).

With the fastest trains, the largest network, and the biggest company worldwide, the CRRC is making aggressive moves into foreign markets. They have opened manufacturing plants in Boston (Barrow, 2014), Malaysia (Barrow, 2015), Argentina (enelsubte.com, 2014), Chicago (Reuters, 2016), and Los Angeles (CRRC, 2014). Furthermore, the Chinese state has been using its high-speed rail capacity as a "powerful means to project broader political influence" (Ker, 2017, p. 3).

6.5 HOW CHINA DIFFERS FROM JAPAN IN INDUSTRIAL POLICIES: A HISTORICAL COMPARISON

Japan's industrial policy of the 1950s and 1960s – often referred to as Japan, Inc. (Abegglen, 1970) – had some similarities with the industrial policy currently embraced by the CCP, but as we intend to argue, there are also some key differences.

The first similarity is that both have successfully followed a strategy of shielding domestic industries from foreign competition while encouraging competition at home. For example, Kiyomiya Hire, Vice President of Fujitsu, which participated in a cooperative project with Hitachi, explained that "Frankly speaking, if we do not do this, we cannot confront our American competitors" (Anchordoguy, 1989, p. 108).

Japan also ran the entire industries as though they were one firm in terms of pooling R&D efforts. This type of cooperation regarding research and development matters was not only known to the Japanese government but encouraged by them through MITI (the Ministry of International Trade and Industry) in various instances. Famously, MITI orchestrated the VLSI (Very Large Scale Integrated) semiconductor alliance between Fujitsu, Hitachi, Mitsubishi Electric, NEC, and Toshiba – firms which were, under ordinary circumstances, competitors. By founding a joint laboratory and funding the project with interest-free loans, Japan was able to catch up with the West in terms of developing silicon wafer substrates, improving computer-aided design technology, and other goals (Sakakibara, 1983). In another case, MITI required a steel firm to purchase a license to use the basic oxygen furnace (BOF), a then-new steelmaking technology.

They also required other steel firms to contribute toward the BOF license – and then distributed the technology to all the contributing firms. This kept the patent holder from playing firms off against one another in order to increase the licensing fee and leveled the playing field for Japanese steel firms by keeping their costs comparable to Western economies (Shibata and Takeuchi, 2006).

Another similarity is that both Japan and China erected non-tariff barriers and forced technology transfers (often illegally or unethically). For example, Texas Instruments (TI) applied for Japanese patents in 1960, and then to establish a wholly owned subsidiary in 1964. Given the importance of TI's technology for the fledgling semiconductor industry and the importance of computers as an economic input good, the Japanese declined to approve the patents until much later – 1977 for some and 1989 for others, in a process that typically only took six to seven years. In the interim, Japanese firms actively stole TI's technology without facing repercussions domestically. TI, obviously displeased, threatened to sue any companies exporting this stolen technology on grounds of patent violations within the destination countries. To appease TI, Japan eventually allowed it to form a joint venture with Sony (Hayes, 1989; US Congressional Office of Technology Assessment, 1991).

A key difference between their industrial policies is that Japanese firms were allowed to rebuff suggestions by MITI, while in China, all firms are required to bend to the will of the CCP. This ability to dissent proved highly valuable to Japan's consumer electronics and automobile industries. For example, MITI would initially not allow Sony to purchase transistors for its radios as this was seen as a waste of valuable foreign currency. In spite of that, Sony's transistor radios went on to be a massive sales success (Lynn, 1998). MITI also suggested on several occasions in the 1950s and 1960s that the auto industry should consolidate. In 1955, they suggested that one firm should export a single subcompact car, and in 1961, they suggested that the industry be consolidated into three firms, each specializing in one type of car. The backlash was so strong, however, that this action, widely seen in retrospect as a mistake, could be avoided by firms (Saxonhouse, 1986). Had MITI's political power been on par with that of the CCP, Japan's success in transistor radios, automobiles, and other fields may have been less than what it was. In comparison, it is difficult to imagine that the CCP would allow firms' preference, public opinion, or even its own laws to stand in the way of policy implementation.

Another key difference is that unlike the Chinese government that has almost the whole country's resources at its disposal (Li and Alon, 2020), the Japanese government cannot mobilize the whole Japanese economy to implement its industrial policies, which are merely "administrative guidance" (Johnson, 1982). The Chinese government controls approximately 56 percent of GDP per annum through taxes, fees, and SOEs (IMF, 2019; National Bureau of Statistics of China, 2016, 2018b). In contrast, during the height of MITI's administrative guidance in the 1960s, Japanese government spending hovered around 10 percent (Tajika and Yui, 2002). The totalitarian nature of the Chinese economic system also means that the CCP enjoys greater control over sectors that are nominally private. According to the Heritage Foundation's Property Rights Index, Japan scores 88 percent (with an Overall Economic Freedom Score of 74, or "mostly free"), while China scores 62 (with an Overall Economic Freedom Score of 58.4, or "mostly unfree") (The Heritage Foundation, 2021).

A third difference is the size of their economies in the world. Given the relative size of China's economy – that is, the largest based on purchasing power in the world (at US\$23 trillion accounting for 18 percent of the world's total output) (CIA, 2020b) as well as its status as the "world's factory" – it is much better positioned than postwar Japan (whose GDP accounted for 3–7 percent of the world's in the 1960s (World Bank, 2020a)) to defend itself against tariffs and other barriers set in place by the international community. Evidence shows that the Chinese government uses access to China's markets as a bargaining chip to coerce foreign countries to go along with its policies and preferences (Dreyer, 2019).

If Japan's industrial policy was successful, then why was it changed? While a comprehensive answer is complex and beyond the scope of this chapter, we make the following observations. One factor was that MITI's ability to steer industrial policy declined. The financial success of Japanese firms meant less debt financing, making interest rate incentives less attractive. Regulatory factors, both domestically and internationally, resulted in the opening of financial markets and reductions in trade barriers. Further, increasing budget deficits meant the government could not financially support industrial development as it once did (U.S. General Accounting Office, 1982).

At the same time as the government's power to implement "administrative guidance" was in decline, Japanese economists note that Japan's single-minded objective to recover from the war gave way to more diverse public opinions. Under pressure from voters, Japan shifted attention to matters such as environmental pollution or the preservation of jobs in industries that were hard-hit by external shocks such as the oil crises (Kobayashi, 1993; Okuno-Fujiwara, 1991). Popular sentiment exerted influence in other ways, too. For example, public outrage hamstrung dumping and collusion efforts undertaken in the television industry; firms were forced to lower domestic prices on color television sets when it became widely known that Japanese were being overcharged and Americans undercharged for these sets (US Congressional Office of Technology Assessment, 1991).

Finally, we should note that there are two key downsides to this type of industrial policy, both in general and as it applies to China in particular. First, there are obviously efficiency losses in preventing the domestic market from accessing superior foreign goods. In Japan, for example, government promotion of domestic supercomputers meant that universities and firms only had access to inferior machines throughout the entirety of the 1980s (US Congressional Office of Technology Assessment, 1991). Second, government support of industries can lead to excess production capacities, such as those being experienced now in Chinese cement and steel, which have been repurposed to service the so-called Belt and Road Initiative (*The Economist*, 2017) (see Chapter 7).

Table 6.1 provides a summary of the upsides and downsides of industrial policies in general, and specific comparisons of how they have been embraced in China and Japan.

These sections of evidence and analysis show that the CCP uses its industrial policy to bolster the competitive advantage of China, Inc. (Li and Farrell, 2020a). The general pattern of China's industrial policy is that first, the CCP identifies certain industries and determines them to be high priorities. Once an industry is designated as strategically important, the party-state will mobilize all the necessary resources from across the country to develop this industry. The party-state will also pick some domestic firms as national champions, and at the same time erect barriers against foreign firms attempting to enter the industry. With a large, protected domestic market, the designated firms will be able to quickly realize scale economies and to lower unit production costs. Once the designated domestic firm becomes efficient, the party-state will support it as it goes out and dominates the world market (Jiang and Li, 2010; Li and Alon, 2020; US-China Economic and Security Commission, 2017; Wen, 2019).

While it is common for countries to use industrial policies to protect domestic industries, the way China uses industrial policy is significantly different. First, unlike the industrial policies of other countries, which are mostly guidelines, China's industrial policy is more like a corporate strategy that approves/disapproves projects and mobilizes the country's resources to help its firms achieve dominance. Second, because of its size, China's industrial policy has a powerful global impact beyond protectionism.

6.6 CHINA, INC.'S GLOBAL STRATEGY

When the Chinese government projects its industrial policy globally, it becomes what I call expansionary mercantilism. While practicing a

Table 6.1. *Industrial policy pros, cons, and examples*

Industrial policy aspect	Benefits	Drawbacks	Examples from China	Examples from Japan
Domestic Protectionism/ Import Substitution	Allows infant industries to learn by doing and become competitive internationally	Protects inefficient firms; worse outcomes for domestic consumers	Solar Power Industry	Automobiles
Technological Appropriation/ Capacity Reorganization	Offers domestic industries an opportunity to "catch up" with leading economies in an expedient way	Creates international tensions; patent laws may be such that these "innovations" cannot be exported	High-Speed Rail	Steel Industry BOF (Basic Oxygen Furnace) Technology
Infant Industry Subsidies	Domestic firms can become internationally competitive	Distortions can create issues such as excess capacity; states can pick the wrong winners; diverts resources from other sectors; policy capture by special interest groups	White lists (e.g., Barwick et al., 2019)	MITI and the Automotive Industry
Administrative Guidance	Allows for the coordination of efforts	The government can be incorrect in its recommendations	National Battery Power Innovation Centre (Kenderdine, 2017)	MITI and Sony's Transistor Radios

Source: Li and Farrell (2020)

protectionist trade policy that maximizes export and minimizes import, the party-state takes it to the next level by using it to influence the world (see Chapters 7 and 8). A *New York Times* article summarizes China's globalization strategy as follows, "China wants to be less dependent on the world for its own needs, while making the world as dependent as possible on China" (Myers and Bradsher, 2020).

The ideological foundation of the CCP's expansionary mercantilism can be traced to Mao Zedong's philosophy that the end justifies the means (see Chapter 4). An Australian researcher on China said, "It [China] wants to follow international rules and norms when it is in its interest, and disregard rules and norms when the circumstances suit it." (quoted from Myers and Bradsher, 2020).

An example of simultaneously following and disregarding the international rules is China's treatment of Australia. In late 2020, China signed a free trade agreement, the Regional Comprehensive Economic Partnership (RCEP), with fifteen countries including Australia (Zhou, 2021). At the same time, China punished Australia by blocking goods from Australia – coal, wine, barley, cotton, and lobsters, in violation of free-trade norms – for Australia's criticism of China's human rights violations and its call to investigate the origin of the Covid-19 outbreak (see Chapter 8).

In late 2020, General Secretary Xi Jinping gave several speeches to promote economic self-reliance, and the party-state announced tax incentives for domestic semiconductor manufacturers in an effort to wean China off its dependence on foreign chips. At the same time, the CCP calls for the world to continue to open to China (Xinhua News Agency, 2020a, b).

As the *New York Times* article on China's global strategy sums it up, "It's globalization with Communist characteristics: The Chinese government promotes the country's openness to the world, even as it adopts increasingly aggressive and at times punitive policies that force countries to play by its rules" (Myers and Bradsher, 2020).

Facing the rapid success of China, Inc.'s global strategy, the international community needs to both understand and effectively deal with it. In Part III of this book, we will discuss how other countries have reacted to China's industrial policy; China's response to other countries' reactions; the prospect that China may change its policies based on other countries' reactions; and strategic and policy considerations for MNCs and governments of democratic countries.

6.7 SUMMARY

Guided by the principles of "treating the entire country as a chessboard" and concentrating the entire country's resources to do big things, the party-state has developed its industrial policy as a corporate strategy. Instead of providing guidelines as most countries do through their industrial policy, the party-state uses its industrial policy to approve or disapprove of projects and mobilizes the country's resources to help its firms achieve dominance. The vast scale and scope of China's markets mean that the effects of China's industrial policy have a powerful global impact.

By reviewing the cases of electronic vehicle batteries, solar panels, and high-speed rail, this chapter shows the general pattern of China's industrial policy. First, the government designates certain industries or sectors as key for the country and assigns them high priority. Then the state will arrange all necessary resources from across the country to develop the key industries. At the same time, the government will protect these industries from foreign competition. The party-state will also pick some domestic firms as national champions and help them acquire necessary technologies. With a large, protected domestic market, the designated firms will be able to quickly realize the necessary scale and to lower unit production costs. Once the designated domestic firm becomes efficient, the party-state will support it as it goes out and dominates the world market.

PART III China, Inc.'s Achilles'
Heel and the World's Response

7 The Chinese Communist Party's Dilemmas and Solutions

All members of the Chinese diplomatic service will continue to rally closely around the CPC[1] Central Committee with Comrade Xi Jinping at its core, earnestly implement Xi Jinping Thought on Socialism with Chinese Characteristics for a New Era, work proactively to advance major-country diplomacy with Chinese characteristics in the new era, and make greater contributions to the building of a community with a shared future for mankind with all countries.

Global Vision and Firm Commitment as a Major Country by Chinese Foreign Minister Wang Yi (Wang, 2020)

7.1 THE CCP'S DOMESTIC HEADACHES

The rule of the CCP over China relies mainly on two institutions: one is political and the other is economic. Politically, the CCP relies on communist ideology and proletarian dictatorship (see Chapter 2 and the "four cardinal principles" in Chapter 5); economically, the CCP relies on capitalistic institutions, such as granting private ownership, allowing market exchanges, and using monetary incentives. The political institution – dictatorship – gives the CCP absolute authority and enables it to coordinate economic activities at will and swiftly. Thus, combining the dictatorship and the capitalistic measures, the CCP organizes the whole country as a giant corporation, and linking China, Inc., to the global market is an indispensable part of China's success. But, at the same time, this arrangement poses a fundamental problem for which, so far, the CCP has been unable to find a satisfactory solution. This problem is the conflict between communist

---

[1] The CPC, which stands for "the Communist Party of China," is the acronym used by the Chinese government for the CCP.

dictatorship and globalization that is based on the existing rules and norms primarily set up by the developed, democratic countries: following the rule of law and respecting human rights.

7.1.1 The Inconsistency and Hypocrisy of the CCP

The dictatorship of the CCP is well documented in the areas of violating human rights; suppressing press freedom; relying on a large police force and technology to intimidate and monitor people; and corruption by government officials.

For example, it sentenced writer and human rights activist Liu Xiaobo to eleven years in prison in 2009 for his call for China to democratize and respect the rule of law. Liu won the 2010 Nobel Peace Prize for "his long and non-violent struggle for fundamental human rights in China." In 2017 Liu was diagnosed with liver cancer. The CCP refused to let Liu leave China for treatment, and Liu died in prison in the same year (Wikipedia, 2019).

The CCP employs a large and technologically sophisticated network of neighborhood and internet surveillance. It also bars Google, Facebook, YouTube, and most NGOs from operating in China.

With the party-state controlling huge resources and party officials having great authority over these resources, corruption is rampant in China (Li, 2019b; Transparency International, 2019; Wedeman, 2017).

All these issues run counter to the CCP's claim to be the benevolent, altruistic vanguard whose only goal is to advance the common people's interest. In order to maintain its moral high ground and its legitimacy to rule permanently, the CCP resorts to hypocrisy.

In 2012 the CCP came up with twelve "Core Socialist Values" and has promoted them with high visibility. These values are: the national values of "prosperity," "democracy," "civility," and "harmony"; the social values of "freedom," "equality," "justice," and the "rule of law"; and the individual values of "patriotism," "dedication," "integrity," and "friendship." The CCP has erected numerous billboards throughout China to propagate them (Wikipedia, 2020c).

However, if anyone in China holds up a sign in public advocating "democracy" "freedom," or "rule of law," they will be arrested. Liu Yuandong was detained for publicly holding up a sign in 2013, and four people were arrested for supporting Liu. Some of them held up signs for "democracy" and "freedom" (Hai, 2013). Zhang Shengyu was sentenced to prison for 15 days for publicly holding up signs containing the words "freedom" and "democracy" in 2016 (Zhang, 2016). Huang Wenxun was detained in 2013 for holding up signs containing the words "democracy, freedom, the constitution, and human rights" (Yang, 2013).

Anticorruption campaigns are an integral part of the CCP's dictatorial rule. The absolute power of the party officials has allowed them to take huge bribes. However, if unchecked, corruption would be out of control and would threaten the party's rule. But without the opportunity to take bribes, officials would have no incentive to work hard for the regime. So, the party must allow some corruption, and, when corruption is too rampant, the party leadership will crack down on it. The symbiotic relationship of corruption and anticorruption has created a uniquely hypocritical scene in China: Officials give anticorruption speeches during the day only to take bribes and indulge in vices (such as receiving sex services) during the night. Many corrupt officials are arrested for corruption while presiding over anticorruption meetings (huanqiuwang, 2015).

The CCP labels any thoughts that it does not like or deems harmful as "Western," and makes "Western" an adjective denoting a negative meaning. Its founding theory, Marxism, is from the West, but the CCP conveniently ignores this fact. Anything the party does not like – such as democracy, free press, or elections – it labels "Western." For Western things that the party relies on or enjoys, such as technologies or luxury goods, the word "Western" disappears.

The following provides further evidence of the hypocrisy of the CCP. Officially, the CCP proudly tells the world that the it is confident, powerful, and fearless. In fact, the CCP is so confident about itself it has created a "confidence doctrine" (自信论, zixinlun) (Wikipedia, 2020b), which is a "signature political philosophy" of CCP General

Secretary Xi Jinping. The doctrine orders Communist Party members, government officials, and the Chinese people to be "confident in our chosen path, confident in our guiding theories, confident in our political system, and confident in our culture." Officially, the doctrine is termed "four matters of confidence" (四个自信, *sigezixin*). The message is loud and clear: we the communists are confident.

However, a CCP document shows otherwise. A 2020 list[2] of industries that the CCP prohibits foreign firms from entering inadvertently reveals that the CCP does not have much confidence and is afraid of foreign influences. Here are some items from the forbidden list (in italics) and my comments:

> *Not allowed: Internet information services, online publishing, online audio and video services, internet cultural operations (except music), internet information announcements, etc.*

The CCP seems to be afraid of the free flow of information. Some Chinese hope that Elon Musk's Starlink satellites, if successful, will enable uncensored internet access for people in China (Zhenxiangchuanmei, 2020).

> *Not allowed: investment in law firms in China.*

Foreign-backed law firms pose a threat to the party-state.

> *Not allowed: investment in research institutes for the social sciences and humanities.*
> *Not allowed: social and public opinion polls and surveys.*
> *Not allowed: investment in news providers.*
> *Not allowed: creating or publishing of books, newspapers, periodicals, audio/video products, and electronic media.*
> *Not allowed: radio broadcasting stations, TV stations, channels, networks, transmission stations, satellite stations, microwave transmission stations, etc.*
> *Not allowed: making TV programs.*

---

[2] I accessed and downloaded the list from images.mofcom.gov.cn on July 5, 2020. The link has since disappeared.

Not allowed: movie production and distribution, etc.
Not allowed: art and cultural performance companies.

These eight "not allowed" are so comprehensive that they completely dispel notions concerning the CCP's confidence.

Not allowed: satellite and TV receiving ground equipment and key parts.

Uh oh, there goes the hope that Musk's Starlink will bring the freedom of visiting the Internet to the Chinese people. If someone in China sets up a dish to connect with Starlink's service, they will be punished.

Printing firms must be majority-owned and controlled by Chinese nationals.

This prohibition shows the CCP's lack of confidence to the extreme. The printing business is mundane, noisy, and polluting. It is a sunset industry that not many want to enter in the first place. And these firms are not content creators or providers; they are just taking orders from publishers to print their materials. Since the CCP already has absolute, total control over content providers and publishing, why does it worry about foreign firms doing the printing? This prohibition reminds me of old communist Romania, where owning a typewriter was illegal, and of the not-so-old China of the early 1990s, when the importing of facsimile machines or copiers was tightly controlled.

These forbidden items lay bare the CCP's lack of confidence, showing that, in spite of the party-state's economic wealth, military might, and the powerful domestic stability maintenance force, the CCP is terrified of freedom of information.

7.1.2   *The CCP's Legitimacy Issue*

Political legitimacy refers to the right of a government to rule and the acceptance of the government by the ruled. According to Lipset (1983), legitimacy "involves the capacity of a political system to engender and maintain the belief that existing political institutions are the most appropriate and proper ones for the society" (p. 64). The CCP's legitimacy, which is derived from Marxist revolutionary theory, is commonly viewed by most Chinese as outdated and therefore is being undermined.

7.1.3 Insiders' Rebellion

Since the founding of the CCP, some party members have become disillusioned with the party. As shown in Chapter 2, the party does not allow party members to freely leave and openly criticize or denounce it; they must be and are punished by the party. The party member with the highest rank who became disillusioned with the party is Zhao Ziyang, the then party general secretary during the 1989 pro-democracy movement centered on Beijing's Tiananmen Square, which included millions of people. He objected to the use of force to put down the mass demonstration. After the military crackdown against the movement, he was removed from his party leadership position and was placed under house arrest. He refused to do self-criticism (see Chapter 2), and, for his refusal, the party never freed him and let him die under house arrest in 2005 (Wikipedia, 2020j).

Ren Zhiqiang is another example of a rebellious insider (see Chapter 2). Ren was born into a family of high-ranking CCP officials and joined the party in his youth. In recent years, Ren has increasingly been critical of the party and the party's leadership. In 2020 he was sentenced to eighteen years in prison for implying that party general secretary Xi Jinping is a clown (Buckley, 2020; Ren, 2020).

A consequence of China's going global that the party might have failed to foresee when it pushed China to open is that globalization provides a safe haven for the rebellious insiders of the party – provided that they can leave China, of course. The case of Cai Xia is such an example (see Chapter 2). Professor Cai began to publicly criticize the party after she landed in the United States (Cai, 2021). This example illustrates the fundamental incompatibility between the party's dictatorial rule and globalization.

7.1.4 *Contradiction between Dictatorship and Globalization*

While the discontent about the lack of political rights and freedom by people in China and the rebellion of CCP insiders are a headache, they can be dealt with relatively easily if the country is closed. The CCP can effectively punish them at will, and can force people to be silent or even turn them into hypocrites.

However, internationally, the ideology and the political system that the party has imposed on China are fundamentally different from, and in conflict with, those of the democracies. This has proven to be very troublesome for the party because China is highly open and is heavily reliant on world trade. Its people travel all over the world, and hundreds of millions of foreigners, many from democracies, visit China. This large-scale and high-frequency interaction between the two systems makes the friction and confrontation particularly acute and highly visible world-wide. Morally, democracy and respect for individual freedom and the rule of law are viewed as just, fair, and superior, whereas dictatorship, repression, and rule through law are viewed as unjust, inhumane, and undignified. Unless the party shuts China off from international exchange – which it cannot afford to do since China's economy depends on trade – the friction and frequent confrontations will continue. China's opening-up has greatly enabled the Chinese people to learn about and experience democracy, as well as the respect for human rights and the rule of law that exists in other countries. Ridiculing the dictatorship and complaining about the lack of freedom, albeit privately, has become a daily routine among millions of Chinese people and a huge headache for the party. For example, the dominant social media app in China, WeChat,[3] has become a convenient platform for Chinese people to criticize the party-state or make sarcastic jokes about the party or party leaders. While we cannot get accurate statistics about the prevalence of criticism, we can indirectly assess this from reports about WeChat

---

[3] WeChat became dominant because the party-state does not allow any foreign competitors to enter China, such as Facebook, Twitter, or others.

accounts being shut or account holders being published for criticizing the party-state. An author reported in the *New York Times* that "Over time, many of my WeChat friends have found their accounts blocked for, according to government censors, 'disseminating malicious rumors'" (Li, 2018). "Malicious rumors" is the Chinese government's dysphemism for information that is critical of the party-state.

7.1.5 The CCP's Solutions

To resolve this friction, the party-state has, theoretically, two main options. The first is to embrace the value of democracy, individual freedom, universal human rights, and the rule of law. This would eventually lead to democratization, a necessary step in enabling China to become a full and responsible member of the international community (i.e., becoming a rule-based country. See Chapter 3). This would also mean that the party would relinquish its absolute rule. But the party has made it clear that it will never do this, as stated by Xi (Gao, 2019), thus ruling out this option.

The second option is to change the world, according to the party's view. If other countries, especially the democracies, accept or at least acquiesce to the ideology and practices of the party – "tell China's story well" (in General Secretary Xi Jinping's words) – and do not criticize its human rights record in international agencies such as the United Nations, then the party-state will gain a more positive image globally. If foreign countries stop criticizing the undemocratic practices in China, the people in China would have less reason to criticize them as well, which would alleviate the headaches of the party and improve the party's legitimacy. This rationale, as I will show in Section 7.2, is an important consideration for the CCP's international strategy.

7.2 THE CCP'S INTERNATIONAL STRATEGY

7.2.1 The CCP's Motivation to Influence the World

Modelski's model of world leadership (Flint, 2006; Modelski, 1987; Rock, 2018) provides a relevant and useful framework to understand the CCP's motivation to influence the world. [4] From a grand historical perspective (the sixteenth century to the twentieth century), he looks at the long cycle of the rise and fall of world leadership. He argues that a world leader is a country that is "dominant and powerful" (Flint, 2006, p. 36), but not a hegemon or superpower that can force other countries to obey. He argues that modern leadership rests on the economic resources of a country and it having attractive institutions, ideas, and practices. Importantly, a powerful country assumes leadership because other countries are "willing followers." In essence, Modelski's world leadership theory evaluates whether a country can be a world leader based on the following criteria (Flint, 2006; Rock, 2018): (1) is the country willing to lead? (2) does it have the power and resources to lead? (3) can it attract followers by providing institutional innovations? For example, from the eighteenth century to the twentieth century the United Kingdom and the United States led the world by offering the ideas of liberal capitalism (the free market, the rule of law and democracy) (Flint, 2006, p. 40). For the CCP, as I will show, the answers to (1) and (2) are positive; however, for (3), the CCP's totalitarian ideology and political system are not appealing, and it has been unable to offer an institutional arrangement to attract followers.

Drawing on world leadership theory and political legitimacy theory (see the subsection on CCP's political legitimacy issue earlier) and using evidence from China, I propose the following reasons why the CCP wants to influence the world: Globally, its communist ideology and totalitarian system hinder its desire to be a world leader; domestically, the Chinese people use global criticism of the CCP's suppression of freedom as support for questioning its legitimacy and demanding political change. Facing these two challenges, the CCP resorts to using both positive (carrots) and negative (stick) incentives to buy support and mute criticism from other countries. This will help the CCP to better realize its ambitions for world

---

[4] This subsection is based on S. Li, 2020c. Leading by Bribing: Evidence from China. *International Journal of Emerging Markets*, in press.

leadership and to strengthen its legitimacy in China. Next I elaborate my argument in detail.

7.2.2 The CCP's International Strategy

In formulating its global strategy, the CCP has the following considerations. First, communism by its definition is expansionary. The victory of communism, according to Marx, Lenin, and Mao, must be a worldwide victory (see Chapter 2). As early as the mid-1950s, after the CCP assumed power, Mao Zedong told the party propaganda organ, the Xinhua News Agency, that "we must put the globe under our control, and let our voice be heard throughout the world" (He, 2019; Wan, 2016). In recent years, bolstered by China's economic success, the party no longer "disguises its claws" (see Chapter 2) and has made its ambition for world leadership very clear. The CCP General Secretary Xi Jinping said that China has contributed "China solution and China power" to the world, and would play its role as "a big responsible country" (South China Morning Post, 2018). In a 2019 *Qiushi* (the main publication of the CCP) article, Xi stated that "We must actively participate in the formulation of international rules and act as participant, promoter, and leader during the changing process of global governance" (Gao, 2019). As summarized by China scholar Minxin Pei, Xi Jinping's "New Era" is "a play for global leadership" (Pei, 2018). The "big idea" of the CCP for world leadership is "building a community with a shared future for humanity" that is "an open, inclusive, clean, and beautiful world" (China International Publishing Group, Academy of Contemporary China and World Studies, and China Academy of Translation, 2019, p. 75).

However, this ambition has been undermined by the CCP's own discord: Its violations of human rights have caught the world's attention, such as the labor camps in Xinjiang, the suppression of political rights in Hong Kong, and the cover-up of the outbreak of Covid-19 in Wuhan, China. Commenting on China, Joseph Nye (2012) wrote, "great powers try to use culture and narrative to create soft power that promotes their national interests, but it's not an easy sell when the message is inconsistent with their domestic realities."

Thus, the second consideration for the CCP's global strategy is how to deal with the fundamental conflict between its totalitarian system and the democratic system that most developed countries have. Successfully dealing with this conflict is not only necessary for the CCP's communist cause but is also vital for putting down democratic discontent, as shown earlier in this chapter. This is why, when the CCP promotes its global leadership, it states that "we must oppose and resist various erroneous views [on China] with a clear stand" and "tell China's story well" (China International Publishing Group et al., 2019, volume 2, pp. 248–251, 254–255). General Secretary Xi vows that "we must never follow the path of Western 'constitutionalism,' 'separation of powers,' or 'judicial independence'" (Gao, 2019).

With these considerations, the CCP's global strategy should serve the goal of global expansion, as dictated by the doctrine of communism; replace, or at least mitigate, the values and norms of democracy and the rule of law; and, by achieving these, improve its legitimacy at home. More specifically, the CCP's global strategy sets several concrete objectives: achieve leadership in international organizations, influence foreign governments, promote a positive image of CCP-led China, and silence criticisms of its human rights violations and aggressive behavior toward Taiwan. To achieve these objectives, the CCP invests a huge amount of resources with great patience, as will be shown later in this chapter.

7.2.3   Capabilities of a State to Support Its Quest for World Leadership

Achieving world leadership requires resources. Logically, in terms of resources, two factors are important in enabling the government of a country to achieve world leadership: the size of the economy under its control, and the degree of its control over the economy.

According to *The World Fact Book of the CIA* (CIA, 2020b), in 2017, the size of the world's economy was US$127 trillion (based on purchasing power parity (PPP)), of which China (with US$23 trillion based on PPP) alone accounted for 18 percent, whereas the US economy was US$21 trillion, making China the world's largest economy, providing a large base on which the party can build to achieve world leadership.

Unlike democracies, which have checks and balances on government spending, the CCP has unchecked power and can mobilize the entire country's resources to achieve its goals (Li and Farrell, 2020b). In other words, the extent to which the CCP can leverage its US$23 trillion economy to buy and influence the world is much higher than the extent to which democratic governments can mobilize their economies to defend themselves. Based on public data, the party-state controls approximately 56 percent of China's GDP through taxes, fees, and state-owned enterprises (in comparison, the US government controls 32 percent) (IMF, 2019; National Bureau of Statistics of China, 2016, 2018a), giving it the largest war chest of any individual country, with which it can influence the world.

The CCP uses the carrot and stick approach to carry out its international strategy. Giving resources to target countries or people can be viewed as using carrots, while punishing countries or people by taking away resources is equivalent to wielding a stick. Section 7.3 provides evidence on how China is expanding its influence worldwide.

7.3   BRIBE THE WORLD, SYSTEMATICALLY

In its quest for global leadership, the Chinese government has turned the relationship between the briber and bribee in corruption upside down.[5] Traditionally, corruption has referred to individuals or organizations that bribe state officials to sell public goods for private gain. In such a relationship, the briber is an individual or an organization such as a private firm, and the bribee is a government official.

[5] This section is based on S. Li, 2019b. *Bribery and Corruption in Weak Institutional Enviroments: Connecting the Dot from a Comparative Perspective* London: Cambridge University Press. S. Li, 2020c. Leading by Bribing: Evidence from China. *International Journal of Emerging Markets*, in press.

In almost all known cases of bribery-corruption, the corrupt official is always the one who *receives*, rather than *pays*, the bribes.

Now, let us switch the roles of the briber and bribee: let the briber be the government of one country, and let the bribee be individuals, organizations, and governments of other countries. In other words, let us add the following to the domain of the bribery-corruption relationship: the government of one country *bribes* the rest of the countries of the world in order to influence their attitudes and behavior. This, I argue, is what the Chinese government is doing systematically in the world. Here is some evidence.

7.3.1 Hanban/Confucius Institutes

The "Hanban," established around 2004, is the party-state's office that was set up to fund Confucius Institutes around the world. According to a 2006 BBC report, the Chinese government initially committed US$10 billion for operating the Confucius Institute program (BBC, 2006 cited from Jensen, 2011). In the United States, the Hanban would make a deal with an American university to provide funding (ranging from US$100,000 to US$400,000) and teachers to set up a Confucius Institute on its campus to teach Chinese language and culture. As of 2017, there were 525 Confucius Institutes and 1,113 Confucius Classrooms in 146 countries (Caixin, 2018; Hanban, 2018). China's per capita income is still low: about US$8,600 based on the official exchange rate in 2017. Why would the Chinese government spend billions to help countries such the United States (per capita income US$59,800) with education, while in its own rural areas, millions of children do not have adequate educational resources?

Perhaps the biggest irony is that the CCP was founded on an anti-Confucius platform in 1921. Its mobilizing slogan was "Down with Confucius!" Since then, the CCP has labelled him the mastermind of all counter-revolutionary and anti-communist forces and has waged many movements in an attempt to eradicate the influence of Confucius. Now, suddenly, and without any logical explanation, while still upholding communism (which is inherently anti-Confucius), the old adversary has become a dear friend.

Actually, we can understand more about this about-face from speeches given by the Chinese officials in charge of ideology and propaganda.

In 2010, Liu Yunshan, then the CCP propaganda head, said,

> We should actively carry out international propaganda battles on issues such as Tibet, Xinjiang, Taiwan, human rights, and Falun Gong. Our strategy is to proactively take our culture abroad ... We should do well in establishing and operating overseas cultural centers and Confucius Institutes.
>
> *(Quoted from Sahlins (2015), p. 6)*

In 2011, Li Changchun, then a CCP leader, explained that,

> The Confucius Institute is an appealing brand for extending our culture abroad. It has made an important contribution toward improving our soft power. The 'Confucius' brand has a natural attractiveness. Using the excuse of teaching Chinese language, everything looks reasonable and logical.
>
> *(Quoted from Sahlins (2015), p. 1)*

Peter Wood, president of the U.S. National Association of Scholars, comments, "The Chinese Communist Party, which organizes and funds the Confucius Institutes through a state agency, the Hanban, is not known for altruistic cultural outreach." In fact, "these institutes have nothing to do with Confucius" (Wood, 2018). According to a study on Confucius Institutes by the National Association of Scholars, "the institutes stifle academic freedom, censor teachers, engage in unlawful religious discrimination, disseminate Chinese propaganda, and violate norms of transparency" (Wood, 2018).

To incentivize American schools to host the Confucius Institute, besides funding, the party-state invites school administrators to lucrative lecturing trips to China, allocates more Chinese students to their campuses, and gives research grants and scholarships to the schools. "For a relatively modest price, the Chinese govern-ment gains enormous influence over major American colleges and universities ... from which it exercises other kinds of influence" (Wood, 2018).

In July 2020, China's Ministry of Education announced that the Hanban had changed its name to the "Ministry of Education Center for Language Education and Cooperation," a move widely viewed as the CCP's rebranding effort to improve Confucius Institute's negative image of censorship and corruption (Zhuang, 2020).

7.3.2 Training Future Foreign Leaders in China

The party-state also sets aside quotas, scholarships, and housing at universities in China for foreign applicants. In 2018, the Chinese government set aside US$5.1 billion in scholarships for foreign stu-dents studying in China. A foreign undergraduate student could receive US$9,108–$10,185 per year, while a foreign doctoral student could receive as much as US$15,353 per year (Radio Free Asia, 2018). In 2019, the state allocated US$5.9 billion for foreign students, a 15 percent increase, while the state budget for Chinese teachers' training saw a 5.6 percent contraction from 2018 (Shaheshang, 2019). In her article, "Beijing is cultivating the next generation of African elites by training them in China," Lily Kuo (2017) observed,

> China is particularly interested in the next generation of African elites. Last year, Beijing announced it would invite 1,000 young African politicians for training in China, after hosting more than 200 between 2011 and 2015. Thousands of African students are pursuing undergraduate and graduate degrees in China on scholarship programs funded by Beijing. As of this year, more Anglophone African students study in China than the United States or the United Kingdom, their traditional destinations of choice.

To make sure that such a strategic intention does not raise any suspicion, "Chinese officials are quick to say these scholarships and trainings are not an attempt to remake Africa in its own image"

(Kuo, 2017). Nevertheless, the intention is sometimes revealed by Chinese officials themselves. An article entitled "China implements strategy in Africa in a low-key style: Review of China-trained African presidents" quoted the Chinese official view of the 1960s, that "if half of all the students from Africa and Latin-America studied in China turned into revolutionaries, they would make a positive impact on the revolutionary course there" (DWnews.com, 2018).

7.3.3 Influencing the Influencers

The Chinese government uses money in various forms to influence the organizations and people who influence public opinions and policies in other countries. The Working Group on Chinese Influence Activities in the United States (2018) reviewed the ways in which the Chinese government used its vast resources to influence the American government at various levels and branches, as well as the Chinese-American community, universities, think tanks, corporations, and the technology and research sectors. The general pattern is that China gives economic resources to American entities so that they will support China's agenda, or will, at least, be less critical of the giver. Here are some cases.

Tung Chee-hwa, vice chairman of Chinese People's Political Consultative Conference and former Hong Kong chief executive, gave money through his China–United States Exchange Foundation (CUSEF) to the Johns Hopkins University School of Advanced International Studies, the Brookings Institution, and elsewhere. Such giving causes self-censorship,

> Researchers understand that their access to China depends on not ruffling feathers. Publishers agree to erase critical articles from journals to gain access to the Chinese markets. By influencing the influencers, China gets Americans to carry its message to other Americans … That's much more effective than having Chinese officials deliver those messages.
>
> (Rogin, 2017)

A strategy to influence the influencers is known as "Blue-Gold-Yellow." "Blue represents large-scale Chinese cyber and internet operations while gold represents China's use of money and financial power. The yellow is part of a plan to use sex to undermine American society" (Gertz, 2017). Based on the report, the last two tactics, gold and yellow, are clearly attempts at bribery and corruption.

7.3.4 Thousand Talents Plan

The "Thousand Talents Plan" recruits experts in research, innovation, and entrepreneurship to work for China (Jia, 2018; The Thousand Talents Plan, Undated, accessed January 9, 2020). The plan gives the invitees two options: one is to work in China on a permanent basis, and the other is to offer them short-term appointments. The short-term program usually targets experts who work full-time at a leading university or research laboratory but do not want to leave their jobs (Jia, 2018). Many of these scholars have prominent posts – for example, in 2020, the US government arrested Harvard University professor Charles Lieber for receiving money (US$50,000/month, US$150,000 annual living expenses, and US$1.5 million to set up a lab in China) from the Thousand Talents Plan and lying about it (Viswanatha and O'Keeffe, 2020).

According to a United States Senate (2019) report,

> ... the Thousand Talents Plan incentivizes individuals engaged in research and development in the United States to transmit the knowledge and research they gain here to China in exchange for salaries, research funding, lab space, and other incentives. China unfairly uses the American research and expertise it obtains for its own economic and military gain.

This arrangement – in which the Chinese government gives money and other benefits to US-based researchers in exchange for their US-funded research results – is similar to the way a mafia group puts a policeman on its payroll in exchange for official information and protection, except that in the Thousand Talents Plan the briber is the government of a country rather than a mafia group.

In late 2018, when the Thousand Talents Plan attracted increasing criticism from the United States, China began to enact the plan more subtly by reducing its online presence, deleting the names of plan participants, and instructing the recruits not to mention the plan in their communications (United States Senate, 2019; Yang and Liu, 2019). This further proves that the Chinese government is aware of the illicit nature of the plan.

7.3.5   The Belt and Road Initiative

China's Belt and Road Initiative (BRI) aims to provide US$4 to 8 trillion in support from the Chinese state (through state-subsidized loans, investments, and gifts), Chinese state-owned enterprises, public–private partnerships, and private investors to participating countries to build infrastructure and other projects (Belt and Road Initiative, Undated). As of 2017, it is estimated to have included more than sixty-eight countries, accounting for 65 percent of the world's population and 40 percent of global GDP (Campbell, 2017; Griffiths, 2017).

The BRI is a main economic vehicle for the CCP to project power worldwide and sway other countries, especially less developed countries, to participate in and support China's international activities (Beech, 2018; Chatterji, 2020; Chaudhury, 2019). The mentality of the CCP leaders in conceiving and designing the relationship between China and the recipient countries of the BRI is how an empire treats its tributary states. Such a mentality is reflected in the designation and layout of the BRF (Belt and Road Forum) compound at Yanxi Lake on the outskirts of Beijing. At the heart of the compound is the BRF conference center, which resembles a place where an emperor would receive the leaders of tributary states. It is an imposing and even intimidating structure that has four roof corners projecting upward with sharp ends. The building materials include massive amounts of precious metal and rare wood, permeated with the colors red and purple – colors for the emperor according to Chinese tradition.

FIGURE 7.1 The Belt and Road Forum Conference Center.
The circle is the logo plate of the Belt and Road Forum.
Source: Author

According to the architect, Liu Lei, the design of the conference center is based on the style of the Han and Tan Dynasties, two of the most powerful eras in Chinese history. The upward projecting roof tips on two sides symbolize wings of a giant bird ready to soar (Sina.com, 2014) (see Figure 7.1). The compound also features a dozen villas to accommodate the visiting heads of tributary states.

Typical financial and economic arrangements for the initiative are these: The Chinese government will fund the infrastructure construction by issuing loans, which will be paid back by the recipient country, and which are secured by land or other valuable assets or rights of the recipient country. A report by Fitch Ratings believes that the Chinese government's "political motivation for projects could trump commercial logic and real demand for infrastructure" (Peter Wells, 2017). "Most analysts agree that, for all its rhetoric about trade and development, [the Belt and Road] is primarily a political project." Its aim is "to win friends and influence people" (Griffiths, 2017).

More recent reports have shown evidence or suspicions that some of the projects were purposely overpriced, so that a portion of the funds could be used for payment to officials in host countries.

According to a report by the Center for a New American Security, "Belt and Road projects have often involved payoffs to politicians and bureaucrats. Projects that are financially or environmentally unsound are sometimes approved as a direct result" (Kliman, Doshi, Lee, and Cooper, 2019, p. 6). Such corruption has been reported in Malaysia, Bangladesh, the Philippines, Equatorial Guinea, Sri Lanka, and Pakistan (Kliman et al., 2019; Wright and Hope, 2018; Yang, 2019).

7.3.6   Foreign Aid

China provided US$350 billion in aid to 140 countries from 2000 to 2014 and was the world's largest giver of aid from 2009 to 2014 (AIDDATA, 2017). China's rapid rise in foreign aid is particularly striking, given that in 2007, the mid-point of the 2000 to 2014 span, per capita income in China was still low, at US$2,695 (World Bank, 2019b), and 27 million to over 100 million Chinese people were below the poverty line (defined by the World Bank as US$1.9/day). This is why global generosity by the Chinese government raises suspicion in the world and angers many people in China (Kilby, 2017; Voice of America, 2018). The Chinese people have coined a term for this generous giving by the CCP: "da sa bi." Its literal meaning is "greatly throwing money," but it sounds like the Beijing colloquial term "da sha bi," which means "a great fool" (Voice of America, 2018).

The aid database, AIDDATA, classifies aid as "official development assistance" (ODA), "other official flows" (OOF), and "vague official flows" (VOF). ODA is "primarily intended for development and welfare," or commonly known as "aid"; OOF is "primarily intended for commercial and representational purposes"; and VOF is the type with "insufficient information" (AIDDATA, 2017).

The majority of US foreign aid is ODA for development and welfare purposes; this accounts for 85 percent of its total aid. For China, that category only accounts for 23 percent. The bulk of aid from China, rather, is OOF, at 61 percent, and is directed toward commerce and representation in the recipient country. Of the Chinese aid, the purpose of US$81 billion is unknown (in the VOF category). If we assume that those funds are likely to be used also for commerce and representation, then OOF would account for 84 percent of total Chinese aid.

Politically, China requires recipients to support its domestic and international policies, such as supporting the "one China policy" and not criticizing the 1989 Tiananmen Crackdown (Kilby, 2017, p. 17, 26). Economically, the Chinese government tends to mix aid with profitable purposes, and " ... freely comingles aid with market-driven inputs such as FDI (foreign direct investment), imports of raw materials, and export credits" (Hook and Rumsey, 2016, p. 67).

Combining political and economic goals, the Chinese government uses aid to build relationships with foreign leaders who support its agendas and to exchange favors (Kilby, 2017; Li et al., 2019). While democracies view their aid as "altruism by one party; the Chinese Government's approach, neither seeks nor values such a distinction" (Yeh and Wharton, 2016, p. 293).

A *Financial Times* article stated that

> China exports its authoritarian model. There are already signs of this as Chinese companies test powerful commercial surveillance technologies and the country increases pressure on regional allies to extradite individuals back to China on the grounds of security and anti-corruption. Beijing's global-facing strategy will only amplify its ability to use economic might to muzzle freedom of speech and advocacy with its trade partners.
>
> *(Feng, 2018)*

7.3.7 *China versus Democracies in Foreign Aid*

Mature democracies, especially the United States, have also used foreign aid to influence other countries. However, there are several key differences between them and China in aid.

First and most fundamentally, their political and economic systems categorically differ, which defines their different methods of funding foreign aid. One of the most important principles of allocating government resources in democracies is that the branch of government that approves the budget (congress/parliament) is separated from the branch that spends it, the executive. Not only do the two branches keep close checks on each other, but they both must also be accountable to the taxpayers whose votes determine their fates. If the taxpayers/voters believe that their taxes are being used for bribery, they can voice their opposition and ultimately stop it. Thus, in the long run, such bribery of the world by their government can be effectively corrected by the mechanisms that are built into a democracy. Furthermore, in democracies, the line between the government and the economy is categorically clearer than in China: The government cannot take resources from firms for bribery. Neither can it ask firms to bribe on its behalf, whereas the CCP can use resources from any China-based/China-related organizations/individuals for bribery (e.g., the case of Patrick Ho, a businessman, who bribed foreign politicians on behalf of the Chinese state, see (U.S. Department of Justice, 2019b)).

Second, their ideologies differ. The ideology of democracies and their governments is to respect human rights and the rule of law. Projecting this ideology internationally, democracies expect aid recipients to do the same, or democratize if they have not done so (Kilby, 2017). Furthermore, democracies emphasize the altruistic aspect of their aid (Kilby, 2017; Müller, 2013; Yeh and Wharton, 2016). For all these purposes and intentions, aid from democracies is not bribery by states – it is illogical for a democratic state to bribe a country to respect the rule of law or to democratize.

In contrast, despite the CCP having "consistently challenged the Western liberal views of democracy and human rights" (Kilby, 2017, p. 10), it is not proud of its communist ideology and tries to hide it when talking with aid recipients. Without a presentable ideology, the CCP uses feel-good or vague language to promote its aid: some are lofty, such as that for a "community with a shared future for humanity" (China International Publishing Group et al., 2019,

p. 74); some are intended to build relationships, such as for "partner-ship and solidarity" (Kilby, 2017, p. 10), and perhaps most import-antly, some are for resisting criticism by other countries of its poor human rights records and its rule over law. For example, the Chinese government "pushed quite hard to insert" "the principle of non-interference in internal affairs" into an OECD document on aid, a phrase that "sits rather uneasily with" the goal of the document, which is to jointly assess and govern all donors (Kilby, 2017, p. 30). While democracies are concerned with leaders of receiving countries who are corrupt, the CCP does not mind such leaders at all, and in fact welcomes them (BBC, 2011; Kilby, 2017). Unlike democracies, the Chinese government does not value being viewed as altruistic (Wood, 2018; Yeh and Wharton, 2016). In sum, the CCP's intent and practice of bribing the world is categorically different from the aid programs of democracies (Kilby, 2017).

7.4   ACTIVELY PARTICIPATE IN INTERNATIONAL ORGANIZATIONS

The Chinese government also uses resources to influence inter-national organizations. In "How China Swallowed the WTO," the *Wall Street Journal* reported, "Geneva – Inside the cement compound housing the World Trade Organization lies a colorful Chinese garden of cultivated rocks, arches and calligraphy." The garden, continued the writer, was a gift from China (Schlesinger, 2017).

As China rises, the party-state increasingly recognizes the importance of international organizations. "It's China's sense that this is 'our' moment, and we need to take control of these bodies," commented Ashok Malik, senior policy adviser at India's foreign ministry. "If you control important levers of these institutions, you influence norms, you influence ways of thinking, you influence inter-national policy, you inject your way of thinking" (quoted from Trofimov, Hinshaw, and O'Keeffe, 2020).

Indeed, in recent years, China has invested huge resources to gain control over international agencies, and has made impressive achievements. For example, in 2016 a senior CCP official, vice minister of China's Public Security Ministry Meng Hongwei, was elected the president of Interpol. Given the fact that China's police force is the tool of the CCP and is above the law, Meng's election was especially ironic. It also shows the strong, determined effort the party-state has made to gain influence in international agencies. What is more ironic is that Meng was lured back to China from his duty in Paris and was arrested in 2018 on corruption charges. He was given a 13½ year prison term in 2020 (Wikipedia, 2020f).

Currently, China heads four of the fifteen United Nations (UN) and UN-affiliated agencies or groups that collectively act as functional departments of the UN and implement UN policies in areas that are important for the world, such as aviation and telecommunication. The four agencies are the Food and Agriculture Organization (FAO), International Civil Aviation Organization, International Telecommunication Union, and the United Nationals Industrial Development Organization. No other country has its citizens heading more than one UN agency (Trofimov et al., 2020).

China's strategy to exert influence or to gain control at international agencies also involves using bribes. Even though China's economy (US$23 trillion) is bigger than the United States' (US$21 trillion), China's contribution to the UN is a fraction of what the United States gives. According to a *Wall Street Journal* Report, China contributed US$1.3 billion to the UN in 2018, while the United States' annual commitment to the UN was US$10 billion (Trofimov et al., 2020). Apparently, while the CCP does not want to contribute proportionally based on the size of its GDP, it seems to have found a much more effective and efficient way to gain influence in the UN and its agencies and to promote China's interests: using funds directly with selective member countries, the UN Secretary-General, and China's projects such as the Belt and Road Initiative (Rosett, 2020a; Trofimov et al., 2020).

China's victory in putting a CCP official into the chair of the director of FAO gives us a glimpse of how the strategy works. In 2019, when the head of FAO was open for election, China sent its candidate, Qu Dongyu, its vice minister of agriculture, to compete for it. One of Qu's rivals was the Cameroonian candidate Medi Moungui, who had the powerful backing of the African Union. In February, a senior Chinese official visited Cameroon and cancelled its US$78 million worth of debt to China, and Moungui withdrew from the race. Qu won (Lynch and Gramer, 2019).

As the *Wall Street Journal* report (Trofimov et al., 2020) observed, "China has leveraged loans and other assistance to dozens of developing nations in Africa, the Pacific and elsewhere to create voting blocs and defeat Western-backed candidates and proposals at the U.N."

China also uses funds directly with the head of the UN, the Secretary-General. For example, China is the second-largest contributor to the UN peacekeeping budgets. As UN expert Claudia Rosett observes, "China's Peace and Development fund bypasses the common pots of UN funding and channels millions of dollars every year directly from Beijing to the executive office of the UN Secretary-General." And such effort, according to Rosett, "has translated into a stronger UN commitment to the goals and activities of China" (Rosett, 2020a).

Its funding to the UN Secretary-General and its leading roles in several UN agencies has enabled China to effectively promote its Belt and Road Initiative at the UN (Rosett, 2020a; Trofimov et al., 2020). According to the *Wall Street Journal* report,

> Some 30 U.N. agencies and institutions have signed memorandums in support of China's Belt and Road infrastructure project ... As a result, China can present its state-run Belt and Road projects, which mainly employ Chinese firms and often leave poor nations in debt, as benign U.N.-approved assistance.
>
> *(Trofimov et al., 2020)*

Moritz Rudolf, founder of Eurasia Bridges, a German consulting firm that studies China's Belt and Road Initiative, summed up that,

"China has been able to make the U.N. more Chinese ... It's systematic." (quoted from Trofimov et al., 2020).

7.5 WAGE THE GREAT PROPAGANDA WAR

As early as 2008, the CCP had begun to develop "The Great Propaganda War," estimated to cost about 45 billion yuan (US$6.9 billion), with the goal of expanding the CCP's propaganda to the world, improving the CCP/China's image, and disseminating the party's policies and views. A Voice of America report terms the great propaganda war as "brainwashing foreigners in great scale" (Ji, 2020).

7.5.1 *Propaganda Tactics*

The CCP keeps its propaganda tactics top secret and thus we can only rely on anecdotal evidence or secondary sources such as analyses by outside researchers. Radio Free Asia (2020c) reported that in late 2020 a one-page document entitled "Nine Tricks of CCP Propaganda" has been circulating online. The nine tricks are,

> Trick 1: Use mainstream media to deliver basic political information.
> Trick 2: Use mainstream media to send political information to targeted groups or individuals.
> Trick 3: Target and send information to people who are interested in political news.
> Trick 4: Package political information as entertaining information.
> Trick 5: Frequently create topics, both positive and negative [about the CCP/China], and mobilize the internet army to amplify the positive and denounce the negative.
> Trick 6: When information is out of control and a confidence crisis on the CCP occurs, use individuals to publish explosive materials to divert the public's attention.
> Trick 7: Use overseas media under the CCP's control to disseminate information so that it appears to have originated from abroad.
> Trick 8: Release low quality criticism of the CCP attributable to the overseas democracy movement, so that Chinese people who jump over the Great Firewall will be dismayed about the overseas democracy movement.

Trick 9: Support and establish opinion leaders who appear to be critical of the CCP. At critical moments such as a crisis, they will guide the public to support the CCP.

While the first three tricks are basic for the propaganda war, from the fourth trick on, it relies on social media apps, such as WeChat and TikTok, and becomes more and more sophisticated, including techniques such as repackaging and spinning. The CCP will sacrifice their own internet soldiers by making them release fake news and then attacking them. The CCP can also flood YouTube, Twitter, and Facebook with its internet army and fake news.

A 2020 report by the Taiwanese Democracy Lab identified four models that the CCP's internet army uses to attack Taiwan: "The Great Propaganda War" (see the "Nine Tricks"); "Little Pink Reds," which refers to individual CCP supporters; "Content Farms," which are organizations that use a large number of freelance writers to produce a high volume of web content specifically designed to increase online traffic and search results; and local collaborators, who are town and village leaders and local online stars. They can appear to be unrelated to the CCP and are very influential and persuasive as a result of their high credibility in the local community (DW, 2020).

7.5.2   Buy Advertising in Major Media

The CCP spent a large amount of money to buy advertising in major media in the world, especially in the United States. According to US Department of Justice documents, *China Daily*, the CCP's number one English newspaper, spent US$19 million on printing and advertising in US media, of which US$11 million went to the *Washington Post* and the *Wall Street Journal*. Reports also show that the *New York Times* ran paid supplements from *China Daily*. These advertisements appear under the title of "China Watch," which makes it look like real news articles. The contents are invariably promoting the views of the CCP and beautifying China and the party (Hasson, 2020).

7.5.3   *Buy News Media*

A major effort to buy influence by the Chinese government is to acquire and control overseas news media, especially Chinese language media (He, 2019). A researcher observed that China uses four tactics,

> First is the attempt to directly control newspapers, television stations, and radio stations through complete ownership or owning major shares. Second is the government's use of economic ties to influence independent media who have business relations with China. This leverage has had major effects on the contents of broadcasting and publishing, effectively removing all material deemed 'unfavorable' by the Chinese government. Third is the purchasing of broadcast time and advertising space (or more) from existing independent media. Closely related to this is the government's providing free, ready-to-go programming and contents. Fourth is the deployment of government personnel to work in independent media, achieving influence from within their ranks.
>
> *(Mei, 2001)*

One well-known case is the online news portal DWnews.com, which was founded after the 1989 Tiananmen massacre by pro-democracy student leaders who had fled China to the United States and other Chinese-American democracy activists. After it became influential, a Hong Kong businessman, who was known to be both pro-Chinese government and backed by the Chinese government, bought it. Since that change of hands, DWnews.com has played a subtle and important role in the Chinese government's efforts in worldwide propaganda (He, 2019). By now, most of the Chinese media organizations worldwide have either been bought or are under the control or influence of the Chinese government (He, 2019).

A list compiled by a blogger with account c1144706 that includes Chinese news media entities under the CCP's control or sponsorship records 140 entities worldwide, mostly Chinese newspapers (ogate.org, 2020). In October 2019, the CCP held "The Tenth

Forum on the Global Chinese Language Media" in Shijiazhuang, Hebei, China. The list of guests was leaked and showed 427 participants, mostly publishers, editor-in-chiefs, and CEOs, representing 427 Chinese media entities from all over the world who came to the meeting. Most of them were from the United States (China News Agency; Xingaodi, 2020).

7.6 THE UNITED FRONT WORK AT WORK

7.6.1 *The Russian Doll Approach*

As discussed in Chapter 2, the objective of the CCP's United Front Work (UFW) is to make the broadest possible alliance with the CCP at the core (Chinese Communist Party, 2020). The target audience of the UFW is the non-communists; rather, the elites, professionals, and leaders of various segments of foreign and mostly democratic countries, who generally do not support the CCP's ideology or policies. The overseas Chinese population is the CCP's primary target for the UFW's effort because the party can appeal to their origin, culture, or ethnic pride. In Chapter 2, I explained how the CCP intentionally blurs the distinction between China the party and China the people, and here I will show that, using the same strategy, the UFW is very effective in targeting overseas Chinese who do not support or are even critical of the CCP's dictatorship.

Fan Chou, a well-known political commentator on Chinese media, likens the strategy of the CCP's United Front Work to a set of Russian nesting dolls – three to five small hollow wooden dolls of decreasing size. Each doll fits inside of the others sequentially until all of the dolls are contained in the largest doll. The largest doll opens up to reveal the next, smaller doll, and that doll in turn opens up to reveal an even smaller doll, until at the center or core is the smallest doll (Fan, 2020).

In Fan's analogy, at the center of the multi-layered doll, the core, is the *"dang"* (党) – the Chinese Communist Party. The next layer is the *"guo"* (国) – the state, the third layer is the *"zhong"* (中) – China, and the largest, the outside doll, is the *"hua"* (华), which refers to all the people in the world of Chinese origin. So, we can translate *"hua"* as "pan-Chinese" (Liu, 2017).

Of course, the ultimate goal is to persuade the target audience of the UFW to support the party. Most overseas Chinese are against communist dictatorship. For these people, the UFW would tell them that being anti-communist is okay, as long as they accept the Chinese state – the People's Republic of China – and the UFW can still fund them. For these people, the hope is that maybe someday the party will make the country democratic. But many overseas Chinese are also opposed to the Chinese state. To them, the CCP will emphasize the layer of *"zhong"* – China the country – to appeal to them. As long as they identify with China the country, the UFW will still fund them, and tolerate their critical views of the Chinese state. Finally, for the overseas Chinese who do not identify with China the country, such as the second or later generations of overseas Chinese, the UFW will push the largest shell of the doll, *"hua,"* selling them on the concept of pan-Chinese. As long as they identify themselves with overseas Chinese, the UFW will dole out resources to them. Once the targets join the pan-Chinese circle, the UFW will continue to work on them to pull them into the *"zhong," "guo,"* and ultimately, the *"dang"* level – the core. An anecdote further supports my analysis here.

A friend of mine, a Chinese-American professor in social science at a US university, visited China a few years ago. During his visit, at a dinner party, he met some UFW officials, who told him, "we know that some of your articles are critical of our party, but it is okay, we understand."

For foreign people who are not of Chinese origin, the party attracts them with Chinese history and culture. The extension of the Russian doll strategy is to promote Chinese culture, such as through the Confucius Institute. Once foreigners are taught the CCP's version of "Chinese culture" (such as recognizing Taiwan as part of China) and begin to like it, it will be a good start for the UFW.

The next goal is to impress them with China's great achievements, and to gradually link them to the party's wise leadership.

The US–China Peoples' Friendship Association, based in the United States, works closely with the Chinese People's Association for Friendship with Foreign Countries in China, which is a front organization under the CCP's Department of United Front Work, and allows articles critical of the CCP to be published in its main publication, the *US-China Review* (Alon, Farrell, and Li, 2020a). This provides evidence in support of the UFW tactic of tolerating foreigners criticizing the CCP as long as they promote Chinese culture adhering to the party's view, such as the issue that Taiwan is "an internal affair on both sides of the Taiwan Straits" (US–China Peoples Friendship Association, 2020).

7.6.2 Participating in the Politics of Foreign Countries

As discussed earlier in this chapter, the CCP is making a great effort and employing a large amount of resources to influence the influencers in foreign countries. This is done through multiple channels: business, academic institutions, think tanks, and other nonprofit organizations such as friendship associations between China and other countries, Chinese diaspora organizations, and social media apps such as WeChat. A *Newsweek* study spent four months identifying these groups, and compiled a list of 600 such groups in the United States. The total number of such groups in the United States were "all in regular touch with and guided by China's Communist Party – a larger-scale version of a pattern found in other countries around the world" (Tatlow, 2020). According to the *Newsweek* report, "the scope of alleged activities is enormous, involving social and business gatherings, extensive information campaigns and building political and economic ties that can be leveraged to Beijing's gain."

The CCP has done extensive work collecting data and analyzing not only the top leaders of major countries in the world but also local officials in these countries. In a speech to the National Governors

Association in Washington, US State Department Secretary Mike Pompeo warned state governors that

> a Chinese Government-backed think tank in Beijing produced a report that assessed all 50 of America's governors on their attitudes towards China. They labeled each of you 'friendly,' 'hardline,' or 'ambiguous.' I'll let you decide where you think you belong. Someone in China already has. Many of you, indeed, in that report are referenced by name.
>
> *(Pompeo, 2020b)*

In late 2020, the story of a Chinese woman by the name of Fang Fang (who also went by Christine Fang) attracted some attention. She is not the famous author Fang Fang who wrote the *Wuhan Diary* during the outbreak of the coronavirus; she was a foreign student in California. The reason that her story caused a small sensation is that it had two intriguing words: espionage and sex. But in my view, Fang Fang's case is an example of the UFW at work. Fang Fang came to study at California State University East Bay around 2011 and had developed extensive social networks in the United States until she abruptly left in 2015. The reason for her sudden disappearance is unknown, but the media speculate that she was investigated by US authorities and thus was called back by the CCP.

During her stay in the United States, Fang was very active in the public affairs of her school, the local community, California state, other states and at the national level. She served as the president of the school's Chinese Student Association and president of the campus chapter of Asian Pacific Islander American Public Affairs. She developed close ties with many American politicians. According to a report published by Axios, "She also engaged in sexual or romantic relationships with at least two mayors of Midwestern cities over a period of about three years, according to one U.S. intelligence official and one former elected official." Her method of penetrating the American political system was to first to actively participate in campus and local political activities, and through these organizations and events get to know more people who could introduce her to more politicians beyond the local community. The CCP provided her with opportunities in China and access to well-connected Chinese officials. She could then introduce her American friends to these opportunities and Chinese officials, which in turn further enhanced her standing in America. The Axios report comments, "the case demonstrates China's strategy of cultivating relationships that may take years or even decades to bear fruit. The Chinese Communist Party knows that today's mayors and city council members are tomorrow's governors and members of Congress" (Allen-Ebrahimian and Dorfman, 2020).

7.6.3 A Sheer Numbers Game

The work of the United Front Work department is a person-to-person business that relies heavily on interpersonal skills, and can only be carried out by real people. Using computers or Zoom meetings is not effective in cultivating close friendships or intimate relationships. The more agents China can dedicate to the UFW's work, the more targets it can identify and reach. In this numbers game, China, with 1.4 billion people, has a tremendous advantage. The United States has 331 million people, or one-fourth of China's population. If both countries assign the same proportion of their respective workforces to influence the other, China would outnumber the United States by a ratio of four to one. In fact, China has 100 million more people than the OECD (Organization for Economic Cooperation and Development, whose members are democratic countries supporting free-market economies) countries combined.

7.7 PUNISHING CRITICS

7.7.1 Coercive Diplomacy

For foreign countries, companies and individuals that criticize the CCP/China or whose words or actions are deemed offensive by the CCP, the CCP will retaliate with both economic and noneconomic measures, as I will explain in detail. A report by researchers at the

Australian Strategic Policy Institute calls the CCP's effort in punishing its critics worldwide "coercive diplomacy" (Hanson, Currey, and Beattie, 2020).

The term "coercive diplomacy" has been used in foreign policy studies to refer to the attempt to get a foreign entity (such as a country, company, or individual) to change their objectionable behavior by threatening to use or using limited force (Art and Cronin, 2003). However, the Australian report on the CCP's coercive diplomacy warns that the CCP has gone beyond conventional coercive diplomacy and has used methods that pose new and greater challenges to the international community.

The report examined data on the use of coercive diplomacy by the CCP in the past ten years, and identified 152 incidences that affected 27 countries and the European Union, as well as 49 foreign companies. Their data also show a sharp increase in cases since 2018. The regions and countries that are hit the hardest by the CCP's actions are Europe, North America, Australia, New Zealand, and East Asia (South Korea, Japan, and Taiwan).

7.7.2 Types of "Crime"

The most frequently used reason by the CCP to punish foreign entities is that what they say or do "hurts the feelings of the Chinese people" (伤害中国人民的感情). This has become a standard response used by the CCP and its media. Variations of this expression include "hurting the feelings of 1.3 billion people" or "hurting the feelings of the Chinese race" (Wikipedia, 2020e). As of December 2020, a search of the Chinese phrase on Google found more than 6.79 million results.

As the Google search shows, it seems that it is very easy to "hurt the feelings of the Chinese people." What are these "crimes" committed by foreign entities? An examination of 152 cases shows the following offenses:

- Failure to treat Taiwan, Hong Kong, or Macau as part of the People's Republic of China;

- Supporting democracy or human rights in China or Hong Kong;
- Failure to recognize the disputed territories as belonging to the PRC;
- Failure to support deploying Huawei's 5G technology in one's country;
- Criticizing the CCP's suppressing of minorities in Xinjiang;
- Hosting the Dalai Lama or praising him;
- Criticizing the CCP's handling of the Covid-19 pandemic, or calling for investigation into its outbreak.

As can be seen, these issues are all directed toward the political actions, economic policies, or ideology of the CCP; and none of them attacks the Chinese culture or Chinese race. However, by labeling them as "hurting the Chinese people," the CCP's goal is to denounce criticism of the CCP as anti-China and Chinese culture, and, therefore, racism.

7.7.3 Types of Measures Used by the CCP to Punish "Offenders"

According to the Australian report, "The CCP's coercive tactics can include economic measures (such as trade sanctions, investment restrictions, tourism bans and popular boycotts) and non-economic measures (such as arbitrary detention, restrictions on official travel and state-issued threats)" (Hanson et al., 2020). Based on its findings, the report tallied thirty-four state-issued threats, nineteen trade restrictions, seventeen tourism restrictions, fourteen restrictions on official travel, eight arbitrary detentions/executions, five popular boycotts, and three investment restrictions.

7.7.4 The Illusive Nature of the CCP's Punishment

In spite of frequently and increasingly using coercive diplomacy, the CCP has never admitted using it, and has always denied any link between what it sees as offensive and its economic and noneconomic punishment. As Chinese Foreign Ministry spokesperson Hua Chunying stated (Hua, 2019),

> First, as a responsible major country, China stands upright with honor. We never strong-arm others, never seek supremacy, never

withdraw from commitments, never bully others, and never complain. The word 'coercion' has nothing to do with China.

While this provides further evidence of the CCP's hypocrisy and its following Mao's teaching of disregarding rules and laws, such a practice gives the CCP deniability of coercive diplomacy, and most importantly, puts the victim at a loss: they know that they have done something that the CCP does not like, but they can never pinpoint what exactly. To avoid the fury of the CCP in the future, they will be extra cautious and avoid everything and anything that may displease the CCP.

7.7.5 Cases[6]

Norway. In 2010, Chinese writer and social critic Liu Xiaobo was awarded the Nobel Peace Prize in Oslo. Although the decision to award the prize to Liu was made by the Nobel committee independent of the Norwegian government, the CCP severely punished Norway for it. The CCP issued state threats, cancelled the bilateral free-trade negotiations between the two countries, and put restrictions on importing Norwegian salmon, such as tightening the import licensing process, implementing stringent inspection methods, and changing custom clearance practices. China also excluded Norway from its 72-hour stay visa waiver granted to all other European countries. The Chinese government stated that all these measures had nothing to do with awarding the Nobel Peace Prize to Liu. Interestingly, China did not cancel the purchase of a Norwegian hydro company that had the deep-water drilling technology that China needed.

South Korea. In July 2016, South Korea decided to install a missile defense system known as "Terminal High Altitude Area Defense" (THAAD) to protect the country from possible attack from North Korea. The Chinese government was outraged by this decision.

---

[6] Based on F. Hanson, E. Currey, and T. Beattie, 2020. The Chinese Communist Party's Coercive Diplomacy. *Australian Strategic Policy Institute* (www.aspi.org.au/report/ chinese-communist-partys-coercive-diplomacy): Accessed December 12, 2020.

In the same month, the Chinese government issued 27 statements and the *People's Daily*, the CCP's top newspaper, published 265 articles denouncing Seoul's decision (Hanson et al., 2020). In formulating its retaliation strategy, the CCP chose South Korea's entertainment industry, tourism, and consumer goods firms, while carefully avoiding South Korea's technology firms and Korean firms that are part of China's supply chain. The CCP encouraged the Chinese people to boycott Korean products, and restricted travel to South Korea. Consumer good conglomerate Lotte Group and Korean automakers Hyundai and Kia were hit hard, and Chinese visitors to South Korea dropped substantially. As usual, the Chinese government dismissed any link between these sanctions and South Korea's THAAD decision.

Canada. On December 1, 2018, on request by the United States, Canada arrested Huawei's Chief Financial Officer Meng Wanzhou for alleged crimes against the United States, based on the extradition treaty between the two countries. Ten days later, China arrested two Canadian citizens in China, Michael Kovrig and Michael Spavor, on allegations of breaking national security laws. In January, 2019, China changed the fifteen-year sentence given to Canadian citizen Robert Schellenberg in 2014 to the death penalty. China also issued tourism restrictions and trade restrictions on canola and all meat products from Canada. The meat ban coincided with the outbreak of African swine flu that devastated China's pork industry. Pork prices skyrocketed in China, and the CCP was forced to cancel the ban to alleviate the pork shortage in China.

Australia. In April 2020, the Australian government called for an investigation into the origins and handling of the Covid-19 outbreak. In June, a Chinese court sentenced Australian citizen Karm Gillespie to death for drug trafficking. China also threatened to cut tourism and restrict Chinese students from studying in Australia. The Chinese government restricted importing coal, wine, beef, barley, and cotton. In December, "with no clear explanation, China left US$3 million worth of Australian rock lobsters dying in Shanghai customs"

(Myers and Bradsher, 2020). In the same month, the Chinese embassy delivered a fourteen-point list of grievances to three news organizations, accusing Australia of attacks on China, including through making a new foreign interference law that targets China, implementing a ban on Huawei and other investment, and Australia's criticism of China's policy on Xinjiang, Taiwan, and Hong Kong. An embassy official said, "China is angry. If you make China the enemy, China will be the enemy" (Myers and Bradsher, 2020). Analysts believe that China was careful in choosing the products to ban. For example, China was about to reduce barley imported from Australia for diversification and on account of reduced domestic demand before the pandemic, so it was convenient to enact the ban as punishment. China avoided banning wool or iron ore from Australia as it would hurt China more.

Mercedes-Benz. In 2018 Mercedes-Benz used a quotation from Tibetan spiritual leader and Nobel Peace Prize winner the Dalai Lama in its worldwide commercial, which was not specifically targeted towards the Chinese market. According to a Reuters report, "in a 'Monday Motivation' hashtagged post on Instagram, Mercedes showed one of its white cars on a beach along with a quote attributed to the Dalai Lama: 'Look at the situations from all angles, and you will become more open'" (Li and Jourdan, 2018). China condemned it, causing Mercedes to remove it and apologize in response.

It's not Made in China. A South African bottled-water company was called "It's not Made in China," and Chinese social media users called for boycotting it. Since the bottled water was not sold to China, it was not clear how China could boycott it. Is the brand name racially discriminatory? Not really, and the company explained that "because everyone is so used to reading MADE IN CHINA on just about everything, we knew that by saying the opposite and calling ourselves IT'S NOT MADE IN CHINA, we would signal that we wanted to do things a little differently." Interestingly, this brand name reminds us of the concern that the EU and United States have about China's strategy of "Made In China 2025" that could give Chinese firms unfair advantages.

National Basketball Association. In 2019, the general manager of the Houston Rockets, Daryl Morey, posted a tweet supporting the Hong Kong protests. China strongly denounced it, terminating deals with the team and suspending broadcasts of NBA games in China. After the NBA apologized and made donations to China at the beginning of the Covid-19 pandemic, it has been slowly coming back into the Chinese market.

7.7.6   *The Wide Coverage of "Insulting China"*

As we explained earlier, *"hua"* means pan-Chinese. Adding a prefix, *"ru"* (insult), it would be *"ruhua"*(辱华), which is a Chinese phrase that means insulting or humiliating anything Chinese, and is commonly translated into "insulting China." It has been widely used by China to refer to discrimination against the Chinese. Many foreign companies have been accused of *ruhua*, which would cause an outrage in China, and, in turn, these companies would incur substantial losses and would be forced to apologize to China. *Ruhua* has become a popular subject among Chinese netizens, many of whom search for foreign governments, media, public figures, or companies for discriminatory words that fall into the broad *ruhua* domain. A Google search of *ruhua* in Chinese in December 2020 yielded 23 million hits. A Google search of "brands that insulted China" in Chinese (*ruhua pinpai*, 辱华品牌) found many articles. The top article is titled "A black list of firms that insulted China the most: these big brands' little hearts are either stupid or bad" (Zheng and Zhang, 2019). The Chinese government also frequently accuses foreign entities of *ruhua*, which is similar to, but is broader than, the "hurting the feelings of the Chinese people" phrase that the Chinese government has been using.

Across nations, I have not seen citizens or netizens of a country, or the government of a country for that matter, invoke such a phrase to punish foreign entities. A Google search for "insulting the U.S." or "insulting America" produced mostly sarcastic comments, such as "what are some good ways to insult an American" (quora.com).

So why is *ruhua* a big deal for the Chinese government and Chinese citizens/netizens?

First, we need to understand the contents of "insulting China." It can mean any of the following:

Insulting (criticizing) China's political system, past (historical) or present;
Insulting (criticizing) China's economic system, past or present;
Insulting (criticizing) China's culture, past or present;
Insulting (criticizing) the Chinese race.

Logically, for people who believe in democracy, rule of law, and universal human rights, criticizing any political and economic systems, past or present, or expressing views different from the official views in China does not constitute "insulting China." By the same logic, cultures evolve over time and what was accepted before may no longer be appropriate, and thus can be criticized. For example, in the United States we criticize the culture that discriminates against people based on sex or race, which was acceptable in the past but no longer is today because of criticism by the American people. Insulting or discriminating against the Chinese ethnic origin or race is racism and should be denounced.

Based on this classification, what kind of "insulting China" have most foreign companies committed? In Table 7.1 I list the types of "insulting China" by the fifty-two companies included in the Australian report (Hanson et al., 2020).

Of the sixty-eight entries, sixty-six (96 percent) are involved with political issues, such as expressing views critical of or different from the CCP. Fifty-eight (85 percent) are involved with how to classify or views on Taiwan, Hong Kong, Macau, Tibet, or Xinjiang. All these are not discriminatory against the Chinese race. As for the case in No. 13, it was about a company chief economist commenting about China's killing of pigs that were infected with African swine flu, saying it would "matter to a Chinese pig." A number of Chinese consumers interpreted the comments to be referring to Chinese people, rather than livestock, and condemned the company for its

Table 7.1. *Types of "insulting China," 52 companies*

No.	Reason for being accused of "insulting China"	Cases	Percent
1	Referring to Taiwan as a separate country/ region from China	20	29.4
2	Referring to Hong Kong as a separate country/ region from China	15	22.1
3	Mentioning/supporting the Hong Kong pro-democracy protest	12	17.6
4	Referring to Tibet as a separate country/region from China, or mentioning the Dalai Lama	5	7.4
5	Being involved in arms sales to Taiwan	3	4.4
6	Mentioning/supporting Uyghurs in Xinjiang	2	2.9
7	Referring to Macau as a separate country/region from China	1	1.5
8	Mentioning Covid-19/criticizing China's handing of it	3	4.4
9	Being involved in Huawei's Meng Wanzhou's arrest	1	1.5
10	Mentioning the 1989 June 4th Beijing Tiananmen Protest/Crackdown	1	1.5
11	Reporting on Xi Jinping's family's assets	1	1.5
12	Making political jokes about China	1	1.5
13	Making jokes about China/Chinese	1	1.5
14	Brand's name is "Not Made In China"	1	1.5
15	Books found in Japanese hotel rooms that denied the Nanking Massacre	1	1.5
	Total Count	68	100.0
	Note: one firm may be counted for multiple reasons.		

Source: Compiled by author based on data from Hanson et al. (2020)

racist remarks. Except for this case, which may be interpreted as a racist comment, all cases in the table are not discriminatory against the Chinese race. They are mostly about expressing political views or viewing Taiwan and/or Hong Kong as separate from China, which reflects the fact that they have borders between them guarded by troops, use different currencies, and Chinese citizens are required to use travel documents such as passports and visas to visit Taiwan or Hong Kong. In sum, "insulting China" is an accusation with strong racist implications that is frequently used against foreign entities for expressing political views that differ from the views of the CCP.

This evidence shows that the CCP has undertaken a large-scale effort with huge resources to exert its influence and change the views of foreign governments, people, and firms on issues relating to China. As the Australian Report pointed out, "This carrot-and-stick approach reflects 'a new level of assertiveness, confidence and ambition' in the CCP's foreign policy and economic diplomacy" (Hanson et al., 2020). In the next chapter, we will review the impact of the CCP's global strategy and how the democratic countries have reacted to it.

7.8 SUMMARY

China, Inc.'s reliance on the low human rights environment domestically and free trade internationally creates a contradiction that is difficult to resolve. The ideas of democracy, human rights, and rule of law that come into China along with trade encourage Chinese people to demand political changes that threaten the CCP's monopoly. The CCP's strategy to suppress domestic demand for democracy is to expand its influence globally. If the international community acquiesces to the way the CCP rules China, it will not only help mute the demand for political changes in China but will also help the party-state achieve dominance in the world. This chapter reviewed the strategies and tactics used by the CCP to influence the world, including using bribery, waging the great propaganda war, building a broad united front alliance, using the "Russian doll" method, practicing coercive diplomacy, and invoking the "insulting China" tactic to silence criticism.

8   Open Societies versus Closed Regime

Who Needs Whom More?

> It's not just economic ties between China and the United States that are in danger. Europe, too, is increasingly talking of rolling back the deep trade and investment ties it has developed with Beijing in recent decades ... Other countries are also pulling up the drawbridges – all leery that today's unprecedented level of economic integration has gone too far, bringing more pain and less gain.
>
> "The Great Decoupling" *Foreign Policy* (Johnson and Gramer, 2020)

8.1   THE IMPACT OF THE CCP'S GLOBAL STRATEGY

8.1.1   *Effects of Bribery by the Chinese State*

The effort of the Chinese party-state to bribe the world has borne fruit (Li, 2020c).[1] Several foreign students who studied in China on scholarship, mostly from Africa, have become political leaders in their countries or regions (DWnews.com, 2018). For example, former president of Ethiopia Mulatu Teshome went to China on a Chinese government scholarship and received his bachelor's, master's, and doctoral degrees there (Zhang, 2013b). Some elected officials in Taiwan, including former Kaohsiung Mayor Han Kuo-yu, studied in China as well (Wen Wei Po, 2002, 2018).

Studies have shown that countries receiving aid from China tend to vote in alignment with China in the United Nations (Dreher, Fuchs, Parks, Strange, and Tierney, 2016; Pang and Wang, 2018; Strüver, 2016). In July 2019, thirty-seven countries wrote a letter to the United Nations supporting the CCP's policy of putting Uyghurs

---

[1] Based on S. Li, 2020c. Leading by Bribing: Evidence from China. *International Journal of Emerging Markets*, in press.

in labor camps in Xinjiang. Notably, thirty-four of the thirty-seven countries have been recipients of official financing from China since 2000, according to AIDDATA (AIDDATA, 2018; Putz, 2019).

A study using statistical data also shows that there is a strong link between Chinese commercially oriented financial flows, such as the Belt and Road Initiative, and voting alignment with China in the United Nations (Raess, Ren, and Wagner, 2017). According to a report by the Center for a New American Security on the Belt and Road projects, "China's willingness to pay politicians to facilitate these projects not only corrodes democratic institutions but also results in policies that are directly against the public interest of the countries in question" (Kliman et al., 2019, p. 7).

There are signs that influential people and media in the United States "tell China's story well" by refraining from negative coverage or criticism of China.

In 2019, former President Jimmy Carter made a comparison of the governments of the United States and China, saying that the former wasted too much money waging multiple wars, while the latter did not wage any wars (China did wage a war with Vietnam in 1979) and put all of its resources into the economy. "The former president said he understood that Trump is worried about China surpassing the U.S. as the world's top economic superpower. 'I don't really fear that time, but it bothers President Trump and I don't know why'" (Hurt, 2019). The Carter Center has been deeply involved with the government of China. The former president has been invited by the Chinese government to visit China. The leaders of China, Xi Jinping and Li Keqiang, "suggest that The Carter Center dedicate more effort toward improving U.S.-China relations." A prominent businessman who has extensive investment in China is on its board of trustees, and some employees have close ties with the Chinese government. The Center boasts of its role in Chinese government efforts in Africa (The Carter Center, 2020).

In April 2017, the US government's Voice of America (VOA) announced that it would broadcast a three-hour, live-on-air interview with Guo Wengui, a Chinese businessman in exile who wanted to expose corruption in China. The Chinese government strongly objected and threatened to retaliate against the United States if the interview was aired.

> Though the interview had been approved by Voice of America management, the leadership reversed itself under pressure. As the broadcast went forward, Voice of America Director Amanda Bennett, who was traveling in Africa at the time, contacted the Mandarin Service, ordering it to cease the broadcast. The reporting team led by Sasha Gong refused to comply and kept it going as long as they could. Eventually, [the VOA] management pulled the plug – in mid-broadcast ... Later the reporting team was suspended, investigated, and eventually fired.
>
> *(Dale, 2018)*

VOA Director Bennett's family owns the educational test service company Kaplan, Inc., which has business and investments in China (New Channel, Undated (accessed April 22, 2019)). To do business in China, a good relationship with the Chinese government is vital (see Chapter 3 and *The Economist*, 2000). According to a posting at the Broadcasting Board of Governors and the US Agency for Global Media (BBG-USAGM), Changqing Cao, an independent journalist and commentator, "raises questions about Ms. Bennett's family's business operations in China. Cao points out in the video that Kaplan, Inc., which he says does multimillion dollar educational operations in communist China, belongs to a company run by Ms. Bennett's husband" (BBG-USAGM Watch, 2017). One of the investigations by VOA that led to the firing of the Chinese report team members was headed by "James McGregor, chairman of APCO China. APCO is a top Washington lobbying firm with extensive business connections in China" (Dale, 2018).

My personal interviews have also yielded some examples of China's influence. A freelance writer who specializes in the political system and elections in the United States told me that a few years ago many Chinese language media outlets in the United States, Hong Kong, and Taiwan competed for her writing, but now no one wants to take her writing, as a result of the influence of the Chinese government (see Section 7.5.3). A well-established professor and senior administrative officer at my university told me about their invited trips to China in which they had to censor themselves, "We know the drill: don't mention Tibet, Taiwan, or Xinjiang … " Another professor at my school who for seven years had led students to China to study always gave a warning lecture to his students before the trip on what not to say or ask in China, based on the party-state's propaganda line. Apparently, the CCP's international strategy (see Chapter 7) has worked on our campus, judging from these cases.

In 2020, Di Dongsheng, a professor and associate dean at Renmin University's School of International Relations in China, gave a speech on US–China relations that went viral. Di, who is said to be an advisor to CCP General Secretary Xi Jinping, told a cheering Chinese audience, "from 1992 to 2016, we could resolve any frictions between China and the U.S., within two months, because we have people at the top [in the U.S. government]. We have old friends in the core power circle in the U.S." (Radio Free Asia, 2020b).

The adverse effect of this bribe and corruption strategy is long-term. According to experts on China, the CCP is well known for its patience and its long-term orientation in its effort to achieve world dominance (Pillsbury, 2015; Wise, 2011). Unlike the Russian government, whose strategy tends to be short-term and specific, such as interfering in an election with the goal of affecting specifically targeted candidates, the CCP does not, usually, have any specific goals in its effort to bribe and corrupt foreign countries. Rather, it aims to change the culture of the world. It invests, long-term, to nurture a positive attitude toward the party around the world. One of its objectives, as discussed earlier, is to tell the world that the CCP and its government are equivalent to being pan-Chinese. If someone criticizes the party or the government, then that person, according to the party, is engaging in "racial discrimination against

Chinese" (Securefreedom, 2019) and, therefore, must be denounced and shunned (see Sections 7.6.1 and 7.7.6).

8.2 THE CHANGING ATTITUDES OF THE DEMOCRACIES

8.2.1 *A China under Communism Going Global Is More Dangerous than a Closed One*

Four decades ago, when the CCP opened up China, the democratic world welcomed it and enthusiastically helped China to overcome many obstacles to join the world market (see Chapter 1). While China's opening up has indeed greatly helped its economic development and contributed to world trade and investment, it has also brought two major concerns to the international community and especially to the democratic countries. The first is China's failure to make any substantial progress in democracy and the rule of law, as we discussed in Part I, and Chapter 2 in particular. The second concern, which is closely related to the first, is that a China going global under the CCP's dictatorship is more dangerous than a closed one. And this is especially true as China evolves into a giant corporation with wealth that no country in the world can rival.[2]

Building on our earlier discussion on the economic expansion of China, Inc. (Part II, Chapters 5 and 6) and the ideological and political expansion of the CCP (Chapter 7), here I will focus on the vulnerability of the open societies of the democracies to a dictatorial regime that actively participates in world affairs and trade but keeps its own country selectively closed to ensure its absolute rule.

The way in which the CCP decides its openness and closedness is strategic to ensure its total control of China while maximizing the benefit from going global. Domestically, the CCP keeps China's political system closed to foreign influences; it censors all foreign media and foreign entertainment products and severely restricts the

---

[2] China has the largest GDP in the world based on purchase power parity CIA 2020a. The World Factbook. *CIA.gov*, www.cia.gov/cia/publications/factbook/index.html (Accessed 11/16/2020).

activities of all foreign entities: diplomats, NGOs, reporters, and academics. Economically, the CCP selectively grants licenses to foreign companies in select sectors (see Chapter 5). As a *New York Times* article puts it, "China says it remains open to the world, but wants to dictate terms" (Myers and Bradsher, 2020).

While the governments of the democratic countries try to use openness/closedness to maximize their benefit, they are constrained by their own laws and by international rules and norms. For example, the executive branch of the US government wanted to restrict the operations of Chinese social media apps such as WeChat and TikTok, but the other branch of the US government – the court – ruled that such restrictions are unlawful and could not be implemented, on the legal ground of protecting free speech and "the Constitutional rights of WeChat" (Swanson and McCabe, 2020). The US court rulings in these cases are particularly ironic because WeChat does not allow free speech and censors postings, and more ironically, the CCP restricts WeChat's constitutional rights and bans virtually all major social media apps from the United States, including Facebook, YouTube, and Twitter, just to name a few.

And this is precisely what the democracies are concerned about. Globally, the CCP takes full advantage of the open societies of the democracies and their rule-based governance (see Chapter 3) to advance its interests and sweeps the laws of these governments aside if they are in its way. A good example is the CCP's global effort to capture people who escaped from China, codenamed "Operation Fox Hunt." The CCP claims that the people on its hunting list are corrupt officials, but evidence shows that the list can include anyone that the Chinese authorities want to arrest, including "political rivals, dissidents, and critics," according to U.S. Assistant Attorney General for National Security John Demers. The CCP uses "extralegal means and unauthorized, often covert, law enforcement activity" to carry out Fox Hunt (Demers, 2020). Typically, the CCP would send its agents as tourists to the country where the target (the victim) lives, hire some private detectives locally, and harass the victim's family in order to force the victim to go back to China. In October 2020, the US government published a case detailing a two-year illegal effort by the CCP to force a victim in the United States to return to China. The agents coerced the father of the victim to travel from China to the United States to persuade his son to return. They also "targeted John Doe-1's [the victim's] adult daughter for surveillance and online harassment." They "affixed a threatening note to the door of the John Doe'1's residence stating, 'If you are willing to go back to mainland and spend 10 years in prison, your wife and children will be all right. That's the end of this matter!'" (U.S. Department of Justice, 2020a).

Another example is that of the CCP's taking advantage of universities in the democracies to develop its military capabilities. The CCP gives grants to foreign schools and scholars to carry out research projects that can be used by the People's Liberation Army, or sends PLA personnel posing as civilian researchers to foreign universities to participate in research projects that may benefit the PLA (Brady, 2020; U.S. Department of Justice, 2020b). The United States is not alone on this issue. According to various reports, the research and development sector in the United Kingdom has increasingly become heavily reliant on China and is exposed to the Chinese military. According to a report on China's influence on British universities led by former universities minister of the United Kingdom Jo Johnson, in 2000, there were 750 academic papers coauthored by Chinese and British researchers; by 2019, the number had increased drastically to 16,267. In 2021, Civitas, an influential think tank, warned the United Kingdom that its top research schools are too closely linked with the People's Liberation Army of China (Staton, 2021).

In 2020, the vulnerability of the open societies of the democracies has resulted in the largest human crisis in modern history with the outbreak of the Covid-19 virus in China. The CCP concealed vital information about the outbreak and caused the world to lose valuable time to contain it (Alon et al., 2020b; Waldron, 2020). Furthermore, the CCP was able to leverage its low human rights advantage (see Chapter 2) to strictly control and quarantine its population, restrict travel to control the spread of the virus, block efforts to investigate the origin of the virus, retaliate against countries that demanded investigations, and spread false information about the origin of the virus (Modern China Studies, 2020).

The way in which the CCP abuses the rules of open societies is analogous to a boxing match between a rule-abiding athlete and someone who does not follow the rules (i.e., an outlaw). If the athlete knocks down the outlaw, he stops and lets the outlaw get up; however, the outlaw uses illegal moves such as kicking the lower part of the body. If the outlaw overpowers the athlete, the former will continue to kill the latter. When the outlaw violates the rules, the organizer of the match, which is rule-based, cannot punish the outlaw by allowing the athlete to apply the same illegal moves on the former, and the organizer certainly will not and cannot punish the outlaw by killing them even if they illegally killed the athlete. Furthermore, the outlaw has great resources and a powerful state to aid them to run away or to hire the best lawyers to defend them. In repeated games, knowing clearly that their rights will be fully protected and that punishment is limited, the outlaw will become more and more brazen in using illegal and fatal attacks.

This analysis shows the damage to the open societies of the democracies inflicted by a powerful dictatorial regime when it can freely enter these countries and disregard the rule of law. The damage is much greater than a dictatorial regime that does not actively participate in global trade and exchange.

From 1949 (the founding of the People's Republic of China) to 1976 (when Mao Zedong died), the same, dictatorial CCP ruled China with the same political principles, such as banning political participation and suppressing freedom of the press. In many ways, the CCP's rule back then was even more severe and inhumane. Harsh punishments were commonplace, including public execution, forcing persecuted people to take part in mass parades, forcing city residents to relocate to the countryside to do hard labor, and massive purges and imprisonment. While these measures were atrocious for the people in China, they had little effect on other countries because *the CCP kept China closed.*

Now, the very same CCP that adheres to the same ideology and principles is going global, armed with the world's largest GDP and expertise in the rules of the international community and how to evade them. The potential to cause substantial damage to the world, especially to the countries that rely on the rule of law and openness, is much greater.

8.2.2 The Democracies' Misconceptions about Russia and China

For a long time, in terms of the leadership's image and perceived threat, the Chinese regime and its leadership had been viewed more favorably than its Russian counterpart. In a 2013 survey by Pew Research Center, 32 percent of Americans surveyed viewed Russia favorably, which was slightly lower than their favorable views on China (33 percent). Experts also viewed Russia more negatively than China. 52 percent of members of the Council of Foreign Relations believed China would become more democratic, while only 19 percent of them expected Russia would become more democratic (Pew Research Center, 2013). In 2020, surveys by Pew Research Center show that Americans still view China more positively than Russia, with 22 percent and 19 percent viewing China and Russia favorably, respectively (Huang, 2020; Silver, Devlin, and Huang, 2020).

During the US presidential election in 2020, Democratic candidate Joe Biden was asked which country was the biggest threat to America. He replied that Russia is the biggest threat, and China is the biggest competitor (O'Donnell, 2020). For him, the two are categorically different: one is a major threat and the other is merely a competitor. But who are the United States' competitors? The United States competes with its democratic allies, such as Canada, the United Kingdom, Germany, and France. In candidate Biden's view then, China belonged to this group – except it was larger.

The belief that Russia is less democratic and poses a greater threat to the United States and other democracies is a misconception. Since it is widely held by the public, experts, and political leaders, it needs to be clarified.

Russia ended its communist dictatorship in the early 1990s and has embarked on its democratization process since then. While the process has been difficult, Russia is no longer under communism. Now Russia has a multi-party system: about four major parties have members in the federal parliament with one dominant party (United Russia). Russia's democratization has suffered serious backsliding during Putin's reign, but opposition parties do exist. For example, the Russian Communist Party is the largest rival of United Russia.

The Russian court system is heavily influenced by Putin's government. But at least in one known case – the 2012 Pussy Riot case – the court released a political protester against Putin's will (Vasilyeva, 2012). Political protests are part of daily life in Russia. In Moscow's Red Square, many street actors play Lenin, Stalin, and even Putin, and give all sorts of speeches. Press freedom is severely limited and independent media organizations are scarce and constantly harassed. Russia's Press Freedom Score is 49 (1=free, and 100=not free) and it is ranked 149th out of 180 countries. Russia's Political Freedom Score is 20 (1=completely not free; 100=completely free) (Freedom House, 2020).

Economically, Russia is weak and small. Its GDP is US$4 trillion (purchasing power parity, or PPP, adjusted; the United States' is US$21 trillion) (CIA, 2020a). In terms of economic freedom, Russia is ranked 94th out of 180 countries and is considered "moderately free" (Heritage Foundation, 2020).

China, on the other hand, is under communist dictatorship (Chapter 2). The court system is completely controlled by the CCP (Chapter 3). All the judges are appointed by the CCP. There are no opposition parties in China. There has not been a single case in which judges defied the CCP in their rulings. Anyone who criticizes the CCP will be harshly punished. An ID card and security check are required to enter Beijing's Tiananmen Square. Numerous policemen and security guards, in uniform or plainclothes, patrol the square and swiftly arrest anyone who appears to be a Falun Gong practitioner (a faith that is banned by the CCP (Wikipedia, 2020d)) or a *Shangfang* petitioner- (groups that are mistreated by the government and seek justice (Lynch, 2010)). China's Press Freedom Score is 78 and it is ranked 177th out of 180 countries. China's Political Freedom Score is 10 (0=completely not free; 100=completely free) (Freedom House, 2020).

Economically, China is huge and strong: Its GDP is US$23 trillion (PPP adjusted), the largest in the world. In terms of economic freedom, China is ranked 103rd out of 180 countries and is in the "mostly unfree" group (Heritage Foundation, 2020).

In sum, Russia is an infant democracy ruled by a charismatic strongman, with some opposition, limited press freedom, a court system under heavy political influence, and a weak and small economy. China is a communist dictatorship with a huge, powerful, and expanding economy, of which the CCP controls about 56 percent (Li, 2020a) and uses the funds lavishly, without hindrance from a system of checks and balances, to influence the world as a geopolitical whole and the United States in particular (see Chapter 7 and Li, 2020a).

It is very clear that, in every aspect, compared to Russia, China's ruling party is more dictatorial, the Chinese people enjoy less freedom, and China has more resources to expand globally. If both countries spent the same share of their GDP on influencing the United States, China would outspend Russia by about six to one. In terms of population, Russia (146 million people) is about one-tenth the size of China (1.44 billion people). If both countries employed the same percentage of their people to collect intelligence from the United States, China would send ten times more spies to the United States than Russia would. If the United States allocated the same percentage of its people to counter China's espionage, every US agent would face four spies from China.

While I do not want to downplay Putin's damage to Russia's infant democracy or Russia's threat to the United States, it is beyond any doubt that communist China poses a much bigger threat than Russia. As a senior adviser at the U.S. National Security Agency commented when comparing the threat posed by the two countries, "Russia is the hurricane ... China is climate change" (Viswanatha and Volz, 2019).

If communist China is a worse offender of human rights and the rule of law than Russia, why is China viewed more positively than the latter in general? Chapter 7 has answered this question: The CCP has been spending a huge amount of money to promote a false positive image of China and to bribe politicians, academics, and elites worldwide to sing along with the CCP.

8.2.3   The Shift in Attitudes toward China in the Democracies

There has been a shift in sentiments toward China in the democracies, for both the public as well as politicians. Take the case of Joe Biden. In July, 2020, an article on Biden's view of the Trump administration's punitive tariff on China commented, "On China ... businesses can probably hope for a reprieve from the tariffs if Biden is the next president" (Newman, 2020).

Five months later, after he won the election, an article read,

> On China, he [Biden] said he would not act immediately to remove the 25 percent tariffs that Trump imposed on about half of China's exports to the United States – or the Phase 1 agreement Trump inked with China that requires Beijing to purchase some US$200 billion in additional U.S. goods and services during the period 2020 and 2021 – which China has fallen significantly behind on ... 'I'm not going to make any immediate moves, and the same applies to the tariffs,' he said.
>
> (Friedman, 2020)

A report in December 2020 stated that both current and former US Trade Representatives advised President-Elect Joe Biden to be tough on China (Jie, 2020).

Joe Biden's change of attitude toward China is very indicative. In May 2020, as a presidential candidate, Biden dismissed the threat from China: "China is going to eat our lunch? Come on, man" (Spiering, 2020). Some nine months later, in February, 2021, soon after he was sworn in as president, Biden warned the United States about China's threat, "They're going to, you know, if we don't get moving, they're going to eat our lunch" (Macias, 2021).

Policymakers in other democracies increasingly express their concerns about China's expansion and failure to play by international rules and norms. A Google search using "Europe's changing attitude toward China" found many articles about Europe's rising worries concerning China's expansion. The following are some examples:

- "Europe Changes Its Mind on China" (Brookings Institution, July 8, 2020).
- "China, Seeking a Friend in Europe, Finds Rising Anger and Frustration" (*The New York Times*, Sept 17, 2020).
- "How Europe Learned to Fear China" (Politico, April, 2019).
- "Why Europe Is Getting Tough on China" (*Foreign Affairs*, April 2019).

In September 2020, Janka Oertel, the Asia Program Director at the European Council on Foreign Relations, issued a policy brief titled, "The New China Consensus: How Europe Is Growing Wary of Beijing" (Oertel, 2020). It summarized the EU's changing attitudes and concerns about China:

- Since the onset of the Covid-19 crisis, there has been a new convergence of EU member states' assessment of the challenges China poses to Europe.
- The Sino-European economic relationship lacks reciprocity, and there are mounting concerns within the EU about China's assertive approach abroad, as well as its breaches of international legal commitments and massive violations of human rights in Hong Kong and Xinjiang.
- Overall, there is growing skepticism about the future trajectory of the relationship, which provides an opportunity for a more robust and coherent EU policy on China.

Opinion polls also show a substantial change in public attitudes toward China. In October 2020, Pew Research Center released a survey report titled "Unfavorable Views of China Reach Historic Highs in Many Countries" (Silver et al., 2020). "Views of China have

Table 8.1. *Percent who have unfavorable view of China, early 2000s to 2020, 12 countries*

Country\year	Early 2000s	2020
	(%)	(%)
Australia	40	81
UK	16	74
Germany	37	71
Netherlands	34	73
Sweden	40	85
US	35	73
S. Korea	31	75
Spain	21	63
France	42	70
Canada	27	73
Italy	61	62
Japan	42	86
Average	36	74

Source: Compiled by author based on Silver et al. (2020)

grown more negative in recent years across many advanced economies, and unfavorable opinion has soared over the past year," the report noted, "Today, a majority in each of the surveyed countries has an unfavorable opinion of China. And in Australia, the United Kingdom, Germany, the Netherlands, Sweden, the United States, South Korea, Spain and Canada, negative views have reached their highest points since the Center began polling on this topic more than a decade ago." Of the twelve countries surveyed (see Table 8.1), 36 percent viewed China unfavorably in the early 2000s; in 2020 that number had more than doubled to 74 percent (Silver et al., 2020).

8.2.4 Improved Knowledge about the CCP

Increasingly, the international community has begun to better understand the nature and the strategies of the CCP. This change was partly aided by Chinese dissidents who have moved abroad and have a first-hand knowledge and deep understanding of the party (Link, 2021). As discussed in Chapters 2 and 7, a main strategy of the CCP is to make the party and the Chinese people synonymous. Now policymakers in the democracies have begun to realize that the CCP and the Chinese people are not the same. Criticizing the party's policies does not amount to an attack on China the country or China the people. For instance, Mike Pompeo, the then Secretary of U.S. State Department, in his July 2020 speech on China policy commented that, "We must also engage and empower the Chinese people – a dynamic, freedom-loving people who are completely dis- tinct from the Chinese Communist Party" (Pompeo, 2020a). Differentiating and treating the CCP and the Chinese people separ- ately, while theoretically and strategically sound, is difficult. The CCP has been steadfastly integrating itself with the population, which is facilitated by its strong indoctrination program, rising nationalism, and China's economic development. Nevertheless, the growing real- ization in the democracies that the Chinese people and the CCP are not the same has caused fury in the CCP, which suggests that such an effort is impactful. In September CCP General Secretary Xi Jinping gave a high-profile speech to rebuke this new view by the democra- cies, "The Chinese people will never allow any individual or any force to separate the CCP and Chinese people and pit them against each other" (Bloomberg News, 2020).

8.2.5 Growing Concern about China, Inc.'s Global Strategy[3]

The United States' sentiment on China's industrial policy has experi- enced significant changes. For a long time the United States' main concern had been about China's vast supply of low cost, unskilled workers and the products they made, such as textiles and garments (Krugman et al., 2012, p. 233). China's plan to develop strategic

---

[3] Based on S. Li and M. Farrell, 2020a. China's Industrial Policy and Its Implications for International Business. *European Journal of International Management*, in press.

industries with high technological content did not catch much attention in the United States. Similarly, in Europe, Chinese exports were not a concern. In the case of textiles, for example, Chinese low- and medium-quality exports complemented high-quality textiles of European manufacture (Tao and Fu, 2007).

In 2015 when China's party-state published its "Made In China 2025" strategic plan, the United States began to pay serious attention to China's industrial policy (see Chapter 6), as shown in a report on the plan by the U.S. Chamber of Commerce, a powerful group representing American business interests who rarely criticize any governments, especially the Chinese government (U.S. Chamber of Commerce, 2017). Calling the plan "global ambitions built on local protections," the Chamber believes it "constitutes a broader strategy to use state resource to alter and create comparative advantage ... on a global scale" (p. 6), expresses "mounting concerns of American business with plans like MIC 2025" (p. 4), and warns that it will "hamper its [China's] complete integration into the global economy" (p. 4). The chamber calls for monitoring and forecasting how MIC 2025 will "impact critical sectors of the global economy" and for "formulating appropriate policy responses" (p. 6).

Penny Prizker, the U.S. Secretary of Commerce in the Obama administration, was also alarmed,

> Let me state the obvious: this unprecedented state-driven interference would distort the market and undermine the innovation ecosystem. The world has seen the effects of this type of targeted, government-led interference before ... The result has been overcapacity in the global marketplace that has artificially reduced prices, cost jobs in both the U.S. and around the world, and caused significant damage to those industries globally.
> *(Nov 2, 2016, quoted from U.S. Chamber of Commerce, 2017, pp. 7–8)*

A more direct response is from US Senator Marco Rubio, who calls on the United States to form its own industrial policy to counter China's, "it's a call to policymakers to remember that the national interest, not economic growth, is our central obligation ... It's a call to invest and compete in the emerging industries of the future, rather than forfeit them to China" (Rubio, 2019).

Similar sentiment is also expressed in the European Union, although perhaps less loudly. The Mechanical Engineering Industry Association (VDMA), which represents more than 3,200 member companies in the mechanical and systems engineering industry in Germany and Europe, recently openly criticized China's industrial policy, specifically state subsidy distortions and market entry barriers. It called on Germany and the EU to reexamine their trade policies toward China accordingly (Dan, 2020).

They are not alone in criticizing China's industrial policy. In the European Commission's EU-China Strategic Outlook, China is noted as being a competitor who "fails to reciprocate market access and maintain a level playing field" (European Commission, 2019b). European firms have faced similar degrees of forced technology trans-fer, and evidence exists that recent outward foreign direct investment from China into the EU can be directly linked to Made In China 2025 goals (Buysse and Essers, 2019).

In sum, their concerns are that the CCP has made China sys-tematically and fundamentally different from the market economy (see Chapters 5 and 6), and has unfairly dominated key industries globally (Li and Farrell, 2020b; Wen, 2019). Based on these concerns, in early 2018, the US government under President Trump began to use tariffs as weapons to pressure China to reduce the trade deficit, starting what we know today as the trade war (Li and Farrell, 2020c). The Chinese government retaliated by raising tariffs on US goods. Since then, the demand on China from the United States has evolved from balancing trade to making "needed structural changes," in the areas of forced technology transfer, intellectual property protection, nontariff barriers, cyber intrusions, and cyber theft of trade secrets, among others (Churchill and Wu, 2019).

8.2.6   The Relocation of Supply Chains from China

In recent years, as China's labor cost has increased along with its fast economic growth rate, companies have begun to seek other countries in which to set up manufacturing facilities. As early as 2015, Foxconn, a major supplier for Apple, set up its facility in India. In 2018, when the US–China trade war started, the relocation of the supply chain from China accelerated (Li, 2019c). A survey of press reports on firms relocating or considering relocating from China between October 2018 and October 2019 records more than fifty firms, including Apple, Samsung, HP, Dell, Microsoft, Foxconn, Suzuki, and Fuyao Glass (whose much-covered expansion to Ohio was documented in the film *American Factory*) (Hoshi, Nakafuji, and Cho, 2019). In terms of country of origin, most of the firms are Japanese and American. In terms of target countries, South Asian nations (Vietnam, Thailand, Taiwan, India, and Cambodia) are the most frequent destinations, followed by Mexico. Many Japanese firms returned home. According to a survey conducted by the American Chamber of Commerce, "More than 70 percent of U.S. firms operating in southern China are considering delaying further investment there and moving some or all of their manufacturing to other countries as the trade war bites into profits." Furthermore, it is not only foreign firms that are considering leaving China, "Half of their Chinese counterparts share the same consideration" (Wong, 2018). In a survey conducted by Baker McKenzie of 600 firms in the Asia-Pacific region, "93 percent of Chinese companies 'were considering making some change to their supply chains to mitigate the effects of trade tariffs,' and '82 percent of respondents are changing their supply chains to counter the trade war'" (Bermingham, 2019).

In 2020, the outbreak of the Covid-19 pandemic in China virtually shut down the supply chain in China for several months, prompting many countries and companies to make a long-term plan to diversify their supply chain globally in order to reduce their reliance on China as a center for manufacturing. By late 2020, Apple and its suppliers had made significant investments in India to produce not only older models of iPhone but also new models (Mathi, 2020).

In February 2021, US President Biden signed an executive order demanding a comprehensive review of supply chains for critical materials, including semiconductors, pharmaceuticals, and rare-earth minerals, with the aim of encouraging domestic production as well as strengthening ties with other democratic allies (The White House, 2021).

All of these data, reports, and actions suggest that the relocation of supply chains from China has already begun and will continue. Many firms that have not yet made the decision to leave are now considering their options. The relocation of supply chains may take years or decades. The negative effects of this relocation on the Chinese economy, which include job losses and the weakening of China's bargaining power in trade and investment, will be significant and long term (Li, 2019c).

8.3   CHINA VERSUS THE DEMOCRACIES: WHO NEEDS WHOM MORE?

The two biggest events that define the world today are the drastic change in US–China relations that began with the US–China trade war and the Covid-19 outbreak that has devastated the world. The common link in the two events is China, which leads to a key question that the democratic countries must answer: how to protect their way of life – their values, political system, and their markets – from being unduly influenced or even altered by a CCP-led China. To answer this question, which will be the topic of Chapter 9, we need to assess the relationship between China and the democracies: Who needs whom more?

This question can be assessed from multiple dimensions: political, economic, and social. While the three are closely intertwined, to facilitate our analysis, we will treat them as separate and connect them if doing so is necessary and feasible.

8.3.1 Political Considerations by China and the Democracies in Their Relationship

For the CCP/China, the question is: for its political goal, does it need to maintain a positive relationship with the democracies? The ultimate political goal of the CCP is not only to rule China forever but also to expand its rule globally, and overthrow capitalism worldwide. This, of course, is a very long-term goal, and even the CCP understands clearly that it cannot realize it in any foreseeable future. In this sense, the long-term goal is not an attainable goal, but rather an ideology, a fundamental attitude that all CCP members should hold (see Chapter 2).

At the practical level, the CCP's goal is to keep its absolute power in China, and to do so, it must continue to enhance its image and legitimacy. An important way for the CCP to enhance its image and legitimacy is to gain respect and support from other countries, especially the most important countries in the world (see Chapter 7). Let us use its relationship with the United States to analyze this issue.

For the time being, the CCP's leadership hides its ultimate goal of burying the United States (Pillsbury, 2015), the symbol of world capitalism, and sets its goal as gaining recognition, respect, and support from it. The CCP leadership also admires the United States for its achievements and the values for which it stands. This can be supported by the fact that many CCP officials send their children to the United States to study, obtain US residency or passports for their spouses, and migrate to the United States after retiring (China Digital Times, 2012). This can also be seen in the example of the former Chinese president Jiang Zemin, who bragged about how he was at ease during an interview with Mike Wallace of CBS in 2000 (Xiao, 2003), and Xi Jinping's claim that he likes to read about Washington, Lincoln, and Roosevelt (he did not specify which one). Xi also claims to have read the *Federalist Papers* and works by famous US authors such as Mark Twain, Jack London, Walt Whitman, and Henry David Thoreau (Zhu, 2015).

Unfortunately, as a result of its dictatorial rule and its poor human rights records, China has been unable to gain much respect from the United States or other democratic countries. In a July 2019 session of the United Nations Human Rights Council (UNHRC), twenty-two countries issued a joint letter to condemn China's mass detention of Uyghurs and other minorities in the north-western region of China, Xinjiang. As expected, all twenty-two signatories of the letter criticizing China were from democratic countries (Yellinek and Chen, 2019) (see Table 8.2). A few days later, a rebuttal letter appeared, which was eventually signed by fifty countries, praising "China's remarkable achievements" in "protecting and promoting human rights through development." Many of the signatories of the letter supporting China are either Chinese political allies or receive loans or other economic aid from China. Some of them have poor human rights records themselves (see Table 8.2).

Table 8.2 can be viewed as a rough division of two camps based on their principles and attitudes toward China. The first group, or the "Critical Group," consists of democratic countries. While the United States should have been in the Critical Camp, it did not sign the letter because it may "not want to complicate what was already a heated trade struggle with the PRC" (Yellinek and Chen, 2019). But the United States voiced strong criticism of the CCP's Xinjiang policy on multiple occasions, and even appointed Elnigar Iltebir, an American-Uyghur, to be China Director on the U.S. National Security Council, which can be viewed as "a signal of a firm stance on the Uyghur issue" (Yellinek and Chen, 2019). The other camp can be viewed as a "loose coalition of developing states usually referred to as the 'Like-Minded Group of Developing Countries,' or simply the 'Like-Minded Group' (LMG)" (Yellinek and Chen, 2019).

An important question is: Which camp does China like? Some statistics that may help us to answer this question follow.

A list of the foreign countries to which most Chinese students choose to go is a good indicator that they like these countries. Few students would choose a country in which to study if they hated it.

Table 8.2. *Signatories of the two letters*

Signatories to the criticizing China letter (the critical camp)	Signatories to the supporting China letter (the "like-minded" camp)	
Australia	Algeria	Nepal
Austria	Angola	Nigeria
Belgium	Bahrain	North Korea
Canada	Bangladesh	Oman
Denmark	Belarus	Pakistan
Estonia	Bolivia	The Philippines
Finland	Burkina Faso	The Russian Federation
France	Burundi	Saudi Arabia
Germany	Cambodia	Serbia
Iceland	Cameroon	Somalia
Ireland	Comoros	South Sudan
Japan	The Congo	Sri Lanka
Latvia	Cuba	The Sudan
Lithuania	Democratic Republic of Congo	Syria
Luxembourg	Djibouti	Tajikistan
The Netherlands	Egypt	Togo
New Zealand	Equatorial Guinea	Turkmenistan
Norway	Eritrea	Uganda
Spain	Gabon	United Arab Emirates
Sweden	Iran	Uzbekistan
Switzerland	Iraq	Venezuela
United Kingdom	Kuwait	Yemen
	Laos	Zambia
	Mozambique	Zimbabwe
	Myanmar	Palestinian Authority

Source: Yellinek and Chen (2019)

Table 8.3. *Chinese students in foreign countries*

Country	Chinese students	Rank of the number of Chinese students among all foreign students in the country
United States	328,547	1
Australia	97,984	1
United Kingdom	94,995	1
Canada	83,990	1
Japan	74,921	1
South Korea	66,672	1
Germany	30,259	1
France	28,043	2
Russia	20,209	4
New Zealand	16,520	1

Source: China Education Online (2017)

Table 8.3 shows the top ten destination countries for Chinese students in 2016 (China Education Online, 2017).

As can be seen from Table 8.3, nine of the top ten countries are democracies, six are in the Critical Camp (Table 8.2), and only one (Russia) is in the Like-Minded Camp, with the number of Chinese students ranked only fourth. So Chinese students' country preference is quite clear: They overwhelmingly want to go to countries in the camp that criticized the Chinese government.

According to a 2012 survey by Pew Research Center on Chinese attitudes toward other countries, 52 percent of Chinese surveyed like American ideas about democracy, and 43 percent of them viewed America favorably. Seventy-four percent of Chinese believed that people are better off in a free market. The majority of them (59 percent) said they like the pace of modern life. The Pew survey concluded that "many Chinese embrace aspects of America's soft

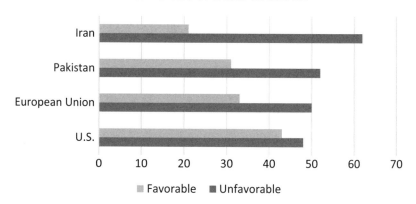

FIGURE 8.1 Chinese views of other countries.
Source: Made by author based on data from Pew Research Center (2012)

power, including U.S. science and technology and American ideas about democracy" (Pew Research Center, 2012). Figure 8.1 presents Chinese attitudes toward Pakistan and Iran, two of the countries that signed the "Like-Minded Letter," and toward the European Union, which provided most of signatories of the Critical Letter. As can be seen, Chinese citizens viewed the United States and EU more favorably than Pakistan and Iran.

Based on these data, we can draw the following profiles of Chinese people and the Chinese government: The Chinese people overwhelmingly like democratic countries more than the "like-minded group of developing countries." The Chinese government heavily relies on the like-minded group for their support – this support is not born of respect, however, but of necessity and strategic convenience. The Chinese government's desire to earn respect from the democracies is evident.

In December 2020, Chinese Foreign Minister Wang Yi remarked that China has no intention to pick a fight with the United States, neither in diplomacy, the media, or any other field. Wang called for cooperation between the world's two largest economies, adding that China's stance on working with the United States remains stable and consistent. "China-U.S. relations have never been a zero-sum game, and the success of either party is not at the expense of the failure of the other party," he said (China Global Television Network, 2020). Obviously, his comment runs counter to the CCP's ideology and ultimate goal of "burying capitalism" (see Chapter 2); but it indeed signals the CCP's strong desire, at least in the short term and out of expediency, to maintain a good relationship with and be respected by the United States.

In conclusion, for the CCP's domestic legitimacy and international respect, China needs to interact with the democratic countries and improve its relationship with them. In contrast, the democracies have little need for the respect or support of China for their domestic legitimacy. In fact, being perceived as being too close to the CCP/China is often viewed as a liability for political leaders in the democracies.

8.3.2 Economic Relationship between China and the Democracies

According to the theory of comparative advantage, free trade (i.e., zero tariffs, zero government subsidies, and zero trade barriers) benefits all trading countries. So, if one country uses trade as a weapon, such as ceasing trade between two countries (delinking), both countries will be hurt economically. But countries still use trade as a weapon to seek concessions or to push trading partners to make changes, such as the trade retaliations by China on Australia and Canada that we reviewed in Chapter 7. Some US policymakers and analysts suggest that the United States should delink from China to protect US interests. If the two countries delink, how will it affect the two economies? Likewise, when criticizing or pressuring China to make changes, European countries must always consider the possibility that China will retaliate and that they may lose their markets in China entirely, which may lead to delinking. How will such a delinking affect China and Europe? These are complex issues and obviously there are no easy answers. In my analysis, I will discuss the scenario that China and the democracies are delinked and in an extreme case of delinking, China is closed. I will also briefly discuss the feasibility of the scenario that China only trades with the "like-minded group of developing countries." While these scenarios are simplified, they help us understand the basic outcome of the economic interaction between China and the democracies.

If, for either internal or external reasons, the CCP closes the country, can China be self-reliant? In theory, the answer is yes: most sizable countries can survive without international trade. From 1949 to the late 1970s, China was essentially closed and self-reliant. North Korea today is still largely closed and self-reliant. But from the economic efficiency perspective, being closed and self-reliant is not a good choice, and the poverty and lack of economic growth in Mao's China and Kim's North Korea serve as strong evidence for that.

Currently, China cannot supply all economic resources and products needed to meet its domestic demand. Many raw materials and commodities such as grain, soybean, oil, copper, ore, wool, and coal need to be imported. China also depends on foreign suppliers for computer chips and many other hi-tech products. China's manufacturing industries also heavily rely on supply chains that are outside of China. All these indicate that China must rely on international trade to sustain and grow its economy. Who are China's main trading partners – are they mostly democratic countries (i.e., the "criticizing China camp") or in the "like-minded group of development countries"?

At least two-thirds of China's international trade is with the United States, Canada, Australia, New Zealand, Europe, and major democratic countries in Asia (India, Japan, South Korea, and Taiwan) (National Bureau of Statistics of China, 2019). The advanced democracies are also the main source that China has relied on for its scientific and technological development (Lau, 2020).

So, China's sustained economic development requires international trade. To keep China open, it needs support from its major trading partners, which are mostly the democracies. Delinking from them will have a substantial negative impact on China.

For the democracies, cessation of trading with China will hurt them as well. If the democracies and China do delink, what are the possible outcomes? For the democracies, products may become more expensive and exports may be reduced in the short run. Can they absorb it without a major economic downturn? The United States' experience during the trade war can shed light on this question. By various estimates and analyses, the impact of higher tariffs and reduced trade between the United States and China on US consumers and GDP is small. The average price level rise resulting from higher tariffs on Chinese goods for US consumers is estimated at about 0.1 percent, and US GDP reduction resulting from the trade war is estimated at between 0.3 percent and 0.7 percent (Hass and Denmark, 2020; Norland, 2018). These impacts have been absorbed by the US economy and consumers without causing major economic downturns. On the positive side, in the long run, the number of manufacturing jobs in the United States will increase since more firms will return, and the United States will reduce its reliance on a single country for vital supplies.

Furthermore, if the democracies can form a new trade alliance based on the rule of law and reciprocity, the size of this group will be large enough to allow members to enjoy the benefits of globalization such as the realization of comparative advantage and economies of scale. Thus, if delinking happens between the democracies and China, the shock would be smaller and the readjustment would be easier for the former than for the latter.

To keep China open, the CCP has an option to build an alliance with countries that economically depend on and politically support China, namely, the "like-minded group of developing countries." This may help the CCP to achieve its dream of building its world without criticism from the democracies. This group should also be large enough to enjoy the benefits of semi-globalization. Of course, if the CCP continues its current practices, such as using favorable laws and disregarding unfavorable ones, it will eventually push its camp members to leave, forcing it back to a more or less closed regime. To avoid this vicious cycle, China still needs some fundamental changes.

An unintended but important benefit of the two-camp arrangement is that it provides a more level playing field for both to compete. In this sense, the leaders of both camps should take this opportunity to show who can lead its camp to better protect human rights and deliver prosperity.

8.3.3   Social Problems for a Closed China: Complete Lack of Opposition Parties

A grave consequence of delinking and China being closed that has not been fully discussed is the loss of the opposition party for China – don't get me wrong: I am not saying that there is another party that can safely exist and freely criticize the CCP *inside* China. Indeed, there is an opposition party, but it is *outside* of China: its members are spread all over the world but mostly in the democratic nations. They are members in the British Parliament, senators or representatives in U.S. Congress, and political and opinion leaders in other democratic countries.

Collectively, these "opposition party" members closely watch how the CCP exercises its power and raise concerns or objections when the CCP harms individual freedom, human rights, or other social welfare of the Chinese people. Governments of democracies also take public actions, such as issuing executive orders and making laws, in an attempt to reduce the negative effects of the CCP's abuse of power.

There have been numerous cases in which political prisoners in China were released and allowed to leave China as a result of international pressure. One of the best-known cases is Wei Jingsheng, a political activist who called for democracy in China in 1978. Wei was sentenced to fifteen years in prison in 1979. In 1993, the CCP released him shortly before the International Olympic Committee voted on the 2000 Summer Games host location, for which Beijing was a contender. Beijing lost to Sydney for hosting the Summer Games, and Wei was arrested again in 1994. In 1995 Wei was sentenced to fourteen years in prison. In 1997, six months before US President Clinton's visit to China, Wei was released and immediately sent to the United States (Zh.wikipedia.org, 2020b). It would not be an exaggeration to say that had the international community (especially the United States) not intervened, Wei would have been very likely to end up dying in a prison or labor camp in China.

International pressure also helps raise awareness of privacy rights amid the Chinese government's big push in using facial recognition for social control. The Chinese government is the biggest user of facial recognition technology in the world, and its "facial recognition database includes nearly every one of China's 1.4 billion citizens" (Lentino, 2019). The way the Chinese government uses facial recognition has been intrusive to people's privacy. Government-installed cameras can catch people jaywalking, taking too much toilet paper in public bathrooms, or in gatherings of social critics. The international community, especially the United States, has criticized such disregard of people's privacy. These criticisms have helped Chinese citizens to push the Chinese government to address it. In 2020, a Chinese citizen, Guo Bing, sued a local zoo for requiring him to provide his facial data and won (Gao, 2020).

When Wang Ran studied in the United States, she was a "Little Pink Red" (*xiao fen hong*, a label for young pro-CCP Chinese nationalists) and defended the CCP against international criticism, she told Radio Free Asia (a news media funded by the U.S. Congress). However, after she went back to China, her parents were taken by the police on what she believes to be fabricated charges. Now she has completely changed her view of the CCP, and, in order to help her cause, agreed to be interviewed by Radio Free Asia, which is labeled as "anti-China" by the CCP (Radio Free Asia, 2020a).

The case of Wang Ran shows that while many "Little Pink Reds" are strongly against "international interferences in China's internal affairs," a phrase frequently used by the Chinese government to denounce international criticism, they may not realize that such international criticism actually helps to improve their own rights in China.

For other countries to be able to play the role of the opposition party in China, the CCP must care about its international image. And the international community must be able to obtain information on China. These imply that China must remain open. If China is closed, the CCP will no longer care about its international image and ignore criticism by other countries, and the *de facto* opposition party will no longer be effective. This will make China become a society that is similar to North Korea and Mao's China. But is this what the CCP wants to do?

Almost totally shut off from the international community, contemporary North Korea (like Mao's China) cannot enjoy the benefits of international trade, and the economy suffers greatly. The Kim regime's absolute rule is maintained by terror: There is a massive prison and labor camp system to intimidate and punish the common people, and frequent purges and executions are undertaken to silence any opposition within the ruling circle. Mao's China featured a different form of terror than we observe in North Korea: political movements (campaigns) (see Chapter 2). Virtually the entire population was mobilized to participate in these movements and people were forced to take sides in the political struggles. The results were chaos and mass killings in many regions.

One analogy to help understand the difference between a totally closed dictatorship and a dictatorship that expands to the outside world is the ringleader Fagin, who ran his thieves' house in London in Charles Dickens' novel *Oliver Twist*. Fagin's gang's internal stability depends on its ability to expand outside of their house – the gang members go out to London to steal. And this is possible because London lets them roam around and does not enforce the law rigorously. If London delinks from Fagin's gang, the closed house of Fagin will force the thieves to fight among themselves and kill each other.

A stagnant cesspool of constant terror and/or infighting is not what the CCP wants to turn China into. So, ironically, while the CCP loathes and reacts strongly against international criticism, the critics (or the "opposition party") benefit the CCP as they play a role in preventing the CCP from turning China into a closed society.

In sum, my analysis shows that politically, the CCP relies on recognition and respect from the democracies; economically, China needs to trade with the major economies of the world, which are mostly democracies, and socially, the de facto opposition party in the democracies keeps China from falling into a closed dictatorship, which will degenerate into infighting (see Figure 8.2). These provide overwhelming and strong support for the idea that *China under the CCP's dictatorship needs the democracies more than the latter needs China*. This conclusion leads to a key point in this chapter: a structural weakness of China, Inc., which has been hidden for decades, is now more exposed.

8.3.4   The Achilles' Heel of China, Inc.

The success of China, Inc., depends on two key conditions: (1), the CCP's dictatorship, and (2) the democracies opening their markets to China and tolerating its violations of rules and laws. This combination produces a Chinese workforce that absolutely obeys the CCP and at the same time is free to circumvent laws internationally, gaining unfair advantages over the open societies of the democracies. The engagement approach (see Chapter 1) – keeping normal business relations with China and asking it to be lawful – is not only ineffective but also allows the CCP to use both bribes and retaliation to train the democracies to behave according to the CCP's preferences (see Chapter 7). Ironically, the success factors, especially China, Inc.'s reliance on the democracies' support or tolerance, are also its Achilles' Heel.

If the democracies change their policies and take effective measures to neutralize the unfair advantages of China, Inc., such as delinking from it, then the way the CCP runs China as a corporation will no longer be successful or sustainable.

Democracies: They mutually benefit from trade.

Dictatorships: They fight each other.

FIGURE 8.2 Dictatorships vs. democracies: Who needs whom more?
Source: Author

Dictatorships need to trade with democracies and take
advantage of their freedoms.

If a dictatorship is closed, the ruling class and
the ruled will infight.

FIGURE 8.2 (*cont.*)

A dictatorship needs democracies to trade with and thrive more than the democracies need the dictatorships.

FIGURE 8.2 *(cont.)*

The CCP clearly realizes this possibility and thus is making a great effort to defend the status quo. In August 2020, China's Foreign Ministry spokesperson, Zhao Lijian, expressed a strong objection in response to US President Trump's intention to delink if China fails to change. Zhao said China and United States should not delink, and the current worsening of their relationship is entirely the United States' fault (Gu, 2020). In September 2020, China's Foreign Minister, Wang Yi, visited Europe to repair China's relationship with it. One of his main points was to oppose delinking (Sohu.com, 2020a). In October, Chinese Ambassador to the United States Cui Tiankai expressed that he "resolutely opposes 'new cold war' and 'delinking'" (Cui, 2020).

Facing China's strong opposition against any changes, the democracies need to review their options and develop an effective strategy to change the unsustainable relationship with China, which is the topic of the next, concluding, chapter.

8.4   SUMMARY

The long and intensifying global expansion of the CCP has made the democratic countries increasingly uncomfortable and concerned. Virtually all the democracies realize that the relationship with China in its current form cannot be sustained. Furthermore, they feel that their open societies are especially vulnerable to the CCP's expansion, which is exacerbated by the lack of reciprocity: While the CCP/China can freely promote its views and enjoy full legal protection in their countries, they are restricted in China, and their citizens can be imprisoned and firms can be shut down in the country without due process. A China going global under dictatorship is more dangerous to the democracies than a closed one. If a dictatorship is closed, it will degenerate into infighting. For political, economic, and social reasons, China depends on its interactions with the democracies more than vice versa. The success of China, Inc., relies on the democracies to allow it to selectively use international rules in its favor and disregard them if needed. This is beginning to change.

9 Policy and Strategic Options for Governments and Firms in the Democracies

> As we compete with China and hold China's government accountable for its abuses on trade, technology, human rights and other fronts, our position will be much stronger when we build coalitions of like-minded partners and allies.
>
> Joe Biden (Delaney, 2020)

9.1 THE CCP'S CHINA: AN ENTIRELY NEW CHALLENGE

The challenge of the CCP is entirely new and the world is still trying to understand it and learn how to deal with it. Before the rise of the CCP, there have been two periods in which dictatorships have attacked or threatened the world.

The first such attack was by the Axis powers, led by fascist Germany, Italy, and Japan in the late 1930s. After years of pursuing a nationalistic industrial policy (see Chapter 6), Germany and Japan had successfully mobilized the resources of their entire country to achieve rapid industrialization and military build-up. Around the late 1930s they began to disregard international rules and invade other countries by military force. The democratic countries first tried to reason with them, made concessions to them, and even signed peace treaties with them, such as the peace treaty between the United Kingdom and Hitler's Germany, hoping that the Axis would change their minds. As we all know, such an appeasement policy was a total failure, and the Axis rapidly expanded worldwide. Eventually, the democracies had to engage in an all-out military confrontation to defeat the Axis in what is now known as World War II.

The second period did not involve an all-out military confrontation, but rather a long period of geopolitical tension known as the

Cold War between the communist camp led by the Soviet Union and the democratic camp led by the United States, spanning from the late 1940s shortly after World War II to the early 1990s when the Soviet Union collapsed. Since its founding, the communist camp[1] was essentially cut off from the developed, democratic world. Their citizens were restricted from freedom of expression and traveling abroad, and had little incentive to work. As a result, these countries suffered constant shortages of virtually all useful products and there was persistent stagnation. The ever-widening gap between the advanced democracies and the communist bloc in living standards and personal freedoms put increasing pressures on the communist rulers in the Eastern European countries. In 1989, Poland and Hungary began to institute competitive elections, and mass protests broke out in Czechoslovakia and East Germany. In November, the infamous Berlin Wall fell. In December 1991, the USSR was declared officially dissolved. Since then, all the formerly communist countries in Eastern Europe and Russia have embarked on democratization, ending the Cold War (see Chapter 8 for Russia's difficult path to democracy).

Now the democratic world is facing the threat of a new dictatorship, the CCP and its China, Inc., that presents challenges that the democratic world has not seen in its fight against the Axis countries in World War II or against the Soviet bloc.

The relationship between the democracies and the Axis countries was that they were enemies of each other, and they were *at war*; each side mobilized their entire population and all resources to defeat the other side, including eliminating and destroying the enemy force. The relationship between the democracies and China is not one of war. In fact, they trade and invest in each other in large scale and volumes. Furthermore, China, Inc., penetrates the democracies with news media, cultural institutions, academic exchange, immigration, and other activities. At the same time, the CCP systematically buys

---

[1] It is also called the Eastern Bloc, which includes the USSR, East Germany, Poland, Romania, Czechoslovakia, Hungary, Bulgaria, Yugoslavia, and Albania.

support from the elites (see Chapter 7), circumvent laws, and undermines the political system of the democracies. So, what kind of relationship do the democracies have with China? It is hard to describe. Before he was elected US President, Joe Biden called China the "biggest competitor" (see Chapter 8); after he became the president, he called China the "most serious competitor" (Churchill, 2021). A 2019 European Union policy paper described China as a "systemic rival" (European Commission, 2019a). Even these terms seem to be offensive to the CCP. China's Foreign Ministry countered that it views Europe as a "strategic partner, not a rival" (Hinshaw, Hua, and Norman, 2020). With close economic ties with China, the democracies find themselves in a very awkward position with the world's largest dictatorship that is poised to change them.

The relationship between the democracies and the Soviet bloc during the Cold War era was adversarial, short of an all-out war. A key difference between the democracies' relationship with the Soviet bloc then and their relationship with China today is that the Soviet bloc was *closed* to the democracies. The two sides did not engage in many economic or cultural exchanges. The officials of the Soviet bloc did not send their children to study in the democracies, nor did they interact with the elites in the democracies through bribery or academic exchange. In fact, the isolation of the Soviet bloc accelerated its demise (see Chapter 8 for the degeneration of closed dictatorships).

In sum, the democracies have the experience to fight dictatorship in a real war or in isolation, but do not have enough experience in dealing with a dictatorship that keeps close ties with the world economically, disregards laws, and closes its country politically. In this chapter, I will present my thoughts on what the democracies can do to develop an effective strategy to protect their political and economic systems and way of life from the expansion of the CCP.

9.1.1   *Understanding the CCP's Attitude-Behavior Pattern*

In formulating policies on China, policymakers in the democratic countries need to understand the CCP (see Chapter 2) and its communication style. The CCP says that Europe is a strategic partner, and China has no intention to pick a fight with the United States and instead wants to cooperate with it (see Chapter 8 and China Global Television Network, 2020). To effectively evaluate to what degree these statements can be trusted, we need to review the characteristics of the CCP and its attitude-behavior patterns. While some of this may have been discussed earlier in the book, these characteristics are worth recapping for policymaking purposes.

The CCP's promises. The history of the CCP shows that when it is weak and needs help, it makes alluring promises. But when it is strong, the promises will be breached. For example, in 1945, four years before seizing power, Mao Zedong promised that the CCP would establish a society like the United States, with freedoms and democracy (Radio France Internationale, 2019). But soon after it seized power in 1949, the CCP made China into one of the most repressive societies with its totalitarian rule. During the 1956 "Hundred Flowers" campaign, the party briefly allowed freedom of speech, but it simply used this to identify and crush those with dissenting views in the ensuing "Anti-Rightist Movement" (Wikipedia, 2020a). In 1997 when Hong Kong was reverted to China, the CCP promised the Hong Kong people "one country, two systems" and a high degree of autonomy for fifty years. In 2020, the CCP imposed a new National Security Law on Hong Kong and took away most of the promised autonomy (Rosett, 2020b). In 2020, the CCP demolished a large number of houses in Xiangtang Village, a suburb of Beijing, leaving many homeowners homeless. The construction of these houses was encouraged and approved by the CCP decades ago when the area was poor and desperately in need of investment. Now the land on which the houses were built has substantially appreciated and the CCP wants to take the land back (Ye, 2020).

The CCP's view on law. CCP General Secretary Xi Jinping stated that "the party's leadership is the fundamental guarantee for the socialist legal system. Ruling by law is to strengthen, not weaken, the party's leadership. The party directs law-making" (Huanqiuwang,

2019). Law for the CCP is a tool for its rule, and can be thought of as "rule by law" instead of "rule of law." As pointed out by Rod Rosenstein, Deputy Attorney General of the United States, in China "the law is an instrument of state power, a mechanism for rulers to maintain control and quash dissent" (U.S. Department of Justice, 2019a). The CCP's use of law is selective and opportunistic. In 2018, Huawei's Chief Financial Officer, Meng Wanzhou, was arrested in Canada by Canadian authorities at the request of the US government on charges of violating US laws. To retaliate against Canada for the arrest, which was (and continues to be) in full compliance with Canadian law, China arbitrarily arrested two Canadian citizens, changed the fifteen-year sentence given to a Canadian citizen to the death penalty, restricted imports of Canadian goods, and issued a tourism warning against Canada. All these acts are not supported by the written laws of China. Furthermore, the Chinese embassy in Canada stated that "The U.S. and Canada, by abusing their bilateral extradition treaty and arbitrarily taking forceful measures against Ms. Meng Wanzhou, gravely violated the lawful rights and interests of the said Chinese citizen" (Zhou, 2020).

The CCP's worship of force and power. The worship of force and equating force to political power are deeply rooted in the culture and practice of the CCP. Mao Zedong had a famous saying, "political power grows out of the barrel of a gun" (Mao, 1927). The CCP has little faith in reasoning, fair play, or following rules. In 1966, the CCP's official newspaper, People's Daily, declared that, "Of all things, power is the center. Having power is having everything" (People's Daily, 1966). Applying the force-power cult to international affairs, the CCP does not care about who is right, but who is more powerful. In Meng's case, it is the United States who caused the arrest, but the CCP picked Canada to retaliate against because it is much less powerful than the United States. Hu Xijin, a CCP official and popular commentator, wrote about how a small place such as Australia would even dare to criticize China. "I feel that it [Australia] is like a piece of chewing gum stuck at the bottom of China's shoe" (Hu, 2020). Gui Congyou,

Chinese ambassador to Sweden who is known as a "wolf warrior" (Wikipedia, 2020i), commented that Sweden criticizing China is like a 48-kilo boxer challenging an 86-kilo boxer (Voice of America).

The CCP's priorities. In 2011, the Chinese government published a whitepaper stating that "China's core interests include national sovereignty, state security, territorial integrity, political system and social stability based on the constitution, and safeguarding sustainable economic and social development" (Chinese Government, 2011). If we peel through these terms and phrases based on the CCP's ultimate objective of maintaining its absolute rule (see Chapter 2 and Zhang and Li, 2020), we can come up with the following priorities for the CCP. The first is social stability, which is the most important for the CCP's rule; next is economic development, which is vital for the CCP to have necessary resources and to gain legitimacy. These two are about survival and therefore are the most important. Internationally, maintaining that issues concerning Taiwan, Tibet, Xinjiang, Hong Kong, and Macau are China's internal affairs is of high priority. Next is to expand China's influence globally. Understanding the priorities of the CCP can help the democracies to leverage their demands more effectively on the CCP to make meaningful changes. The criticism from the democracies mostly focuses on the CCP's human rights record with the hope that this will put pressure on the CCP to improve its record. However, the issue of human rights is not high on the CCP's priorities, and it does not seem to care about its human rights record, making such criticism mostly ineffective. In spite of heavy international condemnation, the CCP has jailed dissidents, cracked down on Hong Kong's democracy movement, and imposed a new National Security Law there. On the other hand, using economic sanctions is more effective in inducing the CCP to make desired changes, as shown by the CCP's great attention and response during the US–China trade war.

The misconception about Xi's personality and the CCP's trajectory. Recent years have witnessed the CCP taking an increasingly tougher stance on both domestic and international affairs. In China, people who criticized the party or merely spoke the truth were sentenced to jail. Zhang Zhan, a lawyer who reported the coronavirus outbreak in Wuhan in early 2020, was sentenced to four years in prison in December of that year (Oxner, 2020). Internationally, the CCP's use of coercive diplomacy has become more frequent (Hanson et al., 2020). This trend emerged along with Xi Jinping's taking over the CCP's reins in 2012. Many analysts attributed the CCP's taking a more domestically repressive and internationally aggressive policy to Xi Jinping's personality (Page, 2020). They believe that when Xi, who is seen as autocratic, is gone, the CCP may revert to a more liberal and milder policy. I think this view is wrong. In this book, I build my case to show that based on the nature of the CCP, its ideology, and its goals, the way in which the CCP rules China and expands globally is logical and inevitable, whoever the party general secretary is. China, Inc., is the invention of the CCP to best achieve its goals. Deng Xiaoping's prescription for the party to "hide its ambition and disguise its claws" (see Chapter 2) implies that once the CCP is strong enough, it will realize its ambition and show its claws. Within the CCP, there has never been any doubt about Deng's prescription and its implication; the only question is *when* the CCP is ready to show its claws. Some in the party feel that Xi showed the claws too hastily (Page, 2020). The democracies should not hope or expect that the CCP will change course after Xi. The domestically repressive and internationally assertive policy is not only built into the political economic institutions but is also in the best interest of the CCP. As China, Inc., gets stronger, such a policy will be more pronounced, regardless of who is at the helm of the party.

China, Inc., blurs the line between military and civilians. Currently, the democracies all have a policy to safeguard their technologies against use by the People's Liberation Army. To implement such a policy, they make a great effort to identify PLA personnel, and bar them from studying or doing research in their academic institutions. They also identify Chinese universities and companies that are linked with the PLA, and prohibit their firms from doing business with these Chinese entities. However, based on the China, Inc., perspective, these measures may not be effective in safeguarding the democracies' technologies from being used by the PLA. China, Inc., can easily reassign other employees and entities who do not have apparent ties with the PLA to engage in exchange with the democracies, achieving the same goals for the PLA – and for the CCP.

9.2 STRATEGIC CONSIDERATIONS FOR THE DEMOCRACIES

9.2.1 *The Need for the Democracies to Take Collective and Concerted Actions*

With the largest population (1.44 billion) and the largest economy (US$23 trillion based on purchase power parity), the relationship between China and most other countries is skewed in favor of the former. As a *Wall Street Journal* article commented, "China's economic might means most countries can't afford to push too hard" (Hinshaw et al., 2020). Furthermore, the CCP controls the gateway to China and makes it clear that only a select number of foreign firms can enter China. If a foreign country criticizes the CCP too much, it will lose its privilege to do business with China. This strategy has worked well for the CCP to deter criticism from other countries.

A card game[2] that I use in my strategy class can illustrate this point. I hold twenty-six black cards and I hand out twenty-six red cards to twenty-six students. A deal (a pairing) between a black card and a red card will be worth US$100, and an unmatched card will be worthless. Accordingly, each student comes to me to make a deal on how we can split the US$100. Since all of the twenty-six red cards can be matched by the twenty-six black cards, and an unmatched card is worthless for the student, as well as for me, the students have the same bargaining power that I do. Furthermore, it would be logical to assume that the students and I would split the US$100 equally.

---

[2] The card game was first introduced by Adam Brandenburger and Barry Nalebuff, 1997. *Co-opetition*. New York: Doubleday.

However, I then publicly throw away two black cards and begin the negotiation (i.e., twenty-six red cards trying match twenty-four black cards). Realizing that two of them will have no match, they are desperate to make any deals with me. In many deals, I only agree to give the student US$1, keeping the lion's share (US$99) for myself!

This game is what the Chinese government is playing with the Fortune 500 companies and with other influential people and entities, including foreign governments. There are many firms and foreign governments that are eager to win opportunities from China, but there is only one China, Inc., the equivalent of openly discarding several cards from my hand in the card game. All foreign politicians and CEOs compete to please the Chinese government, in order to get their chance to do business with China, Inc. As a result, in this "doing business with China" game, the Chinese party-state is holding the whole country hostage in order to play the foreign academics, politicians, governments, firms, and members of international organizations off against each other.

Each foreign firm/government tries to maximize their own benefit by undercutting other countries to make a deal with the CCP, and collectively all foreign firms and governments are worse off. How can they improve their position in the game?

In my class, I ask my students the same question: How can they beat the dealer in the game? They eventually realize that all the twenty-six students must band together to collectively bargain with the teacher. This is what the democracies should do in dealing with China. If they act in unison to deal with China, not only will they be better off in the game, but they will also be effective in pushing China to change.

Since the democracies have more bargaining power in dealing with China than the latter has with the former (see Chapter 8), they should stand firm on their principles in demanding that China change. In order to achieve a more open China under the rule of law, democratic countries must first isolate it, for this is an effective way to force China to change (Li, 2020b).

In 2020, an Inter-Parliamentary Alliance on China (IPAC) was formed by the major democratic countries in the world with the goal of "working toward reform on how democratic countries approach China" (The Inter-Parliamentary Alliance on China, 2020). More than one hundred law-makers – parliament or congress members – from nineteen countries joined it. In 2020, when Australia was singled out by the CCP to retaliate against using economic sanctions (see Chapter 7), the IPAC called for solidarity with the Australian people and led a global campaign to buy Australian wine. While the IPAC is an encouraging start for the legislators of the democracies to work together, the executive branch of the democracies' governments should also form an alliance. A report in December 2020 said that "present and former U.S. Trade Representatives advised president elect Joe Biden to be tough on China, and to unite with allies and join the pan-pacific partnership" (Jie, 2020).

The coalition needs to have a set of principles to govern it. A report on how to counter the CCP's influence in the United States recommended three rules that can be used by the coalition. They are transparency, integrity, and reciprocity (Working Group on Chinese Influence Activities in the United States, 2018). Transparency is an effective tool in exposing and deterring private deals between a member country of the coalition and China. Upholding integrity is a must for all member countries of the coalition. They must all practice democracy, follow the rule of law, and respect human rights. Reciprocity is not only a principle between member states of the coalition but also the coalition's demand on the CCP with respect to their access to China and its markets. Most importantly, all the members of the coalition must agree that if the CCP seriously violates these principles, such as suppressing human rights or practicing coercive diplomacy (see Chapter 7), all members must oppose it; and if a member country is unfairly treated or retaliated against by China, all members of the coalition must take collective action to support the member and oppose the unfair treatment or retaliation by China.

A main challenge for such a coalition is that member countries may breach the agreed collective action by individually making deals with the CCP. How can the coalition effectively curb such behavior? From the game theoretical perspective, political economist Jean-Philippe Platteau (1994, p. 765) laid out conditions under which "generalized morality" can be upheld. For Platteau, generalized morality is necessary to maintain public ordering in a society. The conditions he listed are applicable to the coalition of the democratic countries we discuss here. Listed are his conditions, modified by me for the coalition:

> (1) A large number of member countries must adhere to the coalition's principles as laid out in this section; (2) these countries also have sufficient trust in others' predisposition toward upholding the principles; (3) their support for the principles is strong enough not to be easily discouraged by bad experiences while it is easily reinforced by good experiences; (4) cheating members are subject to strong feelings of guilt when they are free riders among many honest members; and (5) honest member countries are willing to sanction breaches of the principles even when their own interests have not been harmed by the observed breach (and despite the fact that an honest member country's sanctioning activities will probably not bring them any direct reward in the future). In other words, in order to make coalition effective, member countries must be willing to oppose the CCP's rule-violation behavior even when they face retaliation from China, and they must also be willing to confront a member country that deviates from the coalition's collective action on China.

As shown in Chapter 8, politically, economically, and socially, the CCP needs to interact with the democracies more than vice versa. The democracies have more bargaining power in dealing with China, and therefore they can and should stand firm on their principles in demanding that China change.

9.2.2   Policy Objectives for the Democracies

Assuming that the democracies can form a coalition, what should be their main policy objective? In other words, what path do the democracies want China to take? Here are some possibilities:

(1) A democratic China based on the rule of law, both in domestic and international affairs. As we all know, this is highly unlikely in the near future.

(2) The CCP adopts limited rule of law and allows some political liberty and more room for unofficial media in China, although it does not allow political participation such as free elections. Foreigners and foreign firms are more secure in China. This sounds more like Hong Kong's system before the new National Security Law of 2020. This may be possible if there is a coalition by the democratic countries that can effectively pressure China to do it.

(3) China becomes more isolated. This will happen if the democracies delink or divest from China. This will have a negative impact on the Chinese economy, and, as shown in Chapter 8, a closed China may substantially undermine the CCP's legitimacy and cause infighting.

(4) The status quo: China remains under the CCP dictatorship and keeps taking advantage of the open societies of the democracies.

Using democracy based on the rule of law as the ideal, option (1) is the best and option (2) is the second best. Both are preferred to the status quo. Since there is no formidable opposition party inside China, internally, the CCP has little incentive to initiate any changes toward (1) or (2). The only viable force that can push the CCP to make such changes is a united alliance of the democracies demanding that the CCP do so.

9.2.3   Ready to Delink: An Effective Strategy
to Achieve the Preferred Goal

As the past experiences have shown, when a democratic country pushes the CCP to make changes, the latter retaliates with coercive diplomacy, including economic and noneconomic sanctions. Such retaliation can severely hurt a single democratic country, as illustrated in Chapter 8. But if the major democracies take unified counter measures against the CCP's retaliation, the latter's usual strategy will not be effective and will hurt China more. To take the united approach, the democracies should follow a "tit for tat" strategy and respond with appropriate punitive measures to effectively pressure the CCP to make desired changes, and they must be ready to go all the way to delink with China. If the major democracies are highly united and take concerted actions, they do not need to actually delink with China in order to pressure the CCP to take meaningful political steps toward making China more open and liberal. In this sense, the willingness to delink from China is a "*credible threat*," a realistic option for the democracies with the full intent and the apparent ability to carry it out.

Based on this analysis, I argue that an effective strategy to push the CCP to make changes toward the rule of law is a "*tit for tat," delink-ready strategy*. From a game perspective, a likely sequence of pushing the CCP to make needed changes is that in the first stage, the democracies push the CCP to make desired changes, and the CCP refuses and retaliates; in stage two, the democracies raise the pressure and start the process of delinking from China, and China becomes more isolated; in stage three, realizing that the democracies' delinking is for real, the CCP begins to make meaningful changes toward establishing the rule of law.

There will be strong resistance against the tit for tat, delink-ready strategy from the multinational corporations and Wall Street investors who have become deeply entangled with the CCP and making money in China. However, pushing the CCP to make meaningful changes is in their best long-term interest, for their profits from China are based on bribery, corruption, and, most importantly, the CCP's whims. They have no security in their markets or property rights in China. Lasting security and profitability can only be achieved if the CCP/China obeys the rule of law.

As shown in Chapter 8, economic sanctions between China and the democracies will hurt the latter too. But this is temporary. In the long-run, democracies can readjust and be better off than maintaining the status quo. Even if the democracies are not effective in forcing China to play by the rules, in the worst case, delinking will provide more protection for their democratic system from being encroached on by the CCP. If delinking does occur, a possible scenario is that China will form its own trading bloc with like-minded countries. But such a bloc is unlikely to be mutually beneficial because of the predatory nature of dictatorships (see Chapter 8).

Using the United States as an example, I did a cost-benefit analysis of different scenarios of China for the democratic countries, from the status quo, a more isolated China, to a more rule-based China. I assessed whether the effects of different Chinas on the major sectors of the United States are positive or negative. The sectors include jobs, consumption, trade balance, the credit market, education, technology, national security, and the CCP's influence. Table 9.1 shows the result of my analysis. For the United States (or other democratic countries), keeping the status quo is the worst option (total score = −4); a more isolated China is more beneficial to the United States (total score = 2), while a more rules-based China is the best, not only for the United States and the democracies but also for China (total score = 10).

This analysis shows that the tit for tat, delink-ready strategy can be effective in pushing the CCP to make needed changes, such as allowing more political liberty and fairer and reciprocal treatment of foreigners and foreign firms. It should be emphasized that the willingness to delink from China is not for the sake of delinking. Delinking itself is not the goal; it is a "credible threat," or an effective means, for all democracies to achieve the goal of making China play by the rules.

9.3 STRATEGIC CONSIDERATIONS FOR MULTINATIONAL FIRMS

9.3.1 The Friction between the Democracies and China Is Long Term

For multinational corporations and business executives, this book offers important background information on China, the CCP, China's reliance on relation-based governance, the advantages and weaknesses of China, Inc., and the CCP's coercive diplomacy. For investors and executives who conduct business in China, the importance of having a good understanding about the CCP cannot be emphasized enough.

Table 9.1. *Cost-benefit analysis for the United States under different scenarios of China*

Impact on the United States	China under different scenarios		
	China keeps status quo	China becomes more isolated	China becomes more rules-based
US jobs	negative	positive	fair
US consumption	positive	negative	fair
US firms doing business w/ China	profit in short term/more dependent on China	less profit in the short run, more independent of China	positive
US trade balance	negative	positive/neutral	Fair
US easy credit	positive	negative/neutral	fair
US college tuition income	positive in profit, negative in national security	negative in profit, positive in national security	positive
US technology / talents	negative	positive/neutral	positive
US security	negative	positive	positive
Curbing CCP influence	negative	positive	positive
Total score[*]	−4	2	10

[*] *Note*: The total score is the sum of positive and negative points, where positive = 2, negative = −2, others=0.
Source: Author

In their long-term strategy, business executives should realize that, given the irreconcilable fundamental differences in ideology between the CCP and the democracies, the CCP's expansionary strategy, and the rise of China, Inc., the friction between the democracies and China may get worse and will certainly be long term. Needless to say, this not-so-optimistic prospect requires them to plan accordingly in terms of diversification of customers and suppliers and establishing alternative production bases.

9.3.2 The Challenge of China, Inc., for Multinational Corporations

The China, Inc., perspective suggests that multinational corporations (MNCs) dealing with Chinese firms need to know that Chinese firms are subunits of China, Inc. Compared to their counterparts in the democracies, firms in China have much less autonomy, and at the same time, enjoy greater state support financially, technologically, and politically. And they may act on behalf of the Chinese state in business dealings with foreign firms. Their operational objectives may not be based on economic efficiency and profit-maximization for their own individual firms, but rather based on the overall strategy of China, Inc. MNC executives should take into consideration the aforementioned unique characteristics of firms in China when doing business with them. As a prudent strategic habit, MNCs should pay close attention to Chinese government policies and treat them as strategic intents by China, Inc., which, in turn, affect the operations of the firms they may deal with.

The cases we reviewed in Chapter 6 should serve as a caution for MNCs entering the Chinese market. They need to be aware that their technologies can be copied and possibly used against them in domestic markets, as in the case of the high-speed rail industry (Shirouzu, Zhang, Feng, Sen, and Mitchell, 2010). Their domestic rivals may enjoy state protection and subsidies, as the case of the domestic electric vehicle battery maker CATL showed (see Chapter 6).

9.3.3 How to Deal with China's Relation-Based Environment

The framework of rule-based versus relation-based government (see Chapter 3) has several important implications for firms dealing with China in investing, marketing, human resource management, and information and communication management. Listed are some of my cautions and suggestions.

Do not take written laws at face value. An important takeaway of the relation-based perspective is that written laws and regulations should not be taken at face value. The degree of enforcement and degree of fairness in enforcement vary greatly from law to law. MNCs must understand and pay close attention to this issue.

Direct vs. indirect investment. When considering investing in China, an MNC needs to distinguish direct investment versus portfolio (indirect) investment. In a relation-based environment such as China, the quality of *publicly available information* on accounting and auditing for firms is poor and often untrustworthy, making portfolio investment such as buying shares of listed companies particularly risky. On the other hand, direct investment, in which the investor also *directly manages* the firm with *first-hand information,* is relatively safer (Li and Filer, 2007).

Different expectations in working relationships. MNC managers interacting with local employees need to be knowledgeable about the different perceptions of working relationships between people from rule-based countries (the democracies) and relation-based countries (China). Rule-based MNC managers usually treat employees at arm's length and expect local employees to "hit the ground running." They place high-level trust in their local employees unless proven otherwise. Local employees in China, who are mostly relation-based, want to build personal relationships with their supervisor before they can fully trust him/her (Maurer and Li, 2006).

Relying on relationships can be a double-edged sword. It is vital for a foreign player (e.g., a foreign firm or foreign businessperson) entering China to cultivate and establish reliable relationships there.

In doing so, the foreign player should realize two caveats. First, using relations to circumvent formal rules may be illegal, even in a relation-based society such as China. Second, when the foreign player uses relations to gain advantage in the local market, its partners and competitors also use relations to try to outcompete it. And local partners or competitors may have stronger relationships within the power circle. In the early 1990s, McDonald's obtained a prime location in Beijing through *guanxi*, only to find that a Hong Kong businessman, Li Ka-shing, who had a stronger *guanxi*, had McDonalds' evicted for Li's real estate development project (*The Economist*, 1994).

9.3.4 Work Closely with Your Home Government

In 2004, the Chinese authorities requested that Yahoo! in China provide personal information about a journalist named Shi Tao, who used Yahoo! Mail to send information abroad. Using this information, the Chinese government sentenced Shi Tao to ten years in prison. The United States was outraged by Yahoo!'s behavior. Congress summoned Yahoo!'s CEO, Jerry Yang, and Congressman Tom Lantos scolded Yang and Yahoo! "technologically and financially you are giants, morally you are pygmies" (*The New York Times*, 2007). Yang apologized for what Yahoo! did and promised to help the victim's family. But he also made the following comment (Yang, 2007),

> We believe governments, because of their enormous leverage, have a vital role to play independently, teaming with other governments and international institutions, and working with companies ... governments – through trade relationships, bilateral and multi-lateral forums, and other diplomatic means – should be a powerful force for creating a global environment where Internet freedom is a priority and where people are not imprisoned for expressing their political views online.

Yang made an important point here. Yahoo!, a private company, is not equipped to fight against the Chinese government; it needs the backing and active involvement of its government – the US government – to counter human rights violations by the Chinese government. Thirteen years have passed since Yang made this suggestion, but the US government has not made any significant progress in supporting its companies to resolve state actions by China that violate human rights or fair trade.

In 2018, the Chinese state ordered foreign airlines to list Taiwan, Hong Kong, and Macau as domestic destinations within China instead of international destinations. Most airlines, including ones based in the United States, obliged for fear of retribution from the Chinese state. The White House called China's demands "Orwellian nonsense," but fell short of taking any state-to-state actions to counter such a "nonsense" (Chan, 2018). Over the years, Hollywood movie producers have been cutting or altering their movies to pass inspection by the CCP's Propaganda Department. Again, the US government did not take any actions to counter the CCP's censoring, but scolded American producers instead. In 2020, U.S. Attorney General William Barr commented that "Hollywood now regularly censors its own movies to appease the Chinese Communist Party" (Barr, 2020). While Barr's criticism of Hollywood on this point is correct and needed, he and policymakers in the democracies should realize that private businesses such as airlines and movie producers are not in the position to fight foreign governments on their own, especially one of the most powerful and repressive governments in the world. While the democratic governments should encourage their firms to stand up to unfair and inhumane actions by a foreign government, they – the governments themselves – should take state actions to correct the wrongdoings by a foreign government.

Likewise, MNCs should also work closely with their home governments on China-related issues. The advantage of China, Inc., is derived from and backed by the most powerful and resourceful state that is bound by no law. Such state action can only be dealt with by other states. When firms from the democracies run into troubles in China, they should not try to work out the problems under the table, or keep silent as the party-state always advises; they should seek help from their governments and the international community.

9.4 CHINA, INC.'S CHALLENGE TO
MANAGEMENT SCHOLARS

Finally, to my fellow researchers in business management, I hope that this book will provide new "food for thought" for your research. The way the party-state manages China is unique and worth studying, as it not only defines firms and people from China but also influences international business and reshapes the theory of the firm. More importantly, the size of the country and the extent to which it influences the world makes studying it necessary and imperative.

Unfortunately, the topic of how the CCP mobilizes the entire country of China as a whole to help Chinese firms gain advantage has not been adequately investigated by scholars of management and international business (IB) (Buckley, Doh, and Benischke, 2017; Delios, 2017; Phan, 2019). As management scholar Andrew Delios (2017, p. 392) pointed out,

> IB scholars have been zealously researching alliance formation and MNC investment into and out of China. More compelling issues such as the rapacious behaviour of the local partners of foreign firms, or the fundamental competitive inequities for foreign firms in China, as created intentionally by biased local policymakers, were hardly explored.

The gap not only weakens our ability to help MNC executives but also hinders our exploration of new theoretical issues. As management scholar Phillip Phan put it, this constitutes "a glaring white space calling out to be filled" (Phan, 2019).

Our China, Inc., perspective is an effort to fill this gap. Here are some possible research themes that my coauthor Matt Farrell and I came up with for scholars of management and international business to consider.[3]

---

[3] Based on S. Li and M. Farrell, 2020c. The Emergence of China, Inc.: Behind and beyond the Trade War. *International Journal of Emerging Markets*, in press.

The first research question is to further delineate China Inc., as we believe it is a more concrete and researchable conceptualization than the so-called China model (Zhang, 2011). Political scientists and economists have attempted to categorize China using the spectrum from communism to capitalism or from dictatorship to democracy and have been unable to come up with a satisfactory concept that can help us grasp the essence of China under the party-state's rule.

China is no longer a communist state as described in classical political science, with a centrally planned economy and communist dictatorship. Labeling China as state-directed capitalism does not catch the essence of China either. The party-state has had great success in integrating all the people and businesses into a giant corporation. Like a corporation that follows its internal regulations and only resorts to laws external to the corporation when necessary, the party-state also follows its internal rules to govern China and only resorts to laws when doing business in other countries when necessary. Further efforts are needed to compare China, Inc., to the old communist regimes and to liberal democracies, to collect more evidence to further build the case, and to refine the concept of China, Inc., in order to make it more operationalizable.

A second research question relates to the theory of the firm. Existing studies on firms in China have examined how SOEs achieve market goals under the CCP's influence (Guo, Huy, and Xiao, 2017). But that is not adequate. The China, Inc., perspective will enable us to look at all firms in China as business units, subsidiaries, joint ventures, or franchisees. For example, if a competitor wants to estimate Huawei's financial resources, it must realize that Huawei is not constrained by its own budget, as the Chinese government can inject (and has injected, see Yap, 2019) funds or other resources just like a company's headquarters can do for a subsidiary. Or, if Huawei or ZTE undertakes a project in a foreign country, whatever they can access can also be accessed by their ultimate headquarters, China's party-state, which in turn may share it with other business units or subsidiaries. In a US Congressional hearing about TikTok, a Chinese social media app that has built a huge following in the United States, Senator Josh Hawley referred to it as "a company compromised by the Chinese Communist Party [that] knows where your children are, knows what they look like, what their voices sound like, what they're watching, and what they share with each other" (Smith, 2019a). In general, the emergence of China, Inc., requires us to examine the firms and the combination of the firm and the state in China to answer the most basic questions asked by the theory of the firm: Why did such a form emerge? Why and how does the party-state organize economic activities in relation to the market and firms? What is the boundary between firms, government, and the market in China? How and why is the party-state structured in its unique way? What are the agency issues arising from China, Inc.? Who are the principals and agents in this giant corporation?

A third research direction is to reexamine and update the economic institutional theory proposed by North (North, 1990). North uses the analogy of sport games to explain the roles of institutions and organizations in a society, where institutions are the rules of the game, and organizations are the players trying to win the game under the rules. The case of China, Inc., presents several new issues pertinent to North's analogy and theory. First, in China, a dominant organization, the CCP, is not only the rule setter and rule enforcer but also a player. In this setting, further institutional change is less likely to be an interactive process between different parties and interest groups through political channels such as mass participation, elections, or lobbying. Second, institutional theory needs to be considered beyond single-country settings. In the international business arena, the institutions-organizations game is now being played globally, in which the rules (institutions) are set collectively by all countries (their governments) and the players are firms from each country. If a country violates the rules (e.g., providing state subsidies, keeping its market closed, or using state intelligence power to acquire technologies for its firms), then how will that country be punished?

A fourth research question is to examine China's industrial policies and how the international business community should deal with them. From the China, Inc., perspective, these policies are not merely state guidance, but rather corporate strategies, in which the party-state identifies some industries, provides national resources for them, raises entry barriers, and assists them in gaining necessary technologies. Once they achieve low cost, such industries are then globalized. Under what conditions can such a policy be implemented? Should other countries emulate such a policy? What are the effects of the policy on other countries? How should other countries and firms deal with the policy and compete with China, Inc.?

I realize that the perspective of China, Inc., is far from comprehensive and the research questions raised here are preliminary and by no means exhaustive. I believe, however, that the political economy behind the frictions between the democracies and CCP-ruled China, as well as the emergence of China, Inc., are increasingly showing a far-reaching impact on management and international business, and therefore are important phenomena for scholars of management and international business to study.

9.5   SUMMARY

Compared to the Axis countries in World War II and the Soviet Union during the Cold War, China under the CCP's rule presents an entirely new challenge to the democracies, because China is closely intertwined with the latter economically and socially. The CCP's taking an increasingly repressive domestic and internationally aggressive stance in recent years cannot be explained by Xi Jinping's autocratic inclination, but by a logical development based on the CCP's institutions, ideology, and objectives. The only way for the democracies to effectively protect themselves from and counter the CCP's expansion is to form an alliance and take collective actions to demand the CCP make meaningful changes toward respecting human rights, the rule of law, and fair and open markets. To be effective, the democracies should adopt a "tit for tat, delink ready" strategy in pushing the

CCP to make desired changes. *Collectively*, the major democracies have more bargaining power than the CCP in their interactions, and thus they should stand firm on their desired changes for China. For multinational corporations, this book offers several tips to help them in formulating their China strategies based on the perspectives of China, Inc., and China's reliance on the relation-based system. Finally, the book provides new research directions for management scholars that may potentially contribute to the theory of the firm and other theoretical issues.

References

Abegglen, J. C. 1970. The Economic Growth of Japan. *Scientific American*, 222(3): 31–37.

Acemoglu, D., Johnson, S., and Robinson, J. 2005. The Rise of Europe: Atlantic Trade, Institutional Change, and Economic Growth. *American Economic Review*, 95(3): 546–579.

Adkisson, R. V. 2014. Quantifying Culture: Problems and Promises. *Journal of Economic Issues*, XLVIII(1): 89–107.

AIDDATA. 2017. China's Global Development Footprint. *College of William and Mary*, Williamsburg, VA (www.aiddata.org/china): Accessed July 21, 2018.

AIDDATA. 2018. AidData's Geocoded Global Chinese Official Finance, Version 1.1.1. *College of William and Mary*, Williamsburg, VA (www.aiddata.org/data/geocoded-chinese-global-official-finance-dataset): Accessed March 14, 2020.

Allen-Ebrahimian, B. and Dorfman, Z. 2020. Exclusive: Suspected Chinese Spy Targeted California Politicians. ***Axios.com***, December 8 (www.axios.com/china-spy-california-politicians-9d2dfb99-f839-4e00-8bd8-59dec0daf589.html?utm_campaign=organic&utm_medium=socialshare&utm_source=twitter&fbclid=IwAR35Igvyo_uwd0G9qC0vnyFQSK4s3XX-URZLPiXBX8zFDcyRoNt4V_l9BnE): Accessed December 18, 2020.

Almond, G. A. and Verba, S. 1965. *The Civic Culture: Political Attitudes and Democracy in Five Nations*. Boston: Little, Brown & Company.

Alon, I., Farrell, M., and Li, S. 2020a. Democracies and Authoritarian Governments: How Their Responses to Covid-19 Differ. *US-China Review*, XLIV(4): 19–21.

Alon, I., Farrell, M., and Li, S. 2020b. Regime Type and COVID-19 Response. *FIIB Business Review*, 9(3): 152–160.

Alon, I., and Li, S. 2019. Rule over Law or Rule of Law? China's IP Theft Dilemma. *The American Spectator*, September 12 (https://spectator.org/rule-over-law-or-rule-of-law-chinas-ip-theft-dilemma/): Accessed September 20, 2019.

Amnesty International. 2018. Third Anniversary of the Lawyers Crackdown in China: Where Are the Human Rights Lawyers? *Amnesty International*, July 9 (www.amnesty.org/en/latest/campaigns/2018/07/china-human-rights-lawyers-crackdown-third-anniversary/): Accessed November 4, 2019.

Anchordoguy, M. 1989. *Computers Inc: Japan's Challenge to IBM*. Cambridge, MA: Harvard University Asia Center.

Andongni. 2019. 70 Days from Taiwan's Election, Airlines in China Provide Half-Priced Tickets. *Radio France Internationale*, November 1 (www.rfi.fr/cn/20191101-距离台湾大选70天-中国大陆航空公司票价打5折): Accessed November 3, 2019.

Art, R. J. and Cronin, P. M. 2003. *The United States and Coercive Diplomacy*. Washington, DC: United States Institute of Peace Press.

Associated Press. 2020. What the U.S.'s "Phase 1" Trade Deal with China Does and Doesn't Do. *MarketWatch*, January 15 (www.marketwatch.com/story/what-the-uss-phase-1-trade-deal-with-china-does-and-doesnt-do-2020-01-15): Accessed February 11, 2020.

Associated Press. 2021. China Asset Management Chief Lai Xiaomin Executed in Bribery Case. *The New York Post*, January 29 (https://nypost.com/2021/01/29/china-asset-management-chief-lai-xiaomin-executed-in-bribery-case/): Accessed March 3, 2021.

Automotive World. 2021. Mercedes-Benz Cars Triples Global Sales of xEVs and Meets the European CO2 Targets for Passenger Cars in 2020. *Automotive World*, January 8 (www.automotiveworld.com/news-releases/mercedes-benz-cars-triples-global-sales-of-xevs-and-meets-the-european-co2-targets-for-passenger-cars-in-2020/#:~:text=Sales%20in%20the%20North%20America,Great%20Britain%20and%20South%20Korea): Accessed March 2, 2021.

Backchina.com. 2012. Zhou Spoke Up to Expose the Problem in China's Financial Sector: *Backchina.com*. (www.epochtimes.com/gb/12/12/18/n3755159.htm): Accessed July 25, 2021.

Bai, L. 2019. 八个百分点有什么依据呢？ *Zhihu.com*, undated (www.zhihu.com/question/20363340): Accessed November 15, 2020.

Baidu. 2010. 一个县有多少机构. *Baidu.com*, December 26 (https://zhidao.baidu.com/question/209727340.html): Accessed November 19, 2020.

Baidu. undated-a. 中国民主党 （大陆地区非法政党. *Baidu Baike*, undated (https://baike.baidu.com/item/%E4%B8%AD%E5%9B%BD%E6%B0%91%E4%B8%BB%E5%85%9A/14770304): Accessed November 19, 2020.

Baidu. undated-b. 党的组织生活. *Baidu Baike* (https://baike.baidu.com/item/%E5%85%9A%E7%9A%84%E7%BB%84%E7%BB%87%E7%94%9F%E6%B4%BB): Accessed November 19, 2020.

Baidu. undated-c. 国进民退. *Baidu Baike* (https://baike.baidu.com/item/%E5%9B%BD%E8%BF%9B%E6%B0%91%E9%80%80): Accessed December 13, 2020.

Baidu Baike. 2012. Jumping into the Sea to Run Business. *baike.baidu.com*. (https://baike.baidu.com/item/%E4%B8%8B%E6%B5%B7%E7%BB%8F%E5%95%86): Accessed December 10, 2020

Baidu Baike. 2015. 国有资产流失. *Baidu Baike*, November 11 (https://baike.baidu .com/item/%E5%9B%BD%E6%9C%89%E8%B5%84%E4%BA%A7%E6%B5% 81%E5%A4%B1): Accessed December 11, 2020.

Baidu Baike. undated. 圈子文化. *Baidu Baike* (https://baike.baidu.com/item/%E5%9C %88%E5%AD%90%E6%96%87%E5%8C%96/12771877): Accessed November 25, 2020.

baike.baidu.com. 2017a. The Photovoltaic Industry. *baike.baidu.com* (https:// baike.baidu.com/item/光伏产业#1_1): Accessed December 8, 2019.

baike.baidu.com. 2017b. Restraining Order on High-Level Consumption *baike. baidu.com*, July 21 (https://baike.baidu.com/item/%E9%99%90%E5%88% B6%E9%AB%98%E6%B6%88%E8%B4%B9%E4%BB%A4/420202): Accessed November 4, 2019.

Ball, J., Reicher, D., Sun, X., and Pollock, C. 2017. The New Solar System: China's Evolving Solar Industry and Its Implications for Competitive Solar Power in the United States and the World: Stanford University, CA (United States).

Barmé, G. R. 2018. For Truly Great Men, Look to This Age Alone: Was Mao Zedong a New Emperor? *China Heritage*, January 27 (http://chinaheritage.net/journal/ for-truly-great-men-look-to-this-age-alone/): Accessed November 29, 2020.

Barr, W. 2020. Attorney General William P. Barr Delivers Remarks on China Policy at the Gerald R. Ford Presidential Museum. *U.S. Department of Justice*, July 16 (www.justice.gov/opa/speech/attorney-general-william-p-barr-delivers- remarks-china-policy-gerald-r-ford-presidential): Accessed December 31, 2020.

Barrow, K. 2014. CNR Selected to Supply New Trains for Boston, *The Railway Gazette*.

Barrow, K. 2015. CRRC Opens Malaysian Rolling Stock Plant.

Barrow, K. 2018. Ten years, 27,000km: China Celebrates a Decade of High-speed. *International Railway Journal*.

Barwick, P. J., Kalouptsidi, M., and Zahur, N. B. 2019. China's Industrial Policy: An Empirical Evaluation. *NBER Working Paper Series*, 26075.

Batke, J. and Ohlberg, M. 2020. Message Control: How a New For-Profit Industry Helps China's Leaders 'Manage Public Opinion'. *China File*, December 20 (www.chinafile.com/reporting-opinion/features/message-control- china): Accessed December 21, 2020.

Baumann, C., Hamin, H., and Yang, S. J. 2016. Work Ethic Formed by Pedagogical Approach: Evolution of Institutional Approach to Education and Competitiveness. *Asia Pacific Business Review*, 22(3): 374–396.

Baumann, C. and Winzar, H. 2017. Confucianism and Work Ethic – Introducing the ReVaMB Model. In *The Political Economy of Business Ethics in East Asia*, 33–60. New York: Elsevier.

BBC. 2011. China Welcomes Zimbabwe's Robert Mugabe as 'Old Friend'. *BBC*, November 17, 2011 (www.bbc.com/news/av/world-asia-china-15769839/china-welcomes-zimbabwe-s-robert-mugabe-as-old-friend): Accessed January 8, 2020.

BBC. 2015a. China TV Anchor Bi Fujian to Be Punished for Mao Insult. *BBC*, August 10 (www.bbc.com/news/world-asia-china-33844095): Accessed November 19, 2020.

BBC. 2015b. Chinese Lawyer Mo Shaoping on His Career, Justice, and Democracy. *BBC*, June 4 (www.bbc.com/news/av/world-asia-33002876): Accessed November 23, 2020.

BBC. 2018a. People's Congress Session Ends: Xi Jinping Emphasizes "the Party Leads Everything." *BBC*, March 20 (www.bbc.com/zhongwen/simp/chinese-news-43468026): Accessed October 18, 2020.

BBC. 2018b. 吴小晖案水落石出 获刑18年没收财产超百亿创纪录. *BBC*, May 10 (www.bbc.com/zhongwen/simp/chinese-news-44064096): Accessed December 11, 2020.

BBG-USAGM Watch. 2017. Video Critical of Voice of America d

Director Gets Thousands of Views in China. *BBG-USAGM Watch*, September 20 (http://bbgwatch.com/bbgwatch/video-critical-of-voice-of-america-director-gets-thousands-of-views-in-china/): Accessed April 15, 2019.

Beech, H. 2018. 'We Cannot Afford This': Malaysia Pushes Back against China's Vision. *The New York Times*, August 20 (www.nytimes.com/2018/08/20/world/asia/china-malaysia.html): Accessed February 28, 2021.

Beijing Daily. 2019. 新型举国体制"新"在何处. *qstheory.cn*, July 15 (www.qstheory.cn/llwx/2019-07/15/c_1124752797.htm): Accessed December 13, 2020.

Belt and Road Initiative. Undated. Belt and Road Initiative. *Belt and Road Initiative* (www.beltroad-initiative.com/belt-and-road/): Accessed March 7, 2021.

Benedict, R. 1961. *Patterns of Culture*. Boston: Houghton Mifflin.

Bermingham, F. 2019. Trade War Forcing 93 per cent of Chinese Companies to Transform Supply Chains, Survey Shows. April 23 (www.scmp.com/print/economy/china-economy/article/3007334/trade-war-forcing-93-cent-chinese-companies-transform-supply): Accessed September 17, 2019.

Beugelsdijk, S. 2007. Entrepreneurial Culture, Regional Innovativeness and Economic Growth. *Journal of Evolutionary Economics*, 17: 187–210.

Bisin, A. and Verdier, T. 2001. The Economics of Cultural Transmission and the Dynamics of Preferences. *Journal of Economic Theory*, 97: 298–319.

Blomkvist, K. and Drogendijk, R. 2016. Chinese Outward Foreign Direct Investments in Europe. *European Journal of International Management*, 10(3): 343–358.

Bloomberg. 2012. Heirs of Mao's Comrades Rise as New Capitalist Nobility. *Bloomberg.com*: December 26.

Bloomberg News. 2020. Xi Says Party Can't Be Split From Masses in Rebuke to U.S. *Bloomberg*, September 3 (www.bloomberg.com/news/articles/2020-09-03/xi-says-he-ll-never-back-down-in-facing-foreign-interference): Accessed November 19, 2020.

Bo, Z. 2015. Who Are China's 'Princelings'? *The Diplomat*, November 24 (https://thediplomat.com/2015/11/who-are-chinas-princelings/): Accessed November 25, 2020.

Boas, F. 1963 (1911). *The Mind of Primitive Man*. New York: Collier Books.

Bombardier, I. 2010. High speed Train CRH1 – China.

Bradsher, K. 2010. China Sees Growth Engine in a Web of Fast Trains, *The New York Times*.

Bradsher, R. 2004. Informal Lenders in China Pose Risks to Banking System, *The New York Times*.

Brady, A.-M. 2020. Holding a Pen in One Hand, Gripping a Gun in the Other. *The Wilson Center*, July (www.wilsoncenter.org/sites/default/files/media/uploads/documents/2020-07-HoldingAPenInOneHand-Brady.pdf): Accessed December 20, 2020.

Brandenburger, A. and Nalebuff, B. 1997. *Co-opetition*. New York: Doubleday.

Brander, J. 1986. Rationale for Strategic Trade and Industrial Policy. In P. Krugman (ed.), *Strategic Trade Policy and the New International Economics*. Cambridge: MIT Press.

Brander, J. and Spencer, B. 1985. Export Subsidies and International Market Share Rivalry. *Journal of International Economics*, 16: 83–100.

Brandt, L. and Rawski, T. 2019. *Policy, Regulation, and Innovation in China's Electricity and Telecom Industries*: London: Cambridge University Press.

Buckley, C. 2020. China's 'Big Cannon' Blasted Xi. Now He's Been Jailed for 18 Years. *The New York Times*, September 22 (www.nytimes.com/2020/09/22/world/asia/china-ren-zhiqiang-tycoon.html): Accessed November 18, 2020.

Buckley, P. J., Doh, J. P., and Benischke, M. 2017. Towards a Renaissance in International Business Research? Big Questions, Grand Challenges, and the Future of IB Scholarship. *Journal of International Business Studies*, 48(9): 1045–1064.

Buysse, K. and Essers, D. 2019. Cheating Tiger, Tech-Savvy Dragon: Are Western Concerns about 'Unfair Trade'and 'Made in China 2025' Justified? *Economic Review/National Bank of Belgium*. Brussels, 2004, currens: 1–23.

Cai, X. 2019. Using Reverse Thinking to Comment on Big Country's Economic Policies. *New Century Net*, October 19 (https://2newcenturynet.blogspot.com/2019/10/blog-post_26.html): Accessed November 4, 2019.

Cai, X. 2021. The Party That Failed: An Insider Breaks with Beijing. *Foreign Affairs*, January/February (www.foreignaffairs.com/articles/china/2020-12-04/chinese-communist-party-failed): Accessed December 17, 2020.

Caixin. 2018. Chart of the Day: The Growth of China's Confucius Institutes. *Caixin*, November 30 (www.caixinglobal.com/2018-11-30/chart-of-the-day-the-growth-of-chinas-confucius-institutes-101354066.html): Accessed March 10, 2020.

Campbell, C. 2017. China Says It's Building the New Silk Road. Here Are Five Things to Know Ahead of a Key Summit. *Time*, May 12 (http://time.com/4776845/china-xi-jinping-belt-road-initiative-obor/): April 21, 2019.

Canada, I. a. R. B. o. 2020. Responses to Information Requests. *Immigration and Refugee Board of Canada*, October (www.justice.gov/eoir/page/file/1328951/download): Accessed November 19, 2020.

The Carter Center. 2020. The Carter Center. *The Carter Center* (www.cartercenter.org/): Accessed December 20, 2020.

Catino, M. 2015. Mafia Rules: The Role of Criminal Codes in Mafia Organizations. *Scandinavian Journal of Management*, 31: 536–548.

CCTV.com. 2019. 《2019中国国有经济发展报告》发布 国有经济布局和结构调整取得重要进展. *CCTV.com*, December 8 (https://news.cctv.com/2019/12/08/ARTIoS4j83bUZJBLdehioRgb191208.shtml): Accessed December 14, 2020.

Central Commission for Disciplinary Inspection. 2018. 坚持四项基本原则，任何时候我都没有让过步！. *Central Commission for Disciplinary Inspection*, May 22 (www.ccdi.gov.cn/yaowen/201805/t20180522_172323.html): Accessed December 13, 2020.

Cha, A. E. 2008. Solar Energy Firms Leave Waste behind in China. *Washington Post*, 9.

Chan, T. F. 2018. Take a Look at the Letter China's Aviation Authority Sent to 36 Foreign Airlines That the White House Called 'Nonsense.' *Business Insider*, May 8 (www.businessinsider.com/letter-china-aviation-authority-sent-to-36-foreign-airlines-2018-5): Accessed December 31, 2020.

Chatterji, S. K. 2020. Wider Connotations of Chinese 'Salami Slicing'. *Asia Times*, October 22 (https://asiatimes.com/2020/10/wider-connotations-of-chinese-salami-slicing/): Accessed February 28, 2021.

Chaudhury, D. R. 2019. Tanzania President Terms China's BRI Port Project Exploitative. *The Economic Times*, July 6 (https://economictimes.indiatimes.com/news/international/world-news/tanzania-president-terms-bri-port-project-exploitative/articleshow/70109612.cms): Accessed February 28, 2021.

Chen, J. 2013. *A Middle Class without Democracy: Economic Growth and the Prospects for Democratization in China*. New York: Oxford University Press.

Chen, Z. 2007. 從中宣部 2007 年宣傳口徑看中共當前走向. *chinanews.co*, March 15 (www.chinanews.co/news/gb/pubvp/2007/03/200703150818.shtml): Accessed November 20, 2020.

Chen, Z. 2012. Political Reform Is the Prerequisite of Sustainable Economic Growth. *Yanhuangchunqiu*, December (www.chinaaffairs.org/gb/detail.asp?id=127515): March 22, 2013.

China Daily. 2010. How to Nicely Tell Foreigners We "Hide Our Capabilities And Bide Our Time?" *China Daily*, June 25(http://language.chinadaily.com.cn/trans/2010-06/25/content_10020700.htm): Accessed February 27, 2019.

China Digital Times. 2012. "裸官"普遍，中共信心大危機. *China Digital Times*, June 4 (https://china-digital-times.github.io/?/id/229336): Accessed December 20, 2020.

China Economic Weekly. 2016. 中国公务员总数首次披露：716.7万人. *Xinhuanet.com*, June 21(www.xinhuanet.com/politics/2016-06/21/c_129077723.htm): Accessed November 19, 2020.

China Education Online. 2017. 中国留学生在世界主要留学目的国人数情况. *eol.cn* (www.eol.cn/html/lx/report2017/yi.shtml#:~:text=%E6%8D%AE%E6%95%99%E8%82%B2%E9%83%A8%E7%9A%84%E6%9C%80%E6%96%B0,%E8%87%AA%E8%B4%B9%E7%95%99%E5%AD%A649.82%E4%B8%87%E4%BA%BA%E3%80%82&text=%E5%A6%82%E5%9B%BE1%E6%89%80%E7%A4%BA,%E6%80%BB%E4%BA%BA%E6%95%B0%E7%9A%8490%25%E4%BB%A5%E4%B8%8A%E3%80%82): Accessed December 20, 2020.

China Global Television Network. 2020. Wang Yi: China Has No Intention to Pick a Fight with U.S. *China Global Television Network*, December 19 (https://news.cgtn.com/news/2020-12-18/Wang-Yi-China-has-no-intention-to-pick-a-fight-with-U-S–WkmVDuD040/index.html): Accessed December 19, 2020.

China International Publishing Group, Academy of Contemporary China and World Studies, and China Academy of Translation. 2019. *Keywords to Understand China: 19th National Congress of the Communist Party of China*. Beijing: New World Press.

China National Radio. 2014. 邓小平留下丰富外交遗产 "韬光养晦"至今仍有现实意义. www.cnr.cn, August 22 (http://news.cnr.cn/special/dengxiaoping/latest/20140822/t20140822_516278531.shtml): Accessed November 15, 2020.

China News Agency. 第十届世界华文传媒论坛将开幕 400 余家华媒齐聚石家庄. *Overseas China Affairs Office of the State Council* (www.gqb.gov.cn/news/2019/1011/47035.shtml): Accessed December 10, 2020.

China Power Team. 2020. How Well-Off Is China's Middle Class? *ChinaPower*, October 29 (https://chinapower.csis.org/china-middle-class/): Accessed November 18, 2020.

China Watch. 2008. China Watch: An Exchange between Gordon G. Chang and Readers on His March 2008 Piece, "The End of the Chinese Miracle?" *Commentary*, June (www.commentarymagazine.com/articles/china-watch/): Accessed October 17, 2019.

Chinanews.com. 2008. 史海：毛泽东是否说过自己就像个"执伞孤僧"？ *Chinanews.com*, January 4 (www.chinanews.com/cul/news/2008/01-04/1123837.shtml): Accessed November 29, 2020.

Chinese Communist Party. 1995. 中共中央关于制定国民经济和社会发展"九五"计划和2010年远景目标的建议. *China.com.cn*, December 17 (www.china.com.cn/news/zhuanti/zgztk/2008-12/17/content_16961083.htm): Accessed December 16, 2020.

Chinese Communist Party. 2017. *Constitution of the Communist Party of China*. Beijing: Chinese Communist Party.

Chinese Communist Party. 2019. 中共中央关于坚持和完善中国特色社会主义制度推进国家治理体系和治理能力现代化若干重大问题的决定. *Xinhuanet*, November 15 (www.xinhuanet.com/politics/2019-11/05/c_1125195786.htm): Accessed December 13, 2020.

Chinese Communist Party. 2020. 中国共产党统一战线工作条例 (Chinese Communist Party United Front Word Rules). In C. C. Party (ed.): Accessed 2/26/2021. Beijing: Chinese Communist Party. (www.xinhuanet.com/politics/zywj/2021-01/05/c_1126949202.htm).

Chinese Economists. 2019. A Thousand Year Plan: 4.25 Million Will Relocate to Xiongan from Beijing, with a List of Central Level Firms. *eNewsTree.com*, September 27 (https://enewstree.com/discuz/forum.php?mod=viewthread&tid=236210): Accessed November 4, 2019.

Chinese Government. 2000. List of Currently Important Industries, Products, and Technologies to Be Encouraged by the State (1). *Chinese Government*, September 21, 2019 (www.cctv.com/news/china/20000921/481.html): Accessed November 30, 2019.

Chinese Government. 2005. Temporary Regulations to Speed up Industrial Strutural Adjustment *Chinese Government*, December 21 (www.gov.cn/zwgk/2005-12/21/content_133214.htm): Accessed December 1, 2019.

Chinese Government. 2011. 《中国的和平发展》白皮书（全文）. *Chinese Government*, September (www.fmprc.gov.cn/web/zyxw/t855789.shtml): Accessed December 31, 2020.

Chinese Government. 2017. Regulations on Enterprise Naming Restrictions. *State Administration for Industry and Commerce*, July 3, 2017 (http://wsdj.saic.gov.cn/saicfile/mcdj/material/doc_3.pdf): Accessed November 4, 2019.

Chinese Government. 2019a. 2018 Blacklist of Untrustworthy. *Chinese Government*, February 19 (www.gov.cn/fuwu/2019-02/19/content_5366674 .htm): Accessed November 6, 2019.

Chinese Government. 2019b. China's Economic Growth Target Set between 6% and 6.5%. *www.gov.cn*, March 5 (www.gov.cn/zhengce/2019-03/05/content_ 5370859.htm): Accessed November 3, 2019.

Chinese Government. 2019c. Government Officials Punishment Law (Draft for Comment). *The National People's Congress of the PRC*, October 8 to November 6 (www.npc.gov.cn/npc/c8194/201909/89a8074a965d45da82130 5565c491bf9.shtml): Accessed November 4, 2019.

Chisholm, H. 1911. *Jean-Baptiste Colbert*. London: Cambridge University Press.

Churchill, O. 2021. Joe Biden Calls China the 'Most Serious Competitor' to the US, in First Foreign Policy Speech. *Microsoft News*, February 4 (www.msn.com/ en-xl/news/other/joe-biden-calls-china-the-e2-80-98most-serious-competitor-e2-80-99-to-the-us-in-first-foreign-policy-speech-as-president/ar-BB1doJhz): Accessed March 8, 2021.

Churchill, O. and Wu, W. 2019. US Pushes 'Needed Structural Changes' on Forced Technology Transfers and IP Protection during China Trade Talks, but No Sign If Any New Agreements Were Made. *South China Morning Post*, January 9 (www .scmp.com/print/news/china/article/2181436/us-negotiators-push-needed-struc tural-changes-forced-technology-transfers): Accessed September 14, 2019.

CIA. 2020a. The World Factbook. *CIA.gov* (www.cia.gov/cia/publications/fact book/index.html): Accessed November 16, 2020.

CIA. 2020b. The World Factbook www.cia.gov, Accessed April 14, 2019.

Clairmonte, F. 1959. Friedrich List and the Historical Concept of Balanced Growth. *Indian Economic Review*, 4(3): 24–44.

Clinton, B. 2000. Full Text of Clinton's Speech on China Trade Bill. *Paul H. Nitze School of Advanced International Studies of the Johns Hopkins University*, March 9 (www.iatp.org/sites/default/files/Full_Text_of_Clintons_Speech_on_ China_Trade_Bi.htm): Accessed January 1, 2021.

Coase, R. 1937. The Nature of the Firm. *Economica*, 386–405.

Collis, D. and Montgomery, C. 1997. Chapter 5: Organization Limits to Firm Scope. In *Corporate Strategy: Resource and the Scope of the Firm*: Boston: Irwin McGraw-Hill.

CRRC. 2014. Back to the Future Returning Manufacturing to Springfield, Massachusetts. *CRRC Official Website*, (www.crrcgc.cc/ma): Accessed December 9, 2019.

Cui, T. 2020. 中国驻美大使崔天凯：坚决反对"新冷战"和"脱钩". *youtube.com*, October 2 (www.youtube.com/watch?v=KgkuXAJQabs): Accessed December 21, 2020.

Dahl, R. 1971. *Polyarchy: Participation and Opposition*. New Haven: Yale University Press.

Dale, H. C. 2018. A Year Later, Still No Justice for Chinese Voice of America Journalists. *The Heritage Foundation*, May 18 (www.heritage.org/civil-soci ety/commentary/year-later-still-no-justice-chinese-voice-america-journalists): Accessed April 15, 2019.

Dan, L. 2020. German Mechanical Manufacturers Hold Hardline on China. *Radio France Internationale*, January 13 (www.rfi.fr/cn/20200113-%E5%BE%B7% E5%9B%BD%E6%9C%BA%E6%A2%B0%E5%88%B6%E9%80%A0%E5% 95%86%E5%AF%B9%E4%B8%AD%E5%9B%BD%E6%8C%81%E5%BC% BA%E7%A1%AC%E6%80%81%E5%BA%A6): Accessed January 16, 2020.

Delaney, R. 2020. US President-elect Joe Biden Calls for Stronger Trade Coalitions against China, as EU Seems Close to a Deal. *South China Morning Post*, December 29 (www.scmp.com/news/china/diplomacy/article/3115615/us-president-elect-joe-biden-calls-stronger-trade-coalitions): Accessed December 31, 2020.

Delios, A. 2017. The Death and Rebirth (?) of International Business Research. *Journal of Management Studies*, 54(3): 391–397.

Demers, J. C. 2020. Assistant Attorney General John C. Demers Delivers Remarks Announcing People's Republic of China Related Arrests. *U.S. Department of Justice*, October 28 (www.justice.gov/opa/speech/assistant-attorney-general-john-c-demers-delivers-remarks-announcing-peoples-republic): Accessed December 20, 2020.

Deng, X. 1962. 怎样恢复农业生产. Beijing: People's Press.

Deng, X. 1985. 邓小平: 让一部分人先富起来. *News of the Communist Party of China*, October 23 (http://cpc.people.com.cn/GB/34136/2569304.html): Accessed November 14, 2020.

Dettmer, O. 2020. China's Industrial Policy Has Worked Better than Critics Think. *The Economist*, January 2 (www.economist.com/finance-and-economics/2020/ 01/02/chinas-industrial-policy-has-worked-better-than-critics-think): Accessed January 15, 2020.

Dictionary.com. 2005. Propaganda. *Dictionary.com*, (www.dictionary.com/ browse/propaganda): Accessed November 5, 2020.

Diresta, R., Miller, C., Molter, V., Pomfret, J., and Tiffert, G. 2020. *Telling China's Story: The Chinese Communist Party's Campaign to Shape Global Narratives*. Stanford, CA: Hoover Institution.

Dirlik, A. 2012. The Idea of a 'China model': A Critical Discussion. *China Information*, 26(3): 277–302.

Dixit, A. 2004. *Lawlessness and Economics: Alternative Modes of Governance*. Princeton, NJ: Princeton University Press.

Dobbins, J. and Wyne, A. 2018. Engagement vs. Competition: The China Policy Debate. *The Rand Blog*, December 31 (www.rand.org/blog/2018/12/engage ment-vs-competition-the-china-policy-debate.html): Accessed October 19, 2020.

Dou, E. 2017. Jailed for a Text: China's Censors Are Spying on Mobile Chat Groups. *The Wall Street Journal*, December 8 (www.wsj.com/articles/jailed-for-a-text-chinas-censors-are-spying-on-mobile-chat-groups-1512665007): Accessed November 18, 2020.

Dreher, A., Fuchs, A., Parks, B., Strange, A. M., and Tierney, M. J. 2016. Apples and Dragon Fruits: The Determinants of Aid and Other Forms of State Financing from China to Africa. *University of Heidelberg Department of Economics Discussion Paper Series* (620).

Dreyer, J. T. 2010. *China's Political System: Modernization and Tradition* (7th ed.). New York: Longman.

Dreyer, M. 2019. China NBA: How One Tweet Derailed the NBA's China Game Plan. *BBC*, October 10, 2019(www.bbc.com/news/world-asia-china-49995985): Accessed November 4, 2019.

DW. 2020. 报告: 中国假信息深入台湾社群 直播主成协力者. *DW*, October 24 (www .dw.com/zh/%E5%A0%B1%E5%91%8A%E4%B8%AD%E5%9C%8B%E5% 81%87%E8%A8%8A%E6%81%AF%E6%B7%B1%E5%85%A5%E5%8F%B0% E7%81%A3%E7%A4%BE%E7%BE%A4-%E7%9B%B4%E6%92%AD%E4% B8%BB%E6%88%90%E5%8D%94%E5%8A%9B%E8%80%85/a-55383626): Accessed December 10, 2020.

DWnews.com. 2018. China Implements Strategy in Africa in a Low-Key Style: Review of China-Trained African Presidents. *DWnews.com*, October 1 (http:// culture.dwnews.com/history/news/2018-09-30/60088484_all.html): Accessed April 21, 2019.

Earth Policy Institute. 2015. World Solar Photovoltaics Installations, 1996–2013, with Projection to 2015. *Earth Policy Institute*, April 16, 2015 (www.earth-policy.org/?/data_center/C23/): Accessed December 9, 2019.

Econ Journal Watch. 2011. Symposium: Property: A Bundle of Rights? *Econ Journal Watch*, 8(3 (Sept)): https://econjwatch.org/issues/volume-8-issue-3-september-2011.

The Economist. 1994. The Ultimate Takeaway, *The Economist*: 36.

The Economist. 2000. China: Tangled Web. The Economist, 355(8165): CS7 (1page).

The Economist. 2014. Tiger in the Net. *The Economist*, December 11 (www .economist.com/china/2014/12/11/tiger-in-the-net): Accessed November 20, 2020.

The Economist. 2017. What Is China's Belt and Road Initiative? *The Economist,* May 14 (www.economist.com/the-economist-explains/2017/05/14/what-is-chinas-belt-and-road-initiative): Accessed December 9, 2019.

enelsubte.com. 2014. CSR Acquires EMFER and Lands in Argentina. enelsubte.com.

Eun, J.-H. and Lee, K. 2002. Is an Industrial Policy Possible in China? The Case of the Automobile Industry. *Journal of International and Area Studies,* 9(2): 1–21.

European Commission. 2019a. EU–China: A Strategic Outlook. *European Commission,* March 12 (https://ec.europa.eu/commission/sites/beta-political/files/communication-eu-china-a-strategic-outlook.pdf): Accessed December 29, 2020.

European Commission. 2019b. EU–China: A Strategic Outlook. High Representative of the Union for Foreign Affairs, Security Policy. Joint Communication to the European Parliament (12 March).

Fallows, J. 1993. How the World Works. *The Atlantic,* December (www.theatlantic.com/magazine/archive/1993/12/how-the-world-works/305854/): Accessed December 6, 2019.

Fan, C. 2020. The Inescapable Circle of United Front for the Taiwanese. *Apple Daily,* October 11 (https://tw.appledaily.com/forum/20201011/NJ47QP5PIBGRZFXC4M36RR7DRE/): Accessed October 18, 2020.

Feng, B. 2013. Chinese Bodyguards, When Police Won't Do. *The New York Times,* October 8 (https://cn.nytimes.com/lifestyle/20131018/t18bodyguard/en-us/): Accessed November 25, 2020.

Feng, E. 2018. China's Globalisation Paradox. *Financial Times,* July 13.

Flint, C. 2006. *Introduction to Geopolitics.* London: Routledge.

FlorCruz, J. 2012. Q&A: Why the Gu Kailai Trial Is Important, *CNN.com.*

Fogel, R. W. and Engerman, S. L. 1995 (1974). *Time on the Cross: The Economics of American Negro Slavery.* New York: W. W. Norton and Company.

Fong, D. 2018. China's Ghost Towns Haunt Its Economy. *The Wall Street Journal,* June 15 (www.wsj.com/articles/chinas-ghost-towns-haunt-its-economy-1529076819): Accessed November 16, 2020.

Foran, H., Beach, S., Slep, A., Heyman, R., and Wamboldt, M. 2013. *Family Problems and Family Violence.* New York: Springer Publishing Company.

Forsythe, M. 2009. Is China's Economy Speeding off the Rails? *The New York Times.*

Franke, R. H., Hofstede, G., and Bond, M. 1991. Cultural Roots of Economic Performance: A Research Note. *Strategic Management Journal,* 12(Summer): 165–173.

Fraser Institute. 2020. Economic Freedom of the World: 2020 Annual Report. *Fraser Institute* (www.fraserinstitute.org/resource-file?nid=13665&fid=14767): Accessed November 26, 2020.

Freedom House. 2020. Freedom in the World 2020. *Freedom House* (https://free
domhouse.org/countries/freedom-world/scores?sort=asc&order=Total%20Score
%20and%20Status): Accessed November 19, 2020.

Freeman, C. 1995. The National System of Innovation in Historical Perspective.
Cambridge Journal of Economics, 19: 5–24.

Friedman, T. 2020. Biden Made Sure 'Trump Is Not Going to Be President for Four
More Years.' *The New York Times*, December 2 (www.nytimes.com/2020/12/
02/opinion/biden-interview-mcconnell-china-iran.html): Accessed December
17, 2020.

Gambetta, D. 1988. Mafia: The Price of Distrust. In D. Gambetta (ed.), *Trust* ,
pp. 158–210. New York: Basil Blackwell.

Gan, N. 2020. China Is Installing Surveillance Cameras Outside People's Front
Doors . . . and Sometimes Inside Their Homes. *CNN*, April 28 (www.cnn.com/
2020/04/27/asia/cctv-cameras-china-hnk-intl/index.html): Accessed December
14, 2020.

Gao, C. 2019. Xi: China Must Never Adopt Constitutionalism, Separation of
Powers, or Judicial Independence. *The Diplomat*, February 19 (https://
thediplomat.com/2019/02/xi-china-must-never-adopt-constitutionalism-separ
ation-of-powers-or-judicial-independence/): Accessed March 14, 2020.

Gao, F. 2020. 中国"人脸识别首案"宣判 ： 强制刷脸违约. *Radio Free Asia*, November 23
(www.rfa.org/mandarin/yataibaodao/renquanfazhi/gf1-11232020070811.html):
Accessed December 21, 2020.

Gazette, T. R. 2015. Chinese rolling stock manufacturers merge to form CRRC
Corp. *The Railway Gazette*, June 2 (www.railwaygazette.com/news/business/
single-view/view/chinese-rolling-stock-manufacturers-merge-to-form-crrc-corp
.html): Accessed December 9, 2019.

Gertz, B. 2017. Dissident Reveals Secret Chinese Intelligence Plans Targeting U.S.
The Washington Beacon, October 9 (https://freebeacon.com/national-security/
dissident-reveals-secret-chinese-intelligence-plans-targeting-u-s/): Accessed
July 20, 2018.

Girard, B. 2019. The Real Danger of China's National Intelligence Law. *The
Diplomat*, February 23 (https://thediplomat.com/2019/02/the-real-danger-of-
chinas-national-intelligence-law/): Accessed November 4, 2019.

GlobeScan. 2012. Public Remains Concerned over Wealth Inequalities: Global Poll.
GlobeScan, July 5 (https://globescan.com/public-remains-concerned-over-
wealth-inequalities-global-poll/): Accessed November 29, 2020.

Gongshiwang. 2012. Call for Reform Consensus Letter. *Chinaaffairs.org* (December
25).

Granato, J., Inglehart, R., and Leblang, D. 1996. The Effect of Cultural Values on Economic Development: Theory, Hypotheses, and Some Empirical Tests. *American Journal of Political Science*, 40(3): 607–631.

Griffiths, J. 2017. Just What Is This One Belt, One Road Thing Anyway? *CNN*, May 11 (www.cnn.com/2017/05/11/asia/china-one-belt-one-road-explainer/index .html): Accessed April 21, 2019.

Groot, G. 2016. *The Expansion of the United Front under Xi Jinping*: Canberra: ANU Press.

Gu, L. 2020. 北京再严词反对脱钩 似押注美国大选. August 24 (www.rfi.fr/cn/%E4% B8%AD%E5%9B%BD/20200824-%E5%8C%97%E4%BA%AC%E5%86%8D %E4%B8%A5%E8%AF%8D%E5%8F%8D%E5%AF%B9%E8%84%B1%E9% 92%A9-%E4%BC%BC%E6%8A%BC%E6%B3%A8%E7%BE%8E%E5%9B% BD%E5%A4%A7%E9%80%89): Accessed December 21, 2020.

Guancha.cn. 2014. 福喜员工喊冤 指责媒体歪曲事实. *Guancha.cn*, July 24 (www .guancha.cn/society/2014_07_24_249930.shtml): Accessed December 11, 2020.

Guancha.cn. 2015. 最大"高考工厂"安徽毛坦厂中学学生坠楼 家人与校方冲突. *Guancha.cn*, December 31 (www.guancha.cn/Education/2015_12_31_ 346520.shtml): Accessed November 28, 2020.

The Guardian. 2011. How China Dominates Solar Power. *The Guardian*, September 12 (www.theguardian.com/environment/2011/sep/12/how-china-dominates-solar-power): Accessed November 6, 2019.

Guo, Y., Huy, Q. N., and Xiao, Z. 2017. How Middle Managers Manage the Political Environment to Achieve Market Goals: Insights from China's State-Owned Enterprises. *Strategic Management Journal*, 38: 676–696.

Gwartney, J. and Lawson, R. 2012. *Economic Freedom of the World: 2012 Annual Report*. Toronto: The Fraser Institute.

Hai, Y. 2013. 广东民主人士举牌抗议刑拘刘远东. *Voice of America*, April 9 (www .voachinese.com/a/liuyuandong-china-20130409/1637607.html): Accessed December 19, 2020.

Hanban. 2018. Hanban. *Hanban* (http://english.hanban.org/node_7719.htm): Accessed July 20, 2018.

Hanson, F., Currey, E., and Beattie, T. 2020. The Chinese Communist Party's Coercive Diplomacy. *Australian Strategic Policy Institute* (www.aspi.org.au/ report/chinese-communist-partys-coercive-diplomacy): Accessed December 12, 2020.

Harwit, E. T. C. Q. 2007. Building China's Telecommunications Network: Industrial Policy and the Role of Chinese State-Owned, Foreign and Private Domestic Enterprises. *The China Quarterly*, 190: 311–332.

Hass, R. and Denmark, A. 2020. More Pain than Gain: How the US-China Trade War Hurt America. *The Brookings Institute*, August 7 (www.brookings.edu/blog/order-from-chaos/2020/08/07/more-pain-than-gain-how-the-us-china-trade-war-hurt-america/): Accessed December 21, 2020.

Hasson, P. 2020. China's Propaganda Machine Greased by *The New York Times* and Washington Post: Human Rights Watchdog. *The National Interest*, January 15 (https://news.yahoo.com/chinas-propaganda-machine-greased-york-165900364.html): Accessed December 10, 2020.

Hayes, T. C. 1989. U.S. Chip Gets Patent in Japan, *The New York Times*: A. G. Sulzberger.

He, Q. 2019. *Red Infiltration: Uncovering the Global Expansion by China's Media.* Xinbei City, Taiwan: Eight Flags Culture Press.

Heilmann, S. and Shih, L. 2013. The Rise of Industrial Policy in China, 1978–2012. *Harvard-Yenching Institute Working Paper Series*, 17(7): 1–24.

Heritage Foundation. 2020. 2019 Index of Economic Freedom. *Heritage Foundation* (www.heritage.org/index/ranking): Accessed November 19, 2020.

The Heritage Foundation. 2021. 2021 Index of Economic Freedom. *Heritage Foundation* (www.heritage.org/index/ranking): Accessed March 5, 2021.

Hill, C. L. and Hult, G. T. M. 2019. *International Business: Competing in the Global Marketplace* (12th ed.) New York: McGraw Hill.

Hinshaw, D., Hua, S., and Norman, L. 2020. Pushback on Xi's Vision for China Spreads beyond U.S. *The Wall Street Journal*, December 28 (www.wsj.com/articles/pushback-xi-china-europe-germany-beyond-u-s-11609176287?st=bfjml671idjjbat&reflink=article_email_share): Accessed December 28, 2020.

Hofman, B. and Wu, J. 2009. Explaining China's Development and Reform: World Bank.

Hofstede, G. 2001. *Culture's Consequences: Comparing Values, Behaviors, Institutions and Organizations across Nations.* Thousand Oaks, CA: Sage.

Hofstede, G., Hofstede, G. J., and Minkov, M. 2010. *Cultures and Organizations: Software of the Mind: Intercultural Cooperation and Its Importance for Survival* (3rd ed.) New York: McGraw Hill.

Hofstede Insights. 2021. Hofstede Culture Dimensions. *Hofstede Insights* (www.hofstede-insights.com/product/compare-countries/): Accessed March 4, 2021.

Hook, S. W. and Rumsey, J. G. 2016. The Development Aid Regime at Fifty: Policy Challenges Inside and Out. *International Studies Perspectives*, 17(1): 55–74.

Hoshi, M., Nakafuji, R., and Cho, Y. 2019. China Scrambles to Stem Manufacturing Exodus as 50 Companies Leave. *Nikkei Asian Review*, July 18 (https://asia

.nikkei.com/Economy/Trade-war/China-scrambles-to-stem-manufacturing-exodus-as-50-companies-leave): Accessed September 17, 2019.

hotbak.net. 2020. 外汇管制新规2020年，国家外汇管理政策2020年一览. *hotbak.net*, December 2 (www.hotbak.net/key/2020%E5%B9%B4%E5%A4%96%E6%B1%87%E6%94%BF%E7%AD%96.html#:~:text=%E4%BB%8E2020%E5%B9%B41%E6%9C%88,%E7%AD%89%E9%9D%9E%E9%93%B6%E8%A1%8C%E6%94%AF%E4%BB%98%E6%9C%BA%E6%9E%84%E3%80%82): Accessed December 14, 2020.

Hruska, J. 2019. Report: China's New Comac C919 Jetliner Is Built with Stolen Technology. *ExtremeTech*, October 16 (www.extremetech.com/extreme/300313-report-chinas-new-comac-c919-jetliner-is-built-with-stolen-technology): Accessed October 19, 2019.

Hu, X. 2020. 胡锡进：澳大利亚总折腾 像粘在中国鞋底上的口香糖. *huanqiuwang*, April 28 (https://news.sina.com.cn/c/2020-04-28/doc-iirczymi8761478.shtml): Accessed December 30, 2020.

Hua, C. 2019. Foreign Ministry Spokesperson Hua Chunying's Regular Press Conference on October 23, 2019. *Ministry of Foreign Affairs of China*, October 23 (www.fmprc.gov.cn/mfa_eng/xwfw_665399/s2510_665401/t1710130.shtml): Accessed December 12, 2020.

Huang, C. 2020. Views of Russia and Putin Remain Negative across 14 Nations. *Pew Research Center*, December 16 (www.pewresearch.org/fact-tank/2020/12/16/views-of-russia-and-putin-remain-negative-across-14-nations/): Accessed December 20, 2020.

Huang, Y. 2012. The Key to Bringing Democracy to China: It's Naked Self-Interest, Stupid. *Foreign Policy*, November 19 (www.foreignpolicy.com/articles/2012/2011/2019/the_key_to_bringing_democracy_to_china): Accessed March 18, 2013.

huanqiuwang. 2015. 盘点贪官被抓时反应：杨卫泽求饶万庆良要人搀扶. *huanqiuwang*, March 25 (https://china.huanqiu.com/article/9CaKrnJJcQ3): Accessed December 19, 2020.

huanqiuwang. 2019. 习近平谈全面依法治国. *huanqiuwang*, December 8 (https://china.huanqiu.com/article/9CaKrnKodD7): Accessed December 30, 2020.

Human Rights Watch. 2004. Demolished: Forced Evictions and the Tenants' Rights Movement in China. *Human Rights Watch*, 16(4 (C)): 1–43.

Huntington, S. P. 1991. *The Third Wave: Democratization in the Late 20th Century*: Norman, OK: Oklahoma University.

Huoju., S. 2014. No One Is Allowed to Eat from the Party and Break the Party's Wok. *China Digital Times*, October 26 (https://chinadigitaltimes.net/chinese/2014/10/%E6%80%9D%E6%83%B3%E7%81%AB%E7%82%AC-%E4%B9%

A0%E8%BF%91%E5%B9%B3%EF%BC%9A%E7%BB%9D%E4%B8%8D%
E5%85%81%E8%AE%B8%E5%90%83%E5%85%B1%E4%BA%A7%E5%85%
9A%E7%9A%84%E9%A5%AD%E7%A0%B8%E5%85%B1%E4%BA%A7/):
Accessed November 4, 2019.

Hurt, E. 2019. President Trump Called Former President Jimmy Carter to Talk about China. *NPR*, April 15 (www.npr.org/2019/04/15/713495558/president-trump-called-former-president-jimmy-carter-to-talk-about-china): Accessed April 15, 2019.

IMF. 2019. IMF Data. *IMF Data* (https://data.imf.org/?sk=388DFA60–1D26–4ADE-B505-A05A558D9A42&sId=1479331931186): Accessed May 14, 2019.

Insideprison.com. 2006. False Imprisonment in the Adversarial-Inquisitorial System Debate, *Insideprison.com* (www.insideprison.com/false_imprisonment .asp): Accessed December 11, 2020.

International Energy Agency. 2019. Global EV Outlook 2019. *iea.org* (www.iea.org/gevo2019/): Accessed December 3, 2019.

The Inter-Parliamentary Alliance on China. 2020. The Inter-Parliamentary Alliance on China. *The Inter-Parliamentary Alliance on China* (https://ipac .global/): Accessed December 30, 2020.

Jensen, L. M. 2011. Culture Industry, Power, and the Spectacle of China's 'Confucius Institutes.' In T. B. Weston and L. M. Jensen (eds.), *China in and beyond the Headlines*, 280. Lanham, MD: Rowman & Littlefield.

Ji, E. 2020. "大外宣", 大规模对外国人洗脑. *Voice of America*, July 16 (www.voachi nese.com/a/chinese-influence-campaign-become-more-assertive-20200715/ 5504143.html): Accessed December 10, 2020.

Ji, K. 2013. Startup Team: How to Register Your Business. *Zhihu.com*, January 13 (www.zhihu.com/question/19585093): Accessed November 4, 2019.

Jia, H. 2018. China's Plan to Recruit Talented Researchers. *Nature*, 553(7688): S8.

Jiang, F. and Li, X. 2010. Direct Market Intervention and Restrict Competition: The Orientation of China's Industrial Policy and Its Fundamental Defects. *China Industrial Economics*, 270(Sept): 26–36.

Jiang, Y. 2014, June 5. 一座被高考魔化的城 (A City Demonized by the College Entrance Exam), 搜狐大视野>新闻>《发现》 Vol. (http://pic.news.sohu.com/ group-570015.shtml#0): Sohu.com. Accessed Decmebr 20, 2020.

Jie, X. 2020. 美国历任贸易代表集体发声：施压中国, 重返亚太. *Voice of America*, December 19 (www.voachinese.com/a/china-trade-aisa-economy-20201218/ 5705193.html): Accessed December 19, 2020.

Johnson, C. 1982. *MITI and the Japanese Miracle: The Growth of Industrial Policy: 1925–1975*: Stanford, CA: Stanford University Press.

Johnson, I. 2011. High-Speed Trains in China to Run Slower, Ministry Says, *The New York Times*.

Johnson, J. and Lenartowicz, T. 1998. Culture, Freedom and Economic Growth: Do Cultural Values Explain Economic Growth? *Journal of World Business*, 33(4): 332–356.

Johnson, K. and Gramer, R. 2020. The Great Decoupling. *Foreign Policy*, May 14 (https://foreignpolicy.com/2020/05/14/china-us-pandemic-economy-ten sions-trump-coronavirus-covid-new-cold-war-economics-the-great-decoupling/): Accessed December 22, 2020.

Jones, T. Y. and Lim, B. K. 2013. China's New Leader: Reformist or Conservative? *Reuters*, January 11(https://uk.reuters.com/article/china-pol itics-xi-idINDEE90B01D20130112): Accessed November 26, 2020.

Jourdan, A. 2015. U.S. Supplier in China Food Scare Takes Aim at Shanghai Regulator. *Reuters*, January 7(https://fr.reuters.com/article/china-foodsafety-criticism/u-s-supplier-in-china-food-scare-takes-aim-at-shanghai-regulator-idUSL1N0UM14T20150107): Accessed December 11, 2020.

Kalathil, S. and Boas, T. 2003. *Open Networks, Closed Regimes: The Impact of the Internet on Authoritarian Rule*. Washington, DC: Carnegie Endowment for International Peace.

Kato, T. and Long, C. 2006. Executive Compensation, Firm Performance, and Corporate Governance in China: Evidence from Firms Listed in the Shanghai and Shenzhen Stock Exchanges. *Economic Development and Cultural Change*, 54(4): 945–974.

Kaufmann, D., Kraay, A., and Mastruzzi, M. 2020. The Worldwide Governance Indicators. *The World Bank Data*, 2020 (https://info.worldbank.org/govern ance/wgi/Home/Reports): Accessed November 24, 2020.

Kawasaki. 2004. Kawasaki Wins High-Speed Train Order for China.

Kenderdine, T. 2017. China's Industrial Policy, Strategic Emerging Industries and Space Law. *Asia & the Pacific Policy Studies*, 4(2): 325–342.

Kenton, W. 2020. Firm. *Investopedia*, October 23 (www.investopedia.com/terms/f/firm.asp): Accessed December 13, 2020.

Ker, M. 2017. China's High-Speed Rail Diplomacy. *U.S.-China Economic and Security Review Commission*, February 21 (file:///C:/Users/sli/Downloads/China's%20High%20Speed%20Rail%20Diplomacy.pdf): Accessed May 19, 2020.

Kilby, P. 2017. *China and the United States as Aid Donors: Past and Future Trajectories*. Honolulu, HI: East-West Center.

Kiser, E. and Barzel, Y. 1991. The Origins of Democracy in England. *Rationality and Society*, 3(4): 396–422.

Kliman, D., Doshi, R., Lee, K., and Cooper, Z. 2019. Grading China's Belt and Road. *Center for A New American Security*, April (https://s3.amazonaws.com/files .cnas.org/CNAS+Report_China+Belt+and+Road_final.pdf): Accessed April 21, 2019.

Kobayashi, Y. 1993. The Role and Significance of Japanese Industrial Policy: Its Estimation and Recent Issue. *Economic Journal of Hokkaido University*, 22: 69–90.

Kornai, J. 2019. Economists Share Blame for China's 'Monstrous' Turn. *Financial Times*, July 10 (www.ft.com/content/f10ccb26-a16f-11e9-a282-2df48f366f7d): Accessed October 17, 2019.

Kozy, A. 2019. Huge Fan of Your Work: How TURBINE PANDA and China's Top Spies Enabled Beijing to Cut Corners on the C919 Passenger Jet: Part I. *Crowdstrike*, October 14 (www.crowdstrike.com/blog/huge-fan-of-your-work-part-1/): Accessed October 19, 2019.

Kruger, P. 2009. China's Legal Lion. *NYU Law Magazine* (https://blogs.law.nyu .edu/magazine/2009/jerome-cohen-profile/): Accessed November 23, 2020.

Krugman, P. 1992. Does the New Trade Theory Require a New Trade Policy? *World Economy*, 15(4): 423–441.

Krugman, P., Obstfeld, M., and Melitz, M. 2012. *International Economics*. Boston: Addison-Wesley.

Krugman, P. R. 1987. Is Free Trade Passe? *Journal of Economic Perspectives*, 1: 131–144.

Kuo, L. 2017. Beijing Is Cultivating the Next Generation of African Elites by Training Them in China. *Quartz*, December 14 (https://qz.com/1119447/ china-is-training-africas-next-generation-of-leaders/): Accessed July 20, 2018.

Kuran, T. 2009. Explaining the Economic Trajectories of Civilizations: The Systemic Approach. *Journal of Economic Behavior & Organization*, 71: 593–605.

Kwok, V. W.-y. 2009. How Japan Profits from China's Plans, Vol. 2019. *Forbes*.

Landes, D. 1998. *The Wealth and Poverty of Nations: Why Are Some So Rich and Others So Poor*. New York: Norton.

Landes, D. 2006. Why Europe and the West? Why Not China? *Journal of Economic Perspectives*, 20(2): 3-22.

Laomao, S. 2019. 华为任正非：我的导师就是毛主席. *zhihu.com*, May 27 (https:// zhuanlan.zhihu.com/p/67175095): Accessed November 29, 2020.

Lattemann, C., Fetscherin, M., Alon, I., Li, S., and Schneider, A. 2009. CSR Communication Intensity in Chinese and Indian Multinational Companies. *Corporate Governance : An International Review*, 17(4): 426–442.

Lau, K. L. A. and Young, A. 2013. Why China Shall not Completely Transit from a Relation Based to a Rule Based Governance Regime: A Chinese Perspective. *Corporate Governance: An International Review*, 21(6): 577–585.

Lau, L. 2020. 中国面临的最大风险是再次与世界其他国家隔绝. *Sina.com*, October 14 (https://finance.sina.com.cn/review/jcgc/2020-10-14/doc-iiznctkc5561008 .shtml?cre=tianyi&mod=pcpager_fin&loc=17&r=9&rfunc=100&tj=none&tr=9): Accessed December 21, 2020.

Lentino, A. 2019. This Chinese Facial Recognition Start-up Can Identify a Person in Seconds. *CNBC*, May 16 (www.cnbc.com/2019/05/16/this-chinese-facial-recog nition-start-up-can-id-a-person-in-seconds.html): Accessed December 21, 2020.

Lewis, O. 1959. *Five Families: Mexican Case Studies in the Culture of Poverty*. New York: Basic Books.

Li, A. J. 2018. Learning to Survive without WeChat. *The New York Times*, September 20 (www.nytimes.com/2018/09/20/opinion/learning-to-survive-without-wechat-in-china.html?_ga=2.173287584.244173984.1607440079-748572935.1606359212): Accessed December 18, 2020.

Li, H. 1999a. *A History of China's Thought Movement: 1949–1989*. Hong Kong: Cosmos Books.

Li, H., Tang, J., and Zuo, J. 2017a. Government Intervention, Ultimate Control Right and Enterprise Employment Behavior: Research Based on Chinese Private Listed Companies (in Chinese). *Journal of Finance and Economics*, 43(7): 20–31.

Li, J. 2014. 申纪兰被爆料全家都是高官巨富. *New Tang Dynasty Television*, April 17 (www.ntdtv.com/gb/2014/04/17/a1103540.html): Accessed December 15, 2020.

Li, J. 2019a. A US Official Says Tech Giants Alibaba and Tencent Present Similar Risks as Huawei. *Quartz*, September 13, 2019 (https://qz.com/1708662/chinese-tech-giants-tools-of-the-communist-party-us-official/): Accessed November 4, 2019.

Li, M. 2011. High-Speed Rail Forced to Stop Many Short-Haul Routes of Civil Aviation, *Beijing News*.

Li, P.-Y., Huang, K.-F., Xu, K., and Yu, C.-M. J. 2018. The Effect of Local Environment on Innovation: A Comparison of Local and Foreign Firms in China. *European Journal of International Management*, 12(4): 447–471.

Li, P. and Jourdan, A. 2018. Mercedes-Benz Apologizes to Chinese for Quoting Dalai Lama. *Reuters*, February 6 (www.reuters.com/article/us-mercedes-benz-china-gaffe/mercedes-benz-apologizes-to-chinese-for-quoting-dalai-lama-idUSKBN1FQ1FJ): Accessed December 13, 2020.

Li, R. 2013a. Seven Subjects off Limits for Teaching, Chinese Universities Told. *South China Morning Post*, May 10 (www.scmp.com/news/china/article/

1234453/seven-subjects-limits-teaching-chinese-universities-told): Accessed November 14, 2020.

Li, S. 1988. The Road to Freedom: Can Communist Societies Evolve into Democracy? *World Affairs*, 150(3): 183.

Li, S. 1999. Relation-Based versus Rule-Based Governance: An Explanation of the East Asian Miracle and Asian Crisis. Paper presented at the American Economic Association Annual Meeting in New York, January. Listed on the Social Science Research Network (http://papers.ssrn.com/paper.taf?abstract_id=200208). Reprinted in *Review of International Economics*, 2003, 11(4): 651–73, American Economic Association Annual Meeting in New York, New York.

Li, S. 2002a. The Coexistence of Booming and Looting in China. *China Brief*, 2(21): 3–6.

Li, S. 2002b. Does East Love *guanxi* More than West? The Evolution of Relation-Based Governance: Contemporary and Historical Evidences. *Global Economic Review*, 31(1): 1–11.

Li, S. 2009. *Managing International Business in Relation-Based versus Rule-Based Countries*. New York: Business Expert Press.

Li, S. 2013. China's (Painful) Transition from Relation-Based to Rule-Based Governance: When and How, Not If and Why. *Corporate Governance: An International Review*, 21(6): 567–576.

Li, S. 2016. *East Asian Business in the New World: Helping Old Economies Revitalize*. New York: Elsevier.

Li, S. 2019a. *Bribery and Corruption in Weak Institutional Enviroments: Connecting the Dot from a Comparative Perspective*. London: Cambridge University Press.

Li, S. 2019b. The Relocation of Supply Chains from China and the Impact on the Chinese Economy. *China Leadership Monitor*, December 1 (www.prcleader .org/): Accessed December 2, 2019.

Li, S. 2020a. Bribing the World, with Chinese Characteristics. *The American Spectator*, June 29 (https://spectator.org/bribing-the-world-with-chinese-charac teristics/): Accessed December 17, 2020.

Li, S. 2020b. Democracies Should Delink from China. *The American Spectator*, October 10 (https://spectator.org/u-s-china-delink-democracy-communism/): Accessed December 20, 2020.

Li, S. 2020c. Leading by Bribing: Evidence from China. *International Journal of Emerging Markets*, in press.

Li, S. and Alon, I. 2020. China's Intellectual Property Rights Provocation: A Political Economy View. *Journal of International Business Policy*, 3: 60–72.

Li, S. and Farrell, M. 2020a. China's Industrial Policy and Its Implications for International Business. *European Journal of International Management*, in press.

Li, S. and Farrell, M. 2020b. The Emergence of China, inc.: Behind and beyond the Trade War. *International Journal of Emerging Markets*, forthcoming.

Li, S. and Filer, L. 2007. The Effects of the Governance Environment on the Choice of Investment Mode and the Strategic Implications. *Journal of World Business*, 42(1): 80–98.

Li, S., Li, S., and Zhang, W. 2000. The Road to Capitalism: Competition and Institutional Change in China. *Journal of Comparative Economics*, 28: 269–292.

Li, S., Park, S. H., and Bao, R. S. 2019. The Transition from Relation-Based to Rule-Based Governance in East Asia. *International Journal of Emerging Markets*, 14 (1): 171–186.

Li, S., Park, S. H., and Li, S. 2004. The Great Leap Forward: The Transition from Relation-Based Governance to Rule-Based Governance. *Organizational Dynamics*, 33(1): 63–78.

Li, S., Park, S. H., and Selover, D. D. 2017b. The Cultural Dividend: A Hidden Source of Economic Growth in Emerging Countries. *Cross Cultural & Strategic Management*, 24(4): 590–616.

Li, S., Selover, D., and Stein, M. 2011. 'Keep Silent, Make Money': The Institutional Pattern of Earnings Manipulation in China. *Journal of Asian Economics*, 22: 369–382.

Li, S., Park, S. H., and Bao, R. S. 2014. How Much Can We Trust the Financial Report? *International Journal of Emerging Markets*, 9(1): 33–53.

Li, S., and Yeh, K. 2008. Mao's Pervasive Influence on Chinese CEOs. *Harvard Business Review* (December): 62–63.

Liang, M. 2019. Is Huawei a Private- or State-Owned Firm? *Independent Chinese Pen Center*, August 4 (www.chinesepen.org/blog/archives/135248): Accessed November 4, 2019.

Lin, J. 2012. *Demystifying the Chinese Economy*. Cambridge: Cambridge University Press.

Lin, N. 2011. Capitalism in China: A Centrally Managed Capitalism (CMC) and Its Future. *Management and Organization Review*, 7(1): 63–96.

Linebarger, P., Chu, D., and Burks, A. 1956. *Far Eastern Governments and Politics: China and Japan* (2nd ed.) Princeton, NJ: D. Van Nostrand.

Ling, C. and Naughton, B. 2016. An Institutionalized Policy-Making Mechanism: China's Return to Techno-industrial Policy. *Research Policy*, 45: 2138–2152.

Link, P. 2021. Seeing the CCP Clearly. *The New York Review of Books*, February 11 (www.nybooks.com/articles/2021/02/11/china-seeing-ccp-clearly/): Accessed March 11, 2021.

Lipset, S. M. 1959. Some Social Requisites of Democracy: Economic Development and Political Legitimacy. *American Political Science Review*, 53(1): 69–105.

Lipset, S. M. 1983. *Political Man: The Social Bases of Politics* (2nd ed.) London: Heinemann.

List, F. 1909 (1841). *The National System of Political Economy*. New York: Longmans, Green, and Co.

Liu, B. 2018. China's Solar Industry Is at a Crossroads. *Chinadialogue*, August 13 (www.chinadialogue.net/article/show/single/ch/10775-China-s-solar-industry-is-at-a-crossroads): Accessed December 8, 2019.

Liu, E. 2019. Industrial Policies in Production Networks. *The Quarterly Journal of Economics*, 134(4): 1883–1948.

Liu, Z. 2017. 簡明統戰學教程. *liuzhongjing.medium.com*, May 8 (https://liuzhongjing.medium.com/%E7%B0%A1%E6%98%8E%E7%B5%B1%E6%88%B0%E5%AD%B8%E6%95%99%E7%A8%8B-8b871f5a4861): Accessed December 12, 2020.

Lu, Y. 2011. 中宣部严控媒体 堵塞不满宣泄渠道. *Voice of America*, January 14 (www.voachinese.com/a/article-20110114-china-s-tighter-grip-media-113594684/776252.html): Accessed November 20, 2020.

Luo, D., She, G., and Chen, J. 2015. A New Re-examination of the Relationship between Economic Performance and Local Leaders' Promotion. *China Economic Quarterly*, 14(3): 1145–1172.

Luo, J. 2016. High-Speed Rail Profit Map: The East Makes a Huge Loss in the Midwest, *China Economic Weekly*.

Lynch, C. and Gramer, R. 2019. Outfoxed and Outgunned: How China Routed the U.S. in a U.N. Agency. *Foreign Policy*, October 23, 2019 (https://foreignpolicy.com/2019/10/23/china-united-states-fao-kevin-moley/): Accessed March 14, 2020.

Lynch, E. M. 2010. Movie Review: Zhao Liang's "Petition: The Court of Complaints." *China Law & Policy*, February 8 (https://chinalawandpolicy.com/tag/shangfang/): Accessed December 20, 2020.

Lynn, L. H. 1998. The Commercialization of the Transistor Radio in Japan: The Functioning of an Innovation Community. *IEEE Transactions on Engineering Management*, 45(3): 220–229.

Macias, A. 2021. Biden Warns China Is Going to 'Eat Our Lunch' if U.S. Doesn't Get Moving on Infrastructure. *CNBC*, February 11 (www.cnbc.com/2021/02/11/biden-says-china-will-eat-our-lunch-on-infrastructure.html): Accessed March 8, 2021.

Macionis, J. J. 2001. *Sociology*. Upper Saddle River, NJ: Prentice Hall.

MacLeod, C. 2015. Chinese Flock to USA to Give Birth to U.S. Citizens. *USA Today*, April 1 (www.usatoday.com/story/news/world/2015/04/01/china-usa-birth-tourists-business-strong/24887837/): Accessed November 18, 2020.

Malinowski, B. 1922. *Argonauts of the Western Pacific*. London: Routledge and Kegan Paul.

Mao, Y. and Su, D. 2012. The Hard-Working Culture Is the Root-Cause of China's Miracle. *Financial Times*, August 23.

Mao, Z. 1927. Political Power Grows Out of the Barrel of a Gun. *Wikipedia*, December 1 (www.rfa.org/mandarin/duomeiti/jishitie/jj-06022021110054.html): Accessed December 30, 2020.

Mao, Z. 1939. Communists Editorial. *People.com.cn* (http://cpc.people.com.cn/GB/64156/64157/4418419.html): Accessed October 18, 2020.

Mao, Z. 1972. *Quotations from Chairman Mao Tsetung*. Peking: Foreign Languages Press.

Marx, K. and Engels, F. 1848 (1906). *Manifesto of the Communist Party*. Chicago: Charles, H. Kerr & Company.

Maslow, A. 1954. *Motivation and Personality*. New York: Harper.

The Masses' Daily. 2001. 政府"干涉"企业购买设备 如此引资要得吗？. *Sina.com*, May 17 (http://finance.sina.com.cn/g/61536.html): Accessed December 14, 2020.

Mathi, S. 2020. Will Apple Ever Choose India over China? *Marker*, September 15 (https://marker.medium.com/will-apple-ever-choose-india-over-china-2ea5a4fad886): Accessed December 23, 2020.

Maurer, S. and Li, S. 2006. Understanding Expatriate Manager Performance: Effects of Governance Environments on Work Relationships in Relation-Based Economies. *Human Resource Management Review*, 16: 29–46.

MBA Lib. circa 2006. State Asset Loss. *MBA Lib* (https://wiki.mbalib.com/wiki/%E5%9B%BD%E6%9C%89%E8%B5%84%E4%BA%A7%E6%B5%81%E5%A4%B1): Accessed December 17, 2020.

McDonald, J. 2010. China to Bid on US High-Speed Rail Projects, *Associated Press*.

McMorrow, R. W. 2015. Membership in the Communist Party of China: Who Is Being Admitted and How? *JSTOR Daily*, December 19 (https://daily.jstor.org/communist-party-of-china/): Accessed November 15, 2020.

Mei, D. 2001. How China's Government Is Attempting to Control Chinese Media in America. *China Brief*, November 21 (https://jamestown.org/program/how-chinas-government-is-attempting-to-control-chinese-media-in-america/): Accessed January 27, 2021.

Meisner, M. 1999. *Mao's China and After*. New York: Free Press.

Merriam-Webster. undated. Culture. *Merriam-Webster* (www.merriam-webster .com/dictionary/culture): Accessed November 28, 2020.

Minter, A. 2014. China's Li Doesn't Believe His Own Numbers. *Bloomberg*, March 5 (www.bloomberg.com/opinion/articles/2014-03-05/china-s-li-doesn-t-believe-his-own-numbers): Accessed November 16, 2020.

Modelski, G. 1987. *Long Cycles in World Politics*. Seattle: University of Washington Press.

Modern China Studies. 2020. News Coverage on What the Chinese State Did for the Covid-19 Outbreak in China. *Modern China Studies*, 27(2): 5–276.

Moore, B. 1966. *Social Origins of Dictatorship and Democracy: Lord and Peasant in the Making of the Modern World*. Boston: Beacon Press.

Moss, T. 2019. The Key to Electric Cars Is Batteries: One Chinese Firm Dominates the Industry. *The Wall Street Journal*, November 3, (www.wsj.com/articles/ how-china-positioned-itself-to-dominate-the-future-of-electric-cars-115728044 89?mod=searchresults&page=1&pos=3): Accessed November 4, 2019.

Mu, F. 2020. 北京再出重手反垄断, 电商巨头可能好景不再. *Voice of America*, November 10 (www.voachinese.com/a/China-ups-scrutiny-of-tech-giants-with-draft-anti-monopoly-rules-20201110/5655214.html): Accessed December 19, 2020.

Müller, A. R. 2013. Self-Interest vs Altruism in East Asia's Development Aid. *The Broker: Connecting Worlds of Knowledge*, July 3 (www.thebrokeronline.eu/ self-interest-vs-altruism-in-east-asia-s-development-aid/): Accessed January 8, 2020.

Mulvaney, D. 2014. Solar Energy Isn't Always as Green as You Think. *IEEE Spectrum*, 26.

Myers, S. and Bradsher, K. 2020. China Says It Remains Open to the World, but Wants to Dictate Terms. *The New York Times*, November 23 (www.nytimes .com/2020/11/23/world/asia/china-xi-jinping-globalization.html): Accessed December 17, 2020.

Nanhaiwang. 2008. 公家钱不拿白不拿? 儋州有人作假申请骗低保. *Sina.com*, January 17 (http://news.sina.com.cn/c/2008-01-17/080313275867s.shtml): Accessed December 11, 2020.

Nathan, A. and Shi, T. 1996. Left and Right with Chinese Characteristics: Issues and Alignments in Deng Xiaoping's China. *World Politics*, 48(4): 522–550.

National Bureau of Statistics of China. 1997. *China Industrial Statistical Yearbook*. Beijing: China Statistical Press.

National Bureau of Statistics of China. 2016. *China Industrial Statistical Yearbook*. Beijing: China Statistical Press.

National Bureau of Statistics of China. 2018a. *China Statistical Yearbook*. Beijing: China Statistical Press.

National Bureau of Statistics of China. 2018b. National Government Revenue and Expenditure, 1990 to 2018. *National Data of NBS* (http://data.stats.gov.cn/english/tablequery.htm?code=AC07): Accessed October 19, 2019.

National Bureau of Statistics of China. 2019. *China Statistical Yearbook*. Beijing: China Statistical Press.

Neihan Shiwusuo. 2019. Injecting Power: State Announced: Huawei and ZTE and Others Receive Tax Exemption! *new.qq.com*, May 23 (https://new.qq.com/rain/a/20190523A0QLMV): Accessed November 4, 2019.

Nesheim, C. 2019. China's 11 Largest Investment Migration Agencies in 2019. *Investment Immigration Insider*, April 30 (www.imidaily.com/china/chinas-11-largest-investment-migration-agencies-in-2019/): Accessed November 18, 2020.

New Channel. Undated. Introduction to New Channel. *New Channel* (www.newchannel.org/jtjj/): Accessed April 22, 2019.

Newman, R. 2020. What Biden Would Do about Trump's China Tariffs. *yahoo! finance*, July 8 (https://finance.yahoo.com/news/what-biden-would-do-about-trumps-china-tariffs-195835075.html): Accessed December 17, 2020.

The New York Times. 2007. Yahoo chief apologizes to Chinese dissidents' relatives. *The New York Times*, No. 7 (www.nytimes.com/2007/11/07/business/worldbusiness/07iht-yahoo.1.8226586.html): Accessed December 31, 2020.

Norland, E. 2018. Trade War Costs to Consumers, Companies and Nations. *Financial Times*, August 14 (www.ft.com/brandsuite/cme-group/trade-war-costs-consumers-companies-nations/index.html): Accessed December 21, 2020.

North, D. 1990. *Institutions, Institutional Change, and Economic Performance*. Cambridge: Cambridge University Press.

North, D. 1991. Institutions. *Journal of Economic Perspectives*, 5(1): 97–112.

Nye, J. 2012. China's Soft Power Deficit. *The Wall Street Journal*, May 9.

O'Donnell, N. 2020. Joe Biden Makes the Case for Why He Should Be President. *CBS News*, October 25 (www.cbsnews.com/news/joe-biden-democratic-presidential-candidate-kamala-harris-60-mintues-interview-norah-odonnell-2020-10-25/): Accessed December 18, 2020.

Oertel, J. 2020. The New China Consensus: How Europe Is Growing Wary of Beijing. *European Council on Foreign Relations*, September 7 (https://ecfr.eu/publication/the_new_china_consensus_how_europe_is_growing_wary_of_beijing/): Accessed December 21, 2020.

ogate.org. 2020. 不看不知道，原来海外有这么多用中国纳税人的钱办的报纸。遍地假外媒、认清假外媒。. *ogate.org*, March 17 (https://ogate.org/show.aspx?name=c1144706_1_1&line=9): Accessed December 10, 2020.

Okuno-Fujiwara, M. 1991. Industrial Policy in Japan: A Political Economy View. In *Trade with Japan: Has the Door Opened Wider?* 271–304. Chicago: University of Chicago Press.

Ostrom, E. 2000. Collective Action and the Evolution of Social Norms. *Journal of Economic Perspectives*, 14(3): 137–158.

Oxner, R. 2020. U.S. and EU Condemn Jailing of Lawyer Who Reported on Coronavirus in Wuhan. *NPR*, December 29 (www.npr.org/2020/12/29/951258654/u-s-and-eu-condemn-jailing-of-lawyer-who-reported-on-coronavirus-in-wuhan): Accessed December 30, 2020.

Page, J. 2020. How the U.S. Misread China's Xi: Hoping for a Globalist, It Got an Autocrat. *The Wall Street Journal*, December 23 (www.wsj.com/articles/xi-jinping-globalist-autocrat-misread-11608735769?mod=searchresults_pos16&page=1): Accessed December 30, 2020.

Pang, X. and Wang, S. 2018. The International Political Significance of Chinese and US Foreign Aid: As Seen in United Nations General Assembly Voting. *Social Science in China*, 39(1): 5–33.

Park, S. H., Li, S., and Tse, D. 2006. Market Liberalization and Firm Performance during China's Economic Transition. *Journal of International Business Studies*, 37(1): 127–147.

Park, S. H., Li, S., and Zhang, R. 2015. Government Stimulus: Pyramids, National Parks, and Ghost Cities. *Forbes.com*, August 27 (www.forbes.com/sites/ceibs/2015/08/27/government-stimulus-pyramids-national-parks-and-ghost-cities/): Accessed December 22, 2020.

Pei, M. 2012. Communist China's Perilous Phase. *The Wall Street Journal*, May 3.

Pei, M. 2018. China in Xi's "New Era": A Play for Global Leadership. *Journal of Democracy*, 29(2): 37–51.

People's Daily. 1966. 横扫一切牛鬼蛇神. *People's Daily*, June 1 (https://baike.baidu.com/item/%E6%A8%AA%E6%89%AB%E4%B8%80%E5%88%87%E7%89%9B%E9%AC%BC%E8%9B%87%E7%A5%9E): Accessed December 30, 2020.

People's Daily. 2004. Rail Track Beats Maglev in Beijing-Shanghai High Speed Railway, *People's Daily*.

People.cn. 2015a. Xinhua News Agency: Words Banned in News Reporting, Such as "Movie King" or "Movie Queen." *People.cn*, November 5 (http://culture.people.com.cn/n/2015/1105/c87423–27782404.html): Accessed November 3, 2019.

People.cn. 2015b. "亚洲最大高考工厂"安徽毛坦厂中学毁誉参半, *People.cn*, Vol. August 7 (http://edu.people.com.cn/n/2015/0807/c244541–27425136.html): Accessed November 5, 2020.

People.cn. 2018. "摸着石头过河"的来历. *People.cn*, April 12 (http://cpc.people.com.cn/n1/2018/0412/c69113–29921565.html): Accessed November 15, 2020.

People.cn. 2020. The News Net of the Chinese Communist Party. (http://cpc .people.com.cn/): Accessed November 20, 2020.

Peter Wells, D. W. 2017. Fitch Warns on Expected Returns from One Belt, One Road. *Financial Times*, January 25 (www.ft.com/content/c67b0c05-8f3f-3ba5-8219-e957a90646d1): Accessed April 21, 2019.

Pew Research Center. 2012. Growing Concerns in China about Inequality, Corruption. *Pew Research Center*, October 16 (www.pewresearch.org/global/ 2012/10/16/growing-concerns-in-china-about-inequality-corruption/): Accessed December 20, 2020.

Pew Research Center. 2013. Public Sees U.S. Power Declining as Support for Global Engagement Slips. *Pew Research Center*, December 3 (www.pewresearch.org/ politics/2013/12/03/public-sees-u-s-power-declining-as-support-for-global-engage ment-slips/): Accessed December 20, 2020.

Phan, P. H. 2019. International Politics and Management Research: A Glaring White Space Calling out to Be Filled. *Academy of Management Perspectives*, 33(1): 1–2.

Pillsbury, M. 2015. *The Hundred-Year Marathon: China's Secret Strategy to Replace America as the Global Superpower*. New York: St. Martin's Press.

Platteau, J. 1994. Behind the Market Stage Where Real Societies Exist – Parts I and II: The Rule of Public and Private Order Institutions. *Journal of Development Studies*, 30(3): 533–577 and 753–817.

Pompeo, M. 2020a. Communist China and the Free World's Future. *U.S. State Department*, July 23 (www.state.gov/communist-china-and-the-free-worlds-future/): Accessed November 19, 2020.

Pompeo, M. 2020b. U.S. States and the China Competition. *U.S. Department of State*, February 8 (www.state.gov/u-s-states-and-the-china-competition/): Accessed December 11, 2020.

Popenoe, D. 1993. American Family Decline, 1960–1990: A Review and Appraisal. *Journal of Marriage and the Family*, 55: 527–555.

Przeworski, A., Alvarez, M., Cheibub, J., and Limongi, F. 2000. *Democracy and Development: Political Institutions and Well-Being in the World, 1950–1990*. Cambridge: Cambridge University Press.

Putz, C. 2019. Which Countries Are for or against China's Xinjiang Policies? *The Diplomat*, July 15 (https://thediplomat.com/2019/07/which-countries-are-for-or-against-chinas-xinjiang-policies/): Accessed March 14, 2020.

Qin, H. 2007. The Low Human Rights Advantage of China's Economic Development. *www.aisixiang.com*, November 2 (www.aisixiang.com/data/ 16401.html): Accessed October 18, 2020.

Qin, H. 2020. 美国近年来发生的"撕裂" 其根本原因是什么？ *eNewsTree.com*, January 3 (http://enewstree.com/discuz/forum.php?mod=viewthread&tid=265630): Accessed January 5, 2021.

Qu, W., Fong, M., and Oliver, J. 2012. Does IFRS Convergence Improve Quality of Accounting Information? Evidence from the Chinese Stock Market. *Corporate Ownership & Control*, 9(4): 1–10.

Radio France Internationale. 2019. 美国独立日 毛泽东颂扬美国民主文章热传. *Radio France Internationale*, July 4 (www.rfi.fr/cn/%E4%B8%AD%E5%9B%BD/20190704-%E7%BE%8E%E5%9B%BD%E7%8B%AC%E7%AB%8B%E6%97%A5-%E6%AF%9B%E6%B3%BD%E4%B8%9C%E9%A2%82%E6%89%AC%E7%BE%8E%E5%9B%BD%E6%B0%91%E4%B8%BB%E6%96%87%E7%AB%A0%E7%83%AD%E4%BC%A0): Accessed December 29, 2020.

Radio France Internationale. 2020. 苏宁张近东：企业小了是个人的, 大了就是社会的国家的. *Radio France Internationale*, December 28 (www.rfi.fr/cn/%E4%B8%AD%E5%9B%BD/20201228-%E8%8B%8F%E5%AE%81%E5%BC%A0%E8%BF%91%E4%B8%9C-%E4%BC%81%E4%B8%9A%E5%B0%8F%E4%BA%86%E6%98%AF%E4%B8%AA%E4%BA%BA%E7%9A%84%EF%BC%8C%E5%A4%A7%E4%BA%86%E5%B0%B1%E6%98%AF%E7%A4%BE%E4%BC%9A%E7%9A%84%E5%9B%BD%E5%AE%B6%E7%9A%84): Accessed December 28, 2020.

Radio Free Asia. 2018. Government Spends a Large Sum to Support Foreign Students with, People Are Upset *Radio Free Asia*, July 18 (www.rfa.org/mandarin/yataibaodao/jingmao/yf1-07182018100345.html/): Accessed July 20, 2018.

Radio Free Asia. 2019a. Beijing and Prague Cut Ties, Clouds over Sino-Czech Relations *Radio Free Asia*, October 31 (www.rfa.org/cantonese/news/czech-penetration-10312019093413.html?searchterm%3Autf8%3Austring=%20%E5%B8%83%E6%8B%89%E6%A0%BC&encoding=simplified): Accessed November 4, 2019.

Radio Free Asia. 2019b. Return to the Public-Private Joint Venture of the 1950s? Hangzhou and other Regions Send Government Representatives to Private Firms. *Radio Free Asia*, September 23 (www.rfa.org/mandarin/yataibaodao/jingmao/ql1-09232019065851.html?searchterm:utf8:ustring=%20%E9%87%8D%E8%BF%94%E4%BA%94%E5%8D%81): Accessed November 4, 2019.

Radio Free Asia. 2019c. 中国"边控"：可限制任何人出入境. *Radio Free Asia*, August 5 (www.rfa.org/mandarin/yataibaodao/junshiwaijiao/yq-08052019122817.html): Accessed December 16, 2020.

Radio Free Asia. 2020a. 從小粉紅到訪民 海歸女碩士受迫害家破人亡. *Radio Free Asia*, May 22 (www.rfa.org/cantonese/news/broken-05222020083146.html): Accessed December 21, 2020.

Radio Free Asia. 2020b. 翟东升视频引美国关注 特朗普转推. *Radio Free Asia*, December 8 (www.rfa.org/mandarin/yataibaodao/junshiwaijiao/bx-1208202 0122246.html): Accessed December 18, 2020.

Radio Free Asia. 2020c. 【耳邊風】揭中共宣傳九招套路 分工細緻有正有反. *Radio Free Asia*, December 10 (www.rfa.org/cantonese/news/ear/ear-propaganda-12092020064535.html): Accessed December 10, 2020.

Raess, D., Ren, W., and Wagner, P. 2017. Chinese Commercially-oriented Financial Flows and UN Voting Realignment. *Working Paper* (www.peio.me/wp-content/uploads/2018/01/PEIO11_paper_62.pdf): Accessed March 14, 2020.

The Railway Gazette. 2014. CNR and CSR Agree Merger Terms, *The Railway Gazette*.

Rapoport, M. 2020. 'They'd Find Fraud, Fraud, Fraud.' *Institutional Investor*, July 22 (www.institutionalinvestor.com/article/b1mlyjys554sgd/They-d-Find-Fraud-Fraud-Fraud): Accessed November 25, 2020.

Rawls, J. 1971. *A Theory of Justice*: Cambridge, MA: Harvard University Press.

Ren, Z. 2020. 剥光衣服坚持当皇帝的小丑. *matters.news*, March 31 (https://matters .news/@freeMyMind/%E4%BB%BB%E5%BF%97%E5%BC%BA%E7%BD% B2%E5%90%8D%E7%82%AE%E8%BD%B0%E4%B9%A0%E8%BF%91% E5%B9%B3%E5%8E%9F%E6%96%87%E5%85%A8%E6%96%87-%E5%89% A5%E5%85%89%E8%A1%A3%E6%9C%8D%E5%9D%9A%E6%8C%81% E5%BD%93%E7%9A%87%E5%B8%9D%E7%9A%84%E5%B0%8F%E4% B8%91-%E5%85%A8-bafyreie4t3z7yz6efjznfd3rsp5wzitn4fbca2rltclxssz62t w2ywlqt4): Accessed December 18, 2020.

Ren, Z., Lian, Y., and Guo, S. 2019. China's Vehicle Battery Development: 2019. *Chainnews.com*, November 10 (www.chainnews.com/articles/232822260944 .htm): Accessed December 3, 2019.

Reporters without Borders. 2020. World Press Freedom Index. *Reporters without Borders* (https://rsf.org/en/ranking): Accessed November 19, 2020.

Reuters. 2015. Over 40 pct of China's Online Sales Counterfeit, Shoddy: Xinhua. *Reuters*, November 2 (www.reuters.com/article/china-counterfeits-idUSL3N1 2Y04C20151103): Accessed December 11, 2020.

Reuters. 2016. China's CRRC Wins $1.3 bln Deal to Supply Chicago Rail Cars. *Reuters*, March 10 (www.reuters.com/article/crrc-usa-idUSL5N16I0LS): Accessed December 9, 2019.

Reuters. 2017. China Renewable Power Waste Worsens in 2016: Greenpeace. *Reuters*, April 19 (www.reuters.com/article/china-renewables-waste/china-renewable-power-waste-worsens-in-2016-greenpeace-idUSL3N1HQ1KE): Accessed December 9, 2019.

Rock, M. Y. 2018. Introduction to Modelski's Model of World Leadership. *Department of Geography, PennState* (www.e-education.psu.edu/geog128/node/646): Accessed March 13, 2020.

Rodrik, D. 2006. What's So Special about China's Exports? *China & World Economy*, 14(5): 1–19.

Rogin, J. 2017. China's Foreign Influence Operations Are Causing Alarm in Washington. *Washington Post*, December 10 (www.washingtonpost.com/opinions/global-opinions/chinas-foreign-influencers-are-causing-alarm-in-washington/2017/12/10/98227264-dc58-11e7-b859-fb0995360725_story.html?noredirect=on&utm_term=.67fd6fa6d83e): Accessed July 20, 2018.

Rosett, C. 2020a. Buying Power: How China Co-opts the UN. *The Spectator*, December 9 (https://spectator.us/buying-power-china-co-opts-un/): Accessed December 11, 2020.

Rosett, C. 2020b. China's Takedown of Hong Kong Is Part of a Strategy of World Domination. *The Dallas Morning News*, December 27 (www.dallasnews.com/opinion/commentary/2020/12/27/chinas-take-down-of-hong-kong-is-part-of-a-strategy-of-world-domination/): Accessed December 29, 2020.

Rubio, M. 2019. American Industrial Policy and the Rise of China. *Broadcast China*, December 12 (www.followcn.com/exclusive-american-industrial-policy-and-the-rise-of-china/): Accessed December 28, 2019.

Sahlins, M. 2015. *Confucius Institutes: Academic Malware*. Chicago: Prickly Paradigm Press.

Sakakibara, K. 1983. From Imitation to Innovation: The Very Large Scale Integrated (VLSI) Semiconductor Project in Japan. Working Paper (Sloan School of Management) 1490-83. Cambridge, MA: Massachusetts Institute of Technology (http://hdl.handle.net/1721.1/47985): Accessed: June 10, 2019.

Saxonhouse, G. R. 1986. Why Japan Is Winning. *Issues in Science and Technology*, 2(3): 72–80.

Schlesinger, J. 2017. How China Swallowed the WTO. *The Wall Street Journal*, November 1 (www.wsj.com/articles/how-china-swallowed-the-wto-1509551308): Accessed August 13, 2018.

Securefreedom. 2019. Hon. Newt Gingrich Speaks at 'Committee on the Present Danger: China' Event. *Youtube.com*, April 9 (www.youtube.com/watch?v=Clp17vgXmOs): Accessed April 16, 2019.

Shaheshang. 2019. Education Ministry Tightens Belt: Big Increase in Foreign Student Scholarship, Decrease in Teachers' Training, Foreign Student Numbers Will Increase in 2019. *Weixin*, April 9 (https://mp.weixin.qq.com/s/gn1yLzreoekMJGnFXZpUng): Accessed May 7, 2020.

Shao, H. 2019. Who Controls the EV Battery Empire in China? *youyou-tech.com*, November 13 (https://youyou-tech.com/2019/11/13/%E8%B0%81%E5%9C% A8%E6%8E%8C%E6%8F%A1%E4%B8%AD%E5%9B%BD%E7%9A%84% E5%8A%A8%E5%8A%9B%E7%94%B5%E6%B1%A0%E5%B8%9D%E5% 9B%BD%EF%BC%9F/): Accessed December 4, 2019.

Shi, Q. 2019. Two Shareholders of Vision China Give Up on Buying ETF, Government's Window Guidance Flexes Muscle *Laohucaijing.com*, November 19 (http://m.laohucaijing.com/home/detail/134697/%E4%B8% AD): Accessed December 8, 2019.

Shibata, T. and Takeuchi, H. 2006. *Japan, Moving toward a More Advanced Knowledge Economy, 2: Advanced Knowledge Creating Companies*: Washington, DC: World Bank Publications.

Shirouzu, N. 2010. Train Makers Rail against China's High-Speed Designs, *The Wall Street Journal*.

Shubbak, M. H. 2019. The Technological System of Production and Innovation: The Case of Photovoltaic Technology in China. *Research Policy*, 48(4): 993–1015.

Silver, L., Devlin, K., and Huang, C. 2020. Unfavorable Views of China Reach Historic Highs in Many Countries. *Pew Research Center*, October 6 (www .pewresearch.org/global/2020/10/06/unfavorable-views-of-china-reach-historic- highs-in-many-countries/): Accessed December 19, 2020.

Sina.com. 2007. 台州商帮抱团造"大船". *Sina.com*, April 10 (http://finance.sina.com .cn/roll/20070410/04061322988.shtml): Accessed November 25, 2020.

Sina.com. 2011. Walmart Fined 20 Times in 5 years. *sina.com*, September 20 (http://finance.sina.com.cn/focus/wrmwnywfbf/): Accessed December 11, 2020.

Sina.com. 2014. 揭秘雁栖湖核心岛:会议中心按九宫格设计布局. *Sina.com*, November 15 (http://news.sina.com.cn/c/2014-11-15/013931147155.shtml): Accessed February 28, 2021.

Smith, A. 2019a. TikTok and China Come under Scrutiny in Congressional Hearing. *nbcnews.com*, November 5 (www.nbcnews.com/politics/congress/ hawley-takes-aim-tiktok-china-congressional-hearing-n1076586): Accessed November 5, 2019.

Smith, M. 2019b. Communism and Religion Can't Coexist. *The Wall Street Journal*, August 29 (www.wsj.com/articles/communism-and-religion-cant-coex ist-11567120938): Accessed December 15, 2020.

Sohu.com. 2017. Four Top Jokes. *Sohu.com*, March 9 (www.sohu.com/a/ 128339677_117717): Accessed November 20, 2020.

Sohu.com. 2020a. 合作抗疫 增信释疑 反对脱钩 中国外长访欧成果丰硕. *Sohu.com*, September 3 (www.sohu.com/a/416176641_119038): Accessed December 21, 2020.

Sohu.com. 2020b. 谁都想把公家财物据为己有的心理分析 *sohu.com*, June 18 (www.sohu.com/a/402661005_120228149): Accessed December 11, 2020.

Solar, J. 2018. China's PV Manufacturers after '531': What Makes a Winner in Overseas Market. *PVTECH*, November 21 (www.pv-tech.org/guest-blog/chinas-pv-manufacturers-after-531-what-makes-a-winner-in-overseas-market): Accessed December 8, 2019.

South China Morning Post. 2018. Xi Jinping: China to Stick to Communist Rule and Its Own Path to Cope with 'Unimaginable' Perils, *South China Morning Post* (www.scmp.com/news/china/politics/article/2178471/xi-china-stick-communist-rule-and-its-own-path-cope-unimaginable): Accessed February 20, 2019.

Spiering, C. 2020. 'C'mon Man!' Joe Biden Scoffs at China Threat. *Breitbart*, May 1 (www.breitbart.com/politics/2019/05/01/cmon-man-joe-biden-scoffs-at-china-threat/): Accessed March 8, 2021.

Statista. 2020. Market Share of Mobile Payments in China from 2011 to 2018. *Statista* (www.statista.com/statistics/1050151/china-market-share-of-mobile-payments/#:~:text=In%202018%2C%20the%20market%20share,their%20main%20means%20of%20payment): Accessed December 14, 2020.

Staton, B. 2021. 'Dependency' of UK Universities on China Creates Risks, Report Says. *Financial Times*, March 3 (www.ft.com/content/8cc66c7f-a80f-4d84-96dc-71c22f01b57f): Accessed March 8, 2021.

Stevenson, A. 2020. China Is Dismantling the Empire of a Vanished Tycoon. *The New York Times*, July 18 (www.nytimes.com/2020/07/18/business/china-xiao-jianhua.html): Accessed December 11, 2020.

Stiglitz, J. 2008. Is There a Post-Washington Consensus Consensus? In N. S. a. J. Stiglitz (ed.), *The Washington Consensus Reconsidering: Towards a New Global Governance*, 41–56. New York: Oxford University Press.

Strauss, V. and Southerl, D. 1994. How Many Died? New Evidence Suggests Far Higher Numbers for the Victims of Mao Zedong's Era. *The Washington Post*, July 17 (www.washingtonpost.com/archive/politics/1994/07/17/how-many-died-new-evidence-suggests-far-higher-numbers-for-the-victims-of-mao-zedongs-era/01044df5-03dd-49f4-a453-a033c5287bce/): Accessed December 15, 2020.

Strüver, G. 2016. What Friends Are Made of: Bilateral Linkages and Domestic Drivers of Foreign Policy Alignment with China. *Foreign Policy Analysis*, 170–191.

Sun, L. 2009. 警惕上层寡头化、下层民粹化. *sohu.com*, March 3 (http://sun-liping.blog.sohu.com/111418763.html): Accessed November 14, 2020.

Swank, D. 1996. Culture, Institutions, and Economic Growth: Theory, Recent Evidence, and the Role of Communitarian Polities. *American Journal of Political Science*, 40(3): 660–679.

Swanson, A. and McCabe, D. 2020. U.S. Judge Temporarily Halts Trump's WeChat Ban. *The New York Times*, September 20 (www.nytimes.com/2020/09/20/busi ness/economy/court-wechat-ban.html): Accessed December 18, 2020.

Tajika, E. and Yui, Y. 2002. Social Expenditures and Economic Growth: Sharing Growth in a Japanese Way. *Forthcoming as a World Bank Publication*.

Tan, W. 2020. Fraud at China's Luckin Is a 'Great Morality Tale' for Investors, Says Analyst. *CNBC*, July 6 (www.cnbc.com/2020/07/06/investing-fraud-at-china-luckin-coffee-fraud-case-warning-for-investors.html): Accessed November 25, 2020.

Tao, Y. and Fu, X. 2007. China's Textile Industry International Competitive Advantage and Policy Suggestion. *Business and Public Administration Studies*, 2(1): 84.

Tatlow, D. K. 2020. Exclusive: 600 U.S. Groups Linked to Chinese Communist Party Influence Effort with Ambition Beyond Election. *Newsweek*, October 26 (www.newsweek.com/2020/11/13/exclusive-600-us-groups-linked-chinese-communist-party-influence-effort-ambition-beyond-1541624.html): Accessed November 21, 2020.

Tempest, R. 1995. U.S. Citizen Detained by China. *Los Angeles Times*, June 27 (www.latimes.com/archives/la-xpm-1995-06-27-mn-17744-story.html): Accessed November 18, 2020.

The Thousand Talents Plan. Undated. The Thousand Talents Plan (Recruitment Program of Global Experts). *Recruitment* (www.1000plan.org/en/about.html): Accessed January 9, 2020.

The Wall Street Journal. 2014. Xi Rides the Tiger. *The Wall Street Journal*, July 30 (www.wsj.com/articles/xi-rides-the-tiger-1406653411): Accessed November 15, 2020.

The White House. 2021. Remarks by President Biden at Signing of an Executive Order on Supply Chains. *The White House*, February 24 (www.whitehouse .gov/briefing-room/speeches-remarks/2021/02/24/remarks-by-president-biden-at-signing-of-an-executive-order-on-supply-chains/): Accessed February 27, 2021.

Tokyo Shimbun. 2011. Chinese High-Speed Rail "Chinese Star" only 160 km out, Abandoned Original Development. *Tokyo Shimbun*, August 5 (https://megalodon .jp/2011-0805-2051-50/www.tokyo-np.co.jp/article/world/news/CK201108050200 0037.html): Accessed December 9, 2019.

Transparency International. 2019. Corruption Perceptions Index. *Transparency International* (www.transparency.org/cpi2019): Accessed March 14, 2020.

Tribe, K. 2007. *Strategies of Economic Order*. Cambridge: Cambridge University Press.

Trivedi, A. 2021. China's Bad Loan Season Descends Again and This Time It May Be Really Bad. *Bloomberg*, February 17 (www.bloombergquint.com/gadfly/even-with-recovery-china-s-bad-loan-season-may-be-really-bad-this-time#:~:text=The%20numbers%20are%20staggering%3A%20After,out%20of%20the%20virus%20slump): Accessed March 4, 2021.

Trofimov, Y., Hinshaw, D., and O'Keeffe, K. 2020. How China Is Taking over International Organizations, One Vote at a Time. September 29 (www.wsj.com/articles/how-china-is-taking-over-international-organizations-one-vote-at-a-time-11601397208?mod=searchresults_pos6&page=1): Accessed December 18, 2020.

Trompenaars, F. and Hampden-Turner, C. 2012. *Riding the Waves of Culture: Understanding Diversity in Global Business* (3rd ed.) New York: McGraw Hill.

U.S. Chamber of Commerce. 2017. Made in China 2025: Global Ambitions Built on Local Protections (www.uschamber.com/sites/default/files/final_made_in_china_2025_report_full.pdf): U.S. Chamber of Commerce. Accessed August 8, 2019.

U.S. Department of Justice. 2019a. *Deputy Attorney General Rod J. Rosenstein Delivers Remarks at the Center for Strategic & International Studies Event on Defending Rule of Law Norms*. Paper presented at the Center for Strategic & International Studies.

U.S. Department of Justice. 2019b. Patrick Ho, Former Head of Organization Backed by Chinese Energy Conglomerate, Sentenced to 3 Years In Prison for International Bribery and Money Laundering Offenses. *U.S. Department of Justice, U.S. Attorney's Office, Southern District of New York*, March 25 (www.justice.gov/usao-sdny/pr/patrick-ho-former-head-organization-backed-chinese-energy-conglomerate-sentenced-3): Accessed January 8, 2020.

U.S. Department of Justice. 2020a. Eight Individuals Charged with Conspiring to Act as Illegal Agents of the People's Republic of China. *U.S. Department of Justice*, October 28 (www.justice.gov/opa/pr/eight-individuals-charged-conspiring-act-illegal-agents-people-s-republic-china): Accessed November 21, 2020.

U.S. Department of Justice. 2020b. Researchers Charged with Visa Fraud after Lying about Their Work for China's People's Liberation Army. *U.S. Department of Justice*, July 23 (www.justice.gov/opa/pr/researchers-charged-visa-fraud-after-lying-about-their-work-china-s-people-s-liberation-army): Accessed December 20, 2020.

U.S. General Accounting Office. 1982. Industrial Policy: Japan's Flexible Approach, Vol. June 23. Washington, DC: U.S. General Accounting Office.

U.S. News & World Report. 2020. Maury High School. *U.S. News & World Report* (www.usnews.com/education/best-high-schools/virginia/districts/norfolk-city-public-schools/maury-high-school-school-20556): Accessed November 28, 2020.

U.S. State Department. 2020. China Travel Advisory. *U.S. State Department*, September 14 (https://travel.state.gov/content/travel/en/traveladvisories/trave ladvisories/china-travel-advisory.html): Accessed December 16, 2020.

United Nations. 1948. Hunam Rights. *United Nations*, 1948 (www.un.org/en/sections/issues-depth/human-rights/): Accessed November 5, 2019.

United States Senate. 2019. Threats to the U.S. Research Enterprise: China's Talent Recruitment Plans. In R. Portman and T. Carper (eds.), *Permanent Subcommittee on Investigations* (www.hsgac.senate.gov/imo/media/doc/2019-11-18%20PSI%20Staff%20Report%20-%20China's%20Talent% 20Recruitment%20Plans.pdf) Washington, DC: United States Senate.

US-China Economic and Security Commission. 2017. US-China Economic and Security Commission 2017 Annual Report. *US-China Economic and Security Commission*, November 15, 2017.

US-China Peoples Friendship Association. 2020. Statement of Principles. *US-China Peoples Friendship Association* (http://uscpfa.org/about-uscpfa): Accessed December 11, 2020.

US Congressional Office of Technology Assessment. 1991. *Competing Economies: America, Europe, and the Pacific Rim: Summary.* Collingdale, PA: DIANE Publishing.

Vasilyeva, N. 2012. 1 of 3 jailed Pussy Riot members freed. *USA Today*, October 10 (www.usatoday.com/story/news/world/2012/10/10/russia-puss-riot/1623955/): Accessed December 20, 2020.

Viswanatha, A. and O'Keeffe, K. 2020. Harvard Chemistry Chairman Charged on Alleged Undisclosed Ties to China. *The Wall Street Journal*, January 28 (www .wsj.com/articles/harvards-chemistry-chair-charged-on-alleged-undisclosed-ties-to-china-11580228768?mod=searchresults): Accessed May 2, 2020.

Viswanatha, A. and Volz, D. 2019. China's Spying Poses Rising Threat to U.S. *The Wall Street Journal*, April 28 (www.wsj.com/articles/chinas-spying-poses-rising-threat-to-u-s-11556359201): Accessed May 11, 2019.

Voice of America. 2020. 中国驻瑞典大使"威胁性言论"激怒驻在国. *Voice of America*, January 22 (www.voachinese.com/a/Sweden-china-threat-01212020/5254697 .html): Accessed December 30, 2020.

Voice of America. 2018. Current Affairs: Angry in Inside and Suspicion Outside, Why Is Spending Money Diplomacy Hated? *Voice of America*, August 2 (www

.voachinese.com/a/voaweishi-20180801-io-why-xi-money-diplomacy-causes-so-many-complaints/4509228.html): Accessed January 7, 2020.

Voice of America. 2019. 国进民退：北京的国企战略部署. *Voice of America*, February 9 (www.voachinese.com/a/china-private-vs-state-owned-businesses-20190208/4778692.html): Accessed December 13, 2020.

Voice of America. 2020. 逃亡美国，仍似在北京的手掌心：一个"红通犯"的自白. *Voice of America*, November 21 (www.voachinese.com/a/5670590.html): Accessed November 21, 2020.

Walder, A. G. 1995. Local Governments as Industrial Firms: An Organizational Analysis of China's Transitional Economy *American Journal of Sociology*, 101 (2): 263–301.

Waldron, A. 2020. COVID-19 Probably Originated in a Wuhan Lab. *GOLOCALProv News*, March 24 (www.golocalprov.com/news/covid-19-prob ably-originated-in-a...-professor-arthur-waldron): Accessed March 11, 2021.

Wan, J. 2016. Mao Zedong Oversees Propaganda: Manage the Globe, Let Our Voice Reach the World. *www.kunlunce.cn*, March 24 (www.kunlunce.com/jczc/mzdsx/2016-03-24/29515.html): Accessed April 14, 2019.

Wang, B., Qi, L., and Yang, S. 2019. China's Housing Market Is Finally Cooling. Some Homeowners Are Furious. *The Wall Street Journal*, November 5 (www.wsj.com/articles/chinas-housing-market-is-finally-cooling-some-homeowners-are-furious-11572949806?mod=searchresults&page=1&pos=1): Accessed November 5, 2019.

Wang, L. and Zheng, J. 2012. China's Rise as a New Paradigm in the World Economy: Preliminaries. *Journal of Chinese Economic and Business Studies*, 10(4): 301–312.

Wang, M. 2016. China's Human Rights Crackdown Punishes Families, Too. *Human Rights Watch*, August 15 (www.hrw.org/news/2016/08/15/chinas-human-rights-crackdown-punishes-families-too#): Accessed November 19, 2020.

Wang, Y. 2020. Global Vision and Firm Commitment as a Major Country. *Ministry of Foreign Affairs of China*, October 2 (www.fmprc.gov.cn/mfa_eng/wjdt_665385/zyjh_665391/t1821549.shtml): Accessed December 10, 2020.

Weber, M. 1958 (1904–1905). *The Protestant Ethics and the Spirit of Capitalism*. New York: Charles Scribner's Sons.

Wedeman, A. 2017. Xi Jinping's Tiger Hunt: Anti-corruption Campaign or Factional Purge? *Modern China Studies*, 24(2).

Wei, L. 2020. Jack Ma Makes Ant Offer to Placate Chinese Regulators. *The Wall Street Journal*, December 20 (www.wsj.com/articles/jack-ma-makes-ant-offer-to-placate-chinese-regulators-11608479629): Accessed February 6, 2021.

Wei, L. and Davis, B. 2018. Beijing Grabs Tech with New Tenacity. *The Wall Street Journal*, September 27(A1) (www.wsj.com/articles/how-china-systematically-pries-technology-from-u-s-companies-1537972066?mod=searchresults_pos1& page=1): Accessed November 5, 2019.

Wei, Z. and Ng, S. 2019. China Embraces Bankruptcy, U.S.-Style, to Cushion a Slowing Economy. *The Wall Street Journal*, November 6, 2019 (www.wsj.com/ articles/china-embraces-bankruptcy-u-s-style-to-cushion-a-slowing-economy-11573058567?emailToken=6c9bdacd74fd64620227b3a162fff64ce8TZlrMEQCg /ftr/A2pr9afRXvDVDeJFFjGV+RsUFuZNbmLLQ94Eim9bT99qOPf3cIGXChP AFBeAHUSsBvArRDgrgVahMCOhnR20N4LsE7mxIAktHwOt8qJon7jxmzJ1& reflink=article_email_share): Accessed November 7, 2019.

Weil, D. 2013 *Economic Growth* (3rd ed.) New York: Pearson.

Wen, G. 2019. Industrial Policies Revisited. *Financial Times (Chinese edition)*, January 17 (www.ftchinese.com/story/001081081?full=y&archive): Accessed January 5, 2021.

Wen Wei Po. 2002. A New Fad: Politicians in Taiwan Come to China for School. *Wen Wei Po*, June 24 (http://paper.wenweipo.com/2002/06/24/CH0206240053 .htm): Accessed April 22, 2019.

Wen Wei Po. 2018. Han Kuo-yu Trained in China? His Spokeperson Clarifies He Went but Did Not Finish. *Wen Wei Po*, November 21 (https://baijiahao.baidu .com/s?id=1617739070228370354&wfr=spider&for=pc&isFailFlag=1): Accessed April 22, 2019.

White House Office of Trade and Manufacturing Policy. 2018. How China's Economic Aggression Threatens the Technologies and Intellectual Property of the United States and the World. *The White House*, June (www.whitehouse .gov/wp-content/uploads/2018/06/FINAL-China-Technology-Report-6.18.18-PDF.pdf): Accessed March 26, 2020.

Wikipedia. 2019. Liu Xiaobo. *Wikipedia*, June 14 (https://en.wikipedia.org/wiki/ Liu_Xiaobo): Accessed June 17, 2019.

Wikipedia. 2020a. Anti-Rightist Campaign. *Wikipedia*, December 2 (https://en .wikipedia.org/wiki/Anti-Rightist_Campaign): Accessed December 15, 2020.

Wikipedia. 2020b. Confidence Doctrine. *Wikipedia*, May 20 (https://en.wikipedia .org/wiki/Confidence_doctrine): Accessed December 17, 2020.

Wikipedia. 2020c. Core Socialist Values. *Wikipedia*, December 1 (https://en .wikipedia.org/wiki/Core_Socialist_Values#:~:text=The%2012%20values%2C %20written%20in,integrity%22%20and%20%22friendship%22.): Accessed December 19, 2020.

Wikipedia. 2020d. Falun Gong. *Wikipedia*, December 9 (https://en.wikipedia.org/ wiki/Falun_Gong): Accessed December 20, 2020.

Wikipedia. 2020e. Hurting the Feelings of the Chinese People. *Wikipedia* (https://en.wikipedia.org/wiki/Hurting_the_feelings_of_the_Chinese_people): Accessed November 13, 2020.

Wikipedia. 2020f. Meng Hongwei. *Wikipedia*, December 3 (https://en.wikipedia.org/wiki/Meng_Hongwei): Accessed December 10, 2020.

Wikipedia. 2020g. One Agency, Two Names. *Wikipedia* (https://zh.wikipedia.org/wiki/%E4%B8%80%E4%B8%AA%E6%9C%BA%E6%9E%84%E4%B8%A4%E5%9D%97%E7%89%8C%E5%AD%90): Accessed November 12, 2020.

Wikipedia. 2020h. The Party Leads Everything. *Wikipedia* (https://zh.wikipedia.org/wiki/%E5%85%9A%E9%A2%86%E5%AF%BC%E4%B8%80%E5%88%87): Accessed November 12, 2020.

Wikipedia. 2020i. Wolf Warrior Diplomacy. *Wikipedia* (https://en.wikipedia.org/wiki/Wolf_warrior_diplomacy): Accessed October 18, 2020.

Wikipedia. 2020j. Zhao Ziyang. *Wikipedia* November 30 (https://en.wikipedia.org/wiki/Zhao_Ziyang): Accessed December 18, 2020.

Wise, D. 2011. *Tiger Trap*. New York: Houghton Mifflin Harcourt.

Withersworldwide. 2019. Attitudes to Wealth. *Withersworldwide*, September 19 (https://marketing.withersworldwide.com/reaction/emsdocuments/Attitudes Wealthreportactual19sep2019.pdf): Accessed November 29, 2020.

Wittmeyer, A. and Wilson, P. 2009. Captain of Maury Football Team Slain in Park Place Shooting. *The Virginian Pilot*, January 5 (www.pilotonline.com/news/crime/article_e7cbecfa-8908-5454-a5ca-b65643e455c0.html): Accessed November 28, 2020.

Wong, C. H. 2019. China Finally Snuffs Out a Beacon of Liberal Thought and Democracy. *The Wall Street Journal*, August 27 (www.wsj.com/articles/china-finally-snuffs-out-a-beacon-of-liberal-thought-and-democracy-11566886519?mod=article_inline): Accessed November 19, 2020.

Wong, C. H. 2020. 'Their Goal Is to Make You Feel Helpless': In Xi's China, Little Room for Dissent. *The Wall Street Journal*, November 27 (www.wsj.com/articles/their-goal-is-to-make-you-feel-helpless-in-xis-china-little-room-for-dissent-11606496176?mod=searchresults_pos2&page=1): Accessed December 15, 2020.

Wong, E. 2013. In China, Widening Discontent among the Communist Party Faithful. *The New York Times*, January 19 (www.nytimes.com/2013/01/20/world/asia/in-china-discontent-among-the-normally-faithful.html): Accessed November 18, 2020.

Wong, S. L. 2018. Many U.S. Firms in China Eyeing Relocation as Trade War Bites: Survey. *Reuters*, October 29 (www.reuters.com/article/us-usa-trade-china-impact/many-u-s-firms-in-china-eyeing-relocation-as-trade-war-bites-survey-idUSKCN1N30ZE): Accessed September 17, 2019.

Wood, P. 2018. China's Pernicious Presence on American Campuses. *The Chronicle of Higher Education*, February 26.

Working Group on Chinese Influence Activities in the United States. 2018. *Chinese Influence & American Interests: Promoting Constructive Vigilance*. Stanford, CA: Hoover Institution Press.

World Bank. 2015. World Governance Index. http://info.worldbank.org/govern ance/wgi/index.aspx#home.

World Bank. 2019a. *Innovative China: New Drivers of Growth*. In P. R. C. Development Research Center of the State Council (ed.). Washington, DC: World Bank.

World Bank. 2019b. *World Development Indicators*, Vol. 2019. Washington, DC: World Bank.

World Bank. 2020a. The World Bank Data-Japan. *The World Bank Data* (https://data.worldbank.org/country/japan?view=chart): Accessed November 16, 2020.

World Bank. 2020b. The World Bank Data: China. *The World Bank Data* (https://data.worldbank.org/country/china?view=chart(1992-2019): Accessed November 16, 2020.

World Health Organization. 2008. China: Melamine-contamination September - October 2008. *World Health Organization*, October 15 (www.who.int/environ mental_health_emergencies/events/Melamine_2008/en/#:~:text=15%20Octob er%202008%20%2D%20More%20than,formula%20and%20related%20dairy %20products): Accessed December 11, 2020.

World Justice Project. 2020. WJP Rule of Law Index: China. *World Justice Project*, 2020 (https://worldjusticeproject.org/rule-of-law-index/country/2020/China): Accessed November 24, 2020.

World Law Direct. 2008. Adversarial System vs. Inquisitorial System: World Law Direct.

Wright, E. O. 1997. *Class Counts: Comparative Studies in Class Analysis*. Cambridge: Cambridge University Press.

Wright, T. and Hope, B. 2018. Malaysia Eyes China Funds in 1MDB Probe. *The Wall Street Journal*, August 1(A8).

Wu, D. 2016. 大学生就业意愿调查与分析. *xzbu.com* (知行部落), 1673-291x (2016) 09-0127-03 (www.xzbu.com/2/view-11244200.html): Accessed December 16, 2020.

Wu, H. 2019. State Assets Loss and Policy Analsysis. *gwyoo.com*, November (www.gwyoo.com/lunwen/jjgl/zcgllw/201911/709860.html): Accessed December 11, 2020.

Wu, X. 2006. 毛式商帮——毛泽东思想武装起来的中国企业家们. *Aisixiang.com*, September 25(www.aisixiang.com/data/11168.html): Accessed December 11, 2020.

Wu, X. 2008. *China: The Era of Grabbing Wealth: Business History, 1993–2008*. Taipei: Yuanliu.

Xiao, B. 2019. "发枪发子弹，是要死人的"–六四军官追述天安门清场. *ABC*, June 1 (www.abc.net.au/chinese/2019-06-02/tiananmen-square-massacre-30-year-anni versary/11169964): Accessed November 15, 2020.

Xiao, G. 2020. The Leadership of the Chinese Communist Party Is Chosen by History and the People. *People.cn*, October 9 (http://theory.people.com.cn/n1/ 2020/1009/c40531-31884659.html): Accessed November 13, 2020.

Xiao, X. 2003. Jiang Zemin: Keep Silent and Make a Big Fortune, *Epochtimes* (www .epochtimes.com/b5/3/9/30/n385627.htm).

Xin, D. 2011. Full Steam Ahead for High-Speed Rail Patents Overseas, *China Daily*.

Xin, Y. 2020. 医保改革动了3.3亿人的"钱袋子" 个人账户大幅缩水为了救济谁？. *Caijing*, September 9 (https://finance.sina.com.cn/wm/2020-09-09/doc-iivhvpwy5800494.shtml): Accessed November 21, 2020.

Xingaodi. 2020. 全球427家中共大外宣媒体名单曝光. *Chinanewscenter.com*, May 1 (https://news.chinanewscenter.com/archives/2240): Accessed December 10, 2020.

Xinhua. 2020. Commentary: Why Does China not Set Specific Economic Growth Target? *Xinhuanet*, May 22 (www.xinhuanet.com/english/2020-05/22/c_ 139079493.htm): Accessed November 16, 2020.

Xinhua News Agency. 2017. Chinese standard EMU named "Fuxing." *Xinhua News Agency*, June 25 (www.xinhuanet.com//photo/2017-06/25/c_ 1121206644_2.htm): Accessed December 9, 2019.

Xinhua News Agency. 2020a. Keynote Speech by Chinese President Xi Jinping at APEC CEO Dialogues. *xinhuanet.com*, November 19 (www.xinhuanet.com/ english/2020-11/19/c_139527192.htm): Accessed December 17, 2020.

Xinhua News Agency. 2020b. 近平谈新形势下自力更生之路. *Xinhuanet.com*, October 13 (www.xinhuanet.com/politics/leaders/2020-10/13/c_1126598960 .htm): Accessed December 17, 2020.

Xinhuanet.com. 2019. 习近平同志《论坚持党对一切工作的领导》主要篇目介绍. *Xinhuanet.com*, October 27 (www.xinhuanet.com/2019-10/27/c_1125158604 .htm): Accessed November 21, 2020.

Xinhuashe (New China News Agency). 2006. Our Government Will Maintain Absolute Control over Seven Major Industries (www.cenn.cn).

Xinxianren. 2015. "听诊器、方向盘、售货员"的时代. *hanshan.info*, May 18 (http:// hanshan.info/home.php?mod=space&uid=78&do=blog&id=6214): Accessed December 11, 2020.

Xu, Q. 2020. 任正非一句"杀出一条血路"，外媒翻译不及格. *Guancha.cn*, June 10 (www.guancha.cn/internation/2020_06_10_553579.shtml): Accessed November 29, 2020.

Yang, H. 2002. 天歌之股权战：新股东精神还是散户闹革命？ *Sina.com*, October 12 (http://finance.sina.com.cn/t/20021012/1101265402.html): Accessed December 12, 2020.

Yang, J. 2007. Testimony of Jerry Yang Chief Executive Officer and Co-Founder, Yahoo! Inc. before the Committee on Foreign Affairs, U.S. House of Representatives. *Committee on Foreign Affairs, U.S. House of Representatives*, November 6 (www.wired.com/images_blogs/threatlevel/files/testimony_yang.pdf): Accessed December 31, 2020.

Yang, J. 2020. Where "the Party Leads All" Came from. *Guangming Wang (gmw. cn)*, May 26 (https://theory.gmw.cn/2020-05/26/content_33860134.htm): Accessed November 12, 2020.

Yang, J. and Wei, L. 2020. China's President Xi Jinping Personally Scuttled Jack Ma's Ant IPO. *The Wall Street Journal*, November 12 (www.wsj.com/articles/china-president-xi-jinping-halted-jack-ma-ant-ipo-11605203556): Accessed November 18, 2020.

Yang, M. 2013. "举牌五君子"之一黄文勋被抓. *Voice of America*, March 12 (www.voachinese.com/a/huangwenxun-20130312/1619811.html): Accessed December 17, 2020.

Yang, S. 2019. How Much Risk Involved in Belt and Road Initiative. *Voice of America*, April 17 (www.voachinese.com/a/China-bri-risks-20190416/4878654.html): Accessed April 21, 2019.

Yang, X. 1988. An Independent Intellectual's Observation of China's Political Reform. In S. Li (ed.), *Chinese Intellectuals on Politics, Society, and Economy*. Taipei: Guiguan Press.

Yang, Y. and Liu, N. 2019. China Hushes Up Scheme to Recruit Overseas Scientists. *Financial Times*, January 9 (www.ft.com/content/a06f414c-0e6e-11e9-a3aa-118c761d2745): Accessed January 8, 2020.

Yang, Z. 2015. Study Party Branch Budget: Five Agencies' Public Fuding Is 3.8 Billion Yuan. *21Caijing*, March 18 (https://m.21jingji.com/article/20150318/herald/f4056081dbc6b15ea9cd9878ad4b4325.html): Accessed November 11, 2020.

Yap, C.-W. 2019. State Support Helped Fuel Huawei's Global Rise. *The Wall Street Journal*, December 25 (www.wsj.com/articles/state-support-helped-fuel-huaweis-global-rise-11577280736?mod=searchresults&page=1&pos=15): Accessed February 11, 2020.

Ye, B. 2020. 北京香堂断水断电强拆继续 维权业主誓言保卫家园. *Voice of America*, December 19 (www.voachinese.com/a/forced-demolition-crisis-in-beijing-continues-as-homeowners-defy-with-no-utilities-but-government-repression-and-heighted-security-20201219/5705784.html): Accessed December 29, 2020.

Yeh, E. T. and Wharton, E. 2016. Going West and Going Out: Discourses, Migrants, and Models in Chinese Development. *Eurasian Geography and Economics*, 57 (3): 286–315.

Yellinek, R. and Chen, E. 2019. The "22 vs. 50" Diplomatic Split between the West and China over Xinjiang and Human Rights. *China Brief*, December 31 (https:// jamestown.org/program/the-22-vs-50-diplomatic-split-between-the-west-and-china-over-xinjiang-and-human-rights/): Accessed December 19, 2020.

Yew, L. T. 2020. Chinese Academic Disciplined after Criticising Xi and Communist Party. *Reuters.com*, August 17 (www.reuters.com/article/us-china-politics-professor/chinese-academic-disciplined-after-criticising-xi-and-communist-party-idUSKCN25D1DG): Accessed November 19, 2020.

Ying, M. 2019. When Stocks Crash, China Turns to Its 'National Team.' *The Washington Post*, May 10 (www.washingtonpost.com/business/when-stocks-crash-china-turns-to-its-national-team/2019/05/06/2e3dbf7a-7018-11e9-9331-30bc5836f48e_story.html): Accessed December 1, 2019.

Yip, H. 2018. China's $6 Billion Propaganda Blitz Is a Snooze. *Foreign Policy*, April 23 (https://foreignpolicy.com/2018/04/23/the-voice-of-china-will-be-a-squeak/): Accessed November 11, 2020.

You, T. 2017. China Launches Its First Self-Developed Bullet Train 'Fuxing' as Beijing Eyes Global High-Speed Rail Market, *Daily Mail*.

Yu, H. 2019a. Personal Interview by Author with Y., a Senior Investment Executive in China. October 28, 2019, Fairfax, VA.

Yu, J. 2012. What Reasons Do We Have to Make Our People not to Complain? *Chinaaffairs.org*: March 3.

Yu, S. and Goh, B. 2020. China Ups Scrutiny of Tech Giants with Draft Anti-monopoly Rules. *Reuters*, November 10 (www.reuters.com/article/ idUSKBN27Q0JB): Accessed December 19, 2020.

Yu, V. 2013. 'Enemy of the People' Historian Song Yongyi Gives as Good as He Gets. *South China Morning Post*, February 19 (www.scmp.com/news/ china/article/1153447/enemy-people-historian-song-yongyi-gives-good-he-gets): Accessed November 18, 2020.

Yu, X. 2019b. Chinese Banks Quietly Lower Daily Limit on Foreign-Currency Cash Withdrawals. *South China Morning Post*, May 3 (www.scmp.com/business/ banking-finance/article/3008795/chinese-banks-quietly-lower-daily-limit-for eign-currency): Accessed November 4, 2019.

Yu, Y. 2017. 解读中国的资本外逃. *Sina.com*, September 27 (https://finance.sina.cn/ zl/2017-09-27/zl-ifymesii5978281.d.html?from=wap): Accessed December 11, 2020.

zh.wikipedia.org. 2020a. 六安市毛坦厂中学. *zhi.wikipedia.org* (https://zh.wikipedia
.org/wiki/%E5%85%AD%E5%AE%89%E5%B8%82%E6%AF%9B%E5%9D%
A6%E5%8E%82%E4%B8%AD%E5%AD%A6): Accessed November 28, 2020.

Zh.wikipedia.org. 2020b. 魏京生. *zhi.wikipedia.org*, October 13 (https://zh
.wikipedia.org/wiki/%E9%AD%8F%E4%BA%AC%E7%94%9F): Accessed
December 21, 2020.

Zhai, K. 2019. Exclusive: China Prods State Firms to Boost Investment in Crisis-
Hit Hong Kong. *Reuters*, September 12 (www.reuters.com/article/us-hongkong-
protests-soe-exclusive/exclusive-china-prods-state-firms-to-boost-invest
ment-in-crisis-hit-hong-kong-idUSKCN1VY08C): Accessed November 4,
2019.

Zhang, C. 2019a. 中国的国有企业对 GDP 和就业的贡献有多大？. *Working Paper*,
July 15 (http://documents1.worldbank.org/curated/en/390691565249400884/
pdf/How-Much-Do-State-Owned-Enterprises-Contribute-to-China-s-GDP-and-
Employment.pdf): Accessed December 14, 2020.

Zhang, H. 2013a. Non-residents Face Hard and Costly Road to Get around the
Hukou Barrier. *South China Morning Post*, September 23 (www.scmp.com/
news/china/article/1315527/non-residents-face-hard-and-costly-road-get-
around-hukou-barrier): Accessed November 21, 2020.

Zhang, J. 2013b. Ethiopian President Educated in Beijing. *beijing.china.org.cn*,
October 24 (http://beijing.china.org.cn/2013-10/24/content_30387833.htm):
Accessed April 22, 2019.

Zhang, J. J. 2011. Seeking the Beijing Consensus in Asia: An Empirical Test of Soft
Power. *Honors Thesis, Duke University* (https://dukespace.lib.duke.edu/
dspace/handle/10161/5383): Accessed October 17, 2019.

Zhang, S. 2016. 张圣雨: 举牌宣扬民主自由是无私奉献的正义之举——我的无罪辩护.
Minzhuzhongguo.org, October 12 (http://minzhuzhongguo.org/MainArtShow
.aspx?AID=70891): Accessed December 19, 2020.

Zhang, W. 2012. Two Wrong Ideas in China, *Chinaaffairs.org* (www.chinaaffairs
.org/gb/detail.asp?id=122258): Accessed March 8, 2013.

Zhang, W. 2019b. The China Model View Is Factually False. *Journal of Chinese
Economic and Business Studies*, 17(3): 287–311.

Zhang, W. and Li, S. 2020. What You Need to Know about the Chinese Communist
Party. *The American Spectator*, June 2 (https://spectator.org/what-you-need-to-
know-about-the-chinese-communist-party/): Accessed June 9, 2020.

Zheng, Y. and Zhang, Z. 2019. 最全辱华企业黑名单: 这些大品牌的小心思, 不是蠢就是
坏. *News Time*, August 13 (https://tfcaijing.com/article/page/4c4b3666725744
6567424c6e777573465a74653071513d3d): Accessed December 13, 2020.

Zhenxiangchuanmei. 2020. 马斯克星链计划能推倒中共防火墙吗？ *bannedbook.org*, July 9 (www.bannedbook.org/bnews/bannedvideo/20200709/1358185.html): Accessed December 18, 2020.

Zhihu.com. 2015. Are There Party Offices in Private- and Foreign-Owned Firms? *Zhihu.com*, July 18–20 (www.zhihu.com/question/32353669): Accessed November 4, 2019.

Zhou, C. 2021. China Ratifies RCEP Trade Deal Three Months Ahead of Schedule, Urges other Members to Follow Suit. *South China Morning Post*, March 9 (www.scmp.com/economy/global-economy/article/3124678/china-ratifies-rcep-trade-deal-three-months-ahead-schedule): Accessed March 10, 2021.

Zhou, L. 2007. Governing China's Local Officials: An Analysis of Promotion Tournament Model. *Economic Research Journal*, 42(7): 36–50.

Zhou, M. 2020. Huawei's Meng Wanzhou Loses Key Decision in Extradition Case. *Nikkei Asia*, May 28 (https://asia.nikkei.com/Spotlight/Huawei-crackdown/Huawei-s-Meng-Wanzhou-loses-key-decision-in-extradition-case): Accessed December 30, 2020.

Zhou, W. and Li, Z. 2018. China Passed State Survilliance and Investigation Law, "Shuanggui" Becomes Legal *BBC*, March 19 (www.bbc.com/zhongwen/simp/chinese-news-43451802): Accessed November 4, 2019.

Zhu, J. and Liu, B. 2020. 中信证券：中产阶级崛起背景下，中国消费市场的新亮点在哪？ *CITIC Securities*, March 3 (https://m.zhitongcaijing.com/content/detail/278848.html): Accessed November 18, 2020.

Zhu, X. 2015. 对照习近平总书记书单（史上最全版），愧煞. *China Digital Times*, September 24 (https://chinadigitaltimes.net/chinese/2015/09/%E6%9C%B1%E5%AD%A6%E4%B8%9C%EF%BC%9A%E5%AF%B9%E7%85%A7%E4%B9%A0%E8%BF%91%E5%B9%B3%E6%80%BB%E4%B9%A6%E8%AE%B0%E4%B9%A6%E5%8D%95%EF%BC%88%E5%8F%B2%E4%B8%8A%E6%9C%80%E5%85%A8%E7%89%88%EF%BC%89%EF%BC%8C/): Accessed December 20, 2020.

Zhuang, P. 2020. China's Confucius Institutes Rebrand after Overseas Propaganda Rows. *South China Morning Post*, July 4 (www.scmp.com/news/china/diplomacy/article/3091837/chinas-confucius-institutes-rebrand-after-overseas-propaganda): Accessed March 7, 2021.

Index